Congressional Primaries and the Politics of Representation

Congressional Primaries and the Politics of Representation

Peter F. Galderisi, Marni Ezra,
and Michael Lyons, Editors

ROWMAN & LITTLEFIELD PUBLISHERS, INC.
Lanham • Boulder • New York • Oxford

ROWMAN & LITTLEFIELD PUBLISHERS, INC.

Published in the United States of America
by Rowman & Littlefield Publishers, Inc.
4720 Boston Way, Lanham, Maryland 20706
http://www.rowmanlittlefield.com

12 Hid's Copse Road
Cumnor Hill, Oxford OX2 9JJ, England

British Library Cataloguing in Publication Information Available

Library of Congress Cataloging-in-Publication Data

Congressional primaries and the politics of representation / edited by Peter F. Galderisi,
Marni Ezra, and Michael Lyons.
   p. cm.
   Includes bibliographical references and index.
   ISBN 0-7425-0766-1 (alk. paper) — ISBN 0-7425-0767-X (pbk. : alk. paper)
   1. Primaries—United States. 2. United States. Congress—Elections. 3. Representative
goverment and representation—United States. I. Galderisi, Peter F. II. Ezra, Marni,
1969–   III. Lyons, Michael, 1947–
JK2071.C63   2001
324.273'0154—dc21   00-055293

Printed in the United States of America

♾™ The paper used in this publication meets the minimum requirements of American
National Standard for Information Sciences—Permanence of Paper for Printed Library
Materials, ANSI/NISO Z39.48–1992.

Contents

Foreword

When I left graduate school in the early 1980s, I rushed pell-mell into a number of research projects on congressional elections. With youthful exuberance and naïveté, I went searching for answers to questions about why turnout varies across congressional primaries, why some primaries are more competitive than others, and how primaries influence general elections. While my efforts were rewarded with a published paper here and there, my scholarly interests soon turned elsewhere. About a year ago my interest in congressional primaries was again piqued when Peter Galderisi, Marni Ezra, and Michael Lyons introduced me to the scholarship in *Congressional Primaries and the Politics of Representation*. I am pleased to report that the state of the literature is vastly improved over that of fifteen years ago, thanks in large part to the persistent and meticulous work of the researchers featured in this volume.

Congressional Primaries and the Politics of Representation contains a rich array of original and timely essays. Broadly speaking, it focuses on two important topics: (1) how primaries influence general elections, and (2) how primaries influence the ideology of representatives. During the 1980s, the first topic was narrowly defined to mean how the division of the primary vote influenced the general election vote. In this book, the influence of primaries on general elections is expanded to include how primaries influence who will run for office and how money is spent. The data and statistical techniques used range well beyond what was available two decades ago and contribute greatly to the significance of the research. In addition, the authors employ a theoretical rigor that is missing in many of the earlier studies. The second topic, termed the politics of representation, is a relatively new line of inquiry, and this volume pulls together much of the best work in the area. The upshot of the research is that primary type and primary competition have a substantial impact on the ideology of the general election victor. Here again, the combination of solid theoretical and empirical analyses enhances the importance of the work.

The book is also valuable because the authors place their work in context. Each of the essays thoroughly reviews the relevant literature and points the direction for future research. Thus, the volume serves as a "road map" to the congressional primary scholarship, guiding readers through research of both the past and the present, and suggesting routes that need to be explored. Indeed, I wish I had had such a resource when I started work in this area years ago.

Galderisi, Ezra, and Lyons are to be congratulated for editing such a fine book. They have assembled many of the leading scholars of congressional elections, and the result is a splendid set of essays that advance our understanding of congressional primaries in many important ways. It is certainly the best single resource on congressional primaries, and I highly recommend the book to everyone interested in American elections.

Tom Rice

Acknowledgments

We would like to thank a number of people for their assistance in the creation and the preparation of this volume. Steve Wrinn provided his usual encouragement and measure of excitement in selecting this collection for publication. Mary Carpenter and the editorial and production staff of Rowman & Littlefield provided invaluable assistance toward the completion of this volume. Special appreciation is extended to Sally Okelberry, who labored through countless revisions, submissions, and administrative proceedings. We also wish to acknowledge the Milton R. Merrill Endowment of Utah State University's Political Science Department for providing monetary support for the original workshop from which this volume grew and for funding the development and final production of this volume. Finally, we wish to thank all of our colleagues, particularly Tom Rice, who reviewed several of these chapters in their formative stages, encouraged their development, and provided much needed criticism and advice.

Part I

The Study of
Congressional Primaries

Introduction: Nomination Politics and Congressional Representation

Peter F. Galderisi, Marni Ezra,
and Michael Lyons

With few exceptions, scholars, journalists, and political professionals concur that presidential primary elections have had a profound impact on the U.S. political system. As a result, presidential nominations have received substantial attention from academics. Congressional primary elections, however, have received much less academic attention, and much less is understood about their broader effects.

The chapters in this book explore the ways in which congressional primaries appear to be changing congressional elections, congressional politics, and U.S. politics in general. They examine how congressional primaries influence the types of candidates who run in general elections, the support those candidates receive, the positions they take, the resources they spend, the media coverage they receive, and the kinds of party nominees that prevail. The chapters consider the ramifications of congressional primaries for voters, the political parties, interest groups, and the day-to-day representation of constituents by congressional incumbents. They suggest that as with presidential primaries, congressional primaries appear to promote the politics of individualism, fragmenting the Congress and reshaping the political parties into institutions that have renewed themselves by learning to serve the individual members of Congress and the candidates.

THE CHALLENGE OF CONGRESSIONAL PRIMARY RESEARCH

Past neglect of congressional primaries seems to result largely from the methodological difficulties associated with the analysis of congressional nominations and from the perception that these contests are unimportant politically because they are seldom competitive.

Many of the methodological difficulties emanate from the innumerable varia-tions in state primary election laws and political party rules. These variations make simple yet consistent classifications of data difficult, and frequently they result in contradictory state-to-state comparisons. The analysis of congressional primaries also involves the location, collection, and coding of staggering quantities of elec-tion-related data from many different sources—vote tallies, contribution listings, party operatives, and interest-group activists, to name just a few. The contributors to this book tackle many of these difficulties, bringing to light analyses based on complex and time-consuming collection of data from sources not easily found or, previous to their efforts, not even in existence.

This book also challenges the perception that congressional primaries are of little significance because they are seldom competitive. The recent evolution of the presidential nominating system demonstrates why this perception may be flawed. Since 1980, and especially since 1992, presidential primaries have be-come progressively less competitive. The earlier presidential primaries have re-mained fairly competitive; but the later primaries are sometimes not contested at all, as large candidate fields have narrowed rapidly in the first two months of the primary season (2000 being no exception). Often, the later primaries have amounted to little more than formalities necessitated by the parties' national convention rules.

Nonetheless, the *existence* of these later, noncompetitive primaries continues to shape the character of the nominating process. The early primaries, and the campaigning that occurs for months prior to these primaries, have come to as-sume so much importance because they establish perceptions of *potential* candi-date strength over the long haul in all the states. To win the nominations, candi-dates must still demonstrate convincingly that they *could* build the organizations, acquire the resources, establish the credibility, contend with the media, and con-nect with the voters to win in a large number of seriously contested primaries over many months, *if* they needed to. The later primaries still matter; what has changed is that they are now decided largely on the basis of expectations, long before any votes are cast.

The chapters presented here make comparable claims about congressional primaries. They suggest that regardless of whether congressional primaries are competitive, the *existence* of these primaries is something that cannot be ignored by incumbents, potential candidates, the parties, or interest groups. For example, consider how the existence of congressional primaries may change the perspec-tives of incumbents. Although losing a primary may be a remote concern for most incumbents, it is probably safe to assume that they would prefer not to be chal-lenged at all. Incumbents can ward off potential primary challenges just as they protect themselves against opposition party challenges—by appearing so formi-dable politically that a challenge seems hopeless. But creating the appearance of invincibility turns into a more complicated task when an incumbent must con-sider a primary in addition to a general election. The incumbent will need to maintain a voting record that is defensible in a low-turnout, intraparty election. Relationships between the incumbent and ideological interest groups within the party coalition will require more attention. And stockpiling a large campaign fund reserve will become an even more pressing concern than it is with only a general election to finance.

Consider also the existence of primaries in relation to congressional recruitment. Given that congressional incumbents almost never lose their seats in primaries, one might conclude superficially that primaries are not having a huge effect on recruitment. But contests involving incumbents have become a relatively minor component of new-member recruitment in the U.S. Congress. Most new members win their first election in an open-seat race. Whether a particular open-seat primary ultimately proves to be competitive, the *existence* of a primary will influence individual decisions to seek a party nomination—it will encourage candidates who have name recognition or a strong base of ideological support, and it will discourage those who lack access to financial resources. A caucus system might often produce similar nominees, but it might also be more friendly, for example, to those with ties to party officeholders and their organizations.

We mean not to imply by any of this that contested congressional primaries are not an extremely important part of the analyses presented in this book. Though relatively few in number, competitive congressional primaries appear to have consequences disproportionate to their number. Events that occur during these primary elections carry over to the general elections. The expenditure of resources during primaries, the media coverage received, and the involvement of interest groups can influence a candidate's ability to win the general election. In addition, the issue positions taken during the primary season (or, strategically, before) may have long-term consequences for congressional representation. When candidates shift their positions in order to win the party nomination, they may be less able to reposition themselves before the general election. As a result, it is possible that they remain in these more extreme positions even after they arrive in Washington.

PRIMARY COMPETITIVENESS AND ELECTION OUTCOMES

The ways in which primaries impact electoral outcomes in the U.S. House and Senate have been studied from a variety of perspectives, most of which, until recently, have focused on the question of primary competitiveness and its effects on a candidate's chances of winning the general election.

Political scientists have tried to determine what causes certain candidates and not others to receive primary challenges. What district, party, and candidate characteristics increase the likelihood that a candidate will face primary opposition? Central to this inquiry is the status of the incumbent in the district.[1] Taken together, these studies show that both the existence of an incumbent and the vulnerability of the incumbent are important factors in determining primary competition. In both open-seat districts and districts where an incumbent is perceived to be vulnerable, the number of challengers as well as the quality of those challengers will increase.

In addition, scholars have examined the role of partisan strength in districts to determine whether those districts dominated by one party receive more or less competition than those with two-party competition.[2] They find that in districts with a dominant party, candidates in the dominant party's primary receive stiffer competition than those of the minority party. Further, in states with two-party competition, there is typically greater competition in the general election than in the primary election of either party.

In a second line of inquiry, commonly referred to as the divisive primary literature, there has been less agreement as to the consequences of being opposed in a primary election. Many of these studies examine different offices, in different election years, using different methodologies, leading to divergent conclusions. As one might expect, the impact of divisiveness will not be the same for all types of offices or all types of candidates. Much of the disagreement may be due simply to different categories of candidates under examination. For those offices where well-known candidates challenge the incumbent (typically presidential, gubernatorial, and many senatorial contests), divisive primaries show mixed results, some finding positive carryover effects, some negative, and others none at all.[3]

However, in House contests in which the challenger is frequently unknown in the district, previous works largely show that challengers who are opposed in the primary either benefit from it[4] or are not affected by it.[5] Incumbents, conversely, are either harmed by primary competition[6] or unaffected by it.[7] These studies provide compelling evidence that primary competition has substantial influence on House contests, and it differs in its impact on incumbents and challengers.

The third collection of inquiries looks more specifically at the ways in which candidates might be harmed or helped by divisive primaries. They extend the second group of studies by looking more closely at voters and activists to ascertain the ways in which campaigns are affected by contentious nomination battles. Instead of examining aggregate vote shares, these studies typically utilize individual level analyses that explore how divisive primaries can harm particular campaigns.

Specifically, party activists who support the losing primary candidate are less likely to campaign for and vote for their party's nominee in the general election,[8] although it is difficult to conclude that their support could always have been expected had no primary taken place.[9] They develop candidate-centered loyalties that are not necessarily transferrable to another candidate from their own party. In addition, voters who supported primary losers feel alienated and are more likely to abstain from voting in the general election or to defect to the opposite party.[10]

OVERVIEW OF THE CHAPTERS

The chapters in this book present some of the latest research and findings on congressional primaries. They update the previous literature, but more important, they go beyond that literature in an attempt to better understand the political and institutional dynamics that determine how primaries, general elections, and popular representation are linked. Using original data sets, many of the chapters explore aspects of primary elections that have been previously neglected in the congressional elections literature.

The congressional election literature focuses almost exclusively on the causes and the consequences of general election results. Yet, as with the presidential arena, primary elections set the stage for the events that unfold during the general election. To win their party's nomination, candidates take ideological and policy positions that may need to be altered to win over voters outside the partisan base. Candidates expend resources on the primary that may be better used for the general election. And candidates receive publicity, both positive and negative, as a result of their primary involvement. All of these affect not only the field on which general elections are played, but also the representational ability of the candidates who win those and the preceding primary elections.

In chapter two, Peter Galderisi and Marni Ezra historically examine the way in which primary elections developed for U.S. House races and the rules and regulations under which primaries are governed. These guidelines differ among the states as a result of their constitutional right to control the "time and place of elections." Significantly, the introduction of the direct primary and its format were not always premised on a progressive urge to reform but, intentionally or not, may have played to the advantage of established party organizations and the dominance of the two-party system.

In part two of the book, Nomination Players, Politics, and Outcomes, four chapters discuss a number of ways that primary elections influence general election contests. Each chapter stresses that what occurs in the general election must be examined in relation to the nomination contest that preceded it. From the decision to run for office, to the money spent to win, the primary's impact does not end with the nomination.

Drawing on data from the Candidate Emergence Study, in chapter three Sandy Maisel and Walter Stone examine the extent to which the existence of a two-stage election process deters many strong potential candidates for the House. They find that the existence of a primary election does in fact negatively impact some potential candidates' views of the likelihood that they will run in the short term.

Using original interview data of primary election candidates and campaign managers, in chapter four Marni Ezra shows that candidates' prospects for the general election can be both helped and harmed by primary competition. Unlike much previous work that found that primary competition detracted from the chances of success in the general election, Ezra shows the different ways that candidates, especially challengers, can also be helped by these competitive contests.

In chapter five, Jay Goodliffe and David Magleby specifically explore spending patterns in primary elections. Using data from the Federal Election Commission, they compare primary spending for different types of candidates. Similar to other work in this area, they find that primary spending helps challengers and that greater competition leads to greater levels of spending.

John Green looks at the involvement and the success of the Christian Right in primary nominations in chapter six. The Christian Right, he finds, is most likely to support primary challenges to incumbents who are out of step with the cultural conservatism of the district. Conversely, the movement rallies to support its friendly incumbents when they face a challenge.

In part three, The Politics of Representation—Primaries and Polarization, four chapters link primary nominations to the politics of representation. Through roll call votes, measures of congressional ideology, and examination of nomination rules, primary elections are associated with ideological positions that members take once elected to office. In many cases, the ideological positions of candidates selected by voters are influenced by the state's election laws. Primary election rules may have consequences that are both unintended and unanticipated by those who created them.

In chapter seven, Barry Burden examines the role that primary elections play in maintaining congressional polarization by shifting party nominees to the extremes of the ideological spectrum. Unlike what we would expect from the Downsian model, Burden shows that candidates do not completely converge after winning their primaries, leaving the House of Representatives more polarized than it would be without primary contests.

In chapter eight, Kristin Kanthak and Rebecca Morton explore how nomination rules may influence U.S. House contests. They show that open primary systems appear to benefit moderate U.S. House candidates, though not in a simple or linear fashion. Significant differences exist between candidates chosen in semi-open primaries and pure open ones, with the latter generally producing candidates with the most extreme positions.

In chapter nine, Thomas Brunell and Bernard Grofman search for a similar relationship between the type of primary in a state and the partisan composition of that state's U.S. Senate delegation. They conclude that states with closed primaries are more likely to have divided party control in their delegations. They also find that states with closed primaries are more likely than states with open primaries to have Senators who diverge ideologically.

Finally, in chapter ten, Elisabeth Gerber analyzes California's new blanket primary and finds significant differences between the new and the old systems. She shows that the blanket primary results in low but sometimes significant crossover voting, that it lowers competition in primaries for the House, and that it is advantageous to moderate candidates.

Taken together these chapters stimulate new lines of research and thinking about congressional primary elections. The contributors attempt to move away from the standard "divisive primary" research that has dominated the discipline to address some of the fundamental linkages and assumptions of that research. They also seek to move the discussion of nominations from the presidential to the congressional level. Extending the standard analysis of electoral politics widely discussed at the presidential and the general election levels, the chapters explore the role of primary election rules, nomination finances, interest group activity, and ideological polarization in changing the dynamics of partisan discourse. They force us to reevaluate the importance of a nominating process that has developed over a century, that helps to define the final general election outcomes, and that influences representation in our democratic regime.

NOTES

1. Julius Turner, "Primary Elections as the Alternative to Party Competition in 'Safe' Districts," *Journal of Politics* 25 (1953): 197–210. Harvey L. Schantz, "Contested and Uncontested Primaries for the U.S. House," *Legislative Studies Quarterly* 4 (1980): 545–62. Richard Born, "The Influence of House Primary Election Divisiveness on General Election Margins, 1962–1976," *Journal of Politics* 43 (1981): 640–61. Paul S. Herrnson and James G. Gimpel, "District Conditions and Primary Divisiveness in Congressional Elections," *Political Research Quarterly* 48, no. 1 (1995): 117–34.

2. Born, "The Influence of House Primary Election Divisiveness." Schantz, "Contested and Uncontested," 1980. William H. Standing and James A. Robinson, "Inter-Party Competition and Primary Contesting: The Case of Indiana," *American Political Science Review* 48 (1954). Turner, "Primary Elections."

3. Andrew Hacker, "Does a 'Divisive' Primary Harm a Candidate's Election Chances?" *American Political Science Review* 59 (1965): 105–10. James E. Pierson and Terry B. Smith, "Primary Divisiveness and General Election Success: A Re-examination," *Journal of Politics* 37 (1975): 555–62. Robert A. Bernstein, "Divisive Primaries Do Hurt: U.S. Senate Races, 1956–1972," *American Political Science Review* 71 (1977): 540–55. Patrick Kenney and T. W. Rice, "The Effect of Primary Divisiveness in Gubernatorial and Senatorial Elections," *Journal of Politics* 46 (1984): 904–15. Patrick Kenney. "Sorting Out the Effects of Primary Divisiveness in Congressional and Senatorial Elections," *Western Political Quarterly* 41 (1988): 765–77. Patrick Kenney and T. W. Rice, "The Effect of Contextual Forces on Turnout in Congress and Primaries," *Social Sciences Quarterly* 67 (1986): 329–36. James I. Lengle, Diana Owen, and Molly W. Sonner, "Divisive Nominating Mechanisms and Democratic Party Electoral Prospects," *Journal of Politics* 57, no. 2 (1995): 370–83. Walter J. Stone, Lonna Rae Atkeson, and Ronald B. Rapoport, "Turning On or Turning Off?" Mobilization and Demobilization Effects of Participation in Presidential Nomination Campaigns, *American Journal of Political Science* 36, no. 3, (1992): 665–91.

4. R. Michael Alvarez, David T. Canon, and Patrick Sellers, "The Impact of Primaries

on General Election Outcomes in the U.S. House and Senate," Social Science Working Paper #932: California Institute of Technology, 1995. Born, "The Influence of House Primary Election Divisiveness." Marni Ezra, "The Benefits and Burdens of Congressional Primary Elections" (unpublished dissertation, American University, 1996). Peter F. Galderisi, "Is the Direct Primary a Threat to Party Maintenance? The Divisive Primary Revisited, Again" (paper delivered at the annual meeting of the Midwest Political Science Association, Milwaukee, April 28–May 1, 1982). Paul S. Herrnson, *Congressional Elections: Campaigning at Home and in Washington* (Washington, D.C.: Congressional Quarterly Press, 1995).

5. Kenney, "Sorting Out the Effects of Primary Divisiveness."

6. Alvarez, Canon, and Sellers, "The Impact of Primaries on General Election Outcomes." Born, "The Influence of House Primary Election Divisiveness." Ezra, "The Benefits and Burdens." Galderisi, "Is the Direct Primary a Threat?" 1982. Herrnson, *Congressional Elections.*

7. Kenney, "Sorting Out the Effects of Primary Divisiveness." Mark C. Westlye, "The Effects of Primary Divisiveness on Incumbent Senators, 1968–1984" (paper presented at the annual meeting of the American Political Science Association, New Orleans, 1985).

8. Walter J. Stone, "Prenomination Candidate Choice and General Election Behavior: Iowa Presidential Activists in 1980," *American Journal of Political Science* 28 (1984): 361–78. Walter J. Stone, "The Carryover Effect in Presidential Elections," *American Political Science Review* 80, no. 1 (1986): 271–78. E. H. Buell Jr. "Divisive Primaries and Participation in Fall Presidential Campaigns: A Study of the 1984 New Hampshire Primary Activists," *American Politics Quarterly* 14 (1986): 376–90. Donald Bruce Johnson and James R. Gibson, "The Divisive Primary Revisited: Party Activists in Iowa," *American Political Science Review* 68 (1974): 67–77. John Comer, "Another Look at the Effects of the Divisive Primary," *American Politics Quarterly* 4, no. 1 (1976): 121–28.

9. Galderisi, "Is the Direct Primary a Threat?" William G. Mayer, *The Divided Democrats: Ideological Unity, Party Reform, and Presidential Elections* (Boulder, Colo. Westview, 1996).

10. Priscilla L. Southwell, "The Politics of Disgruntlement: Nonvoting and Defection among Supporters of Nomination Losers, 1968–1984," *Social Science Journal* 8, no. 1 (1986): 81–95. James I. Lengle, "Divisive Presidential Primaries and Party Electoral Prospects, 1932–1976," *American Politics Quarterly* 8, no. 3 (1980): 261–77.

2

Congressional Primaries in Historical and Theoretical Context

Peter F. Galderisi and Marni Ezra

Much has been written about the creation, the use, and the changing conditions of presidential primaries in the modern era. Initially, however, the use of the direct primary in the presidential contest was limited. Only twenty states held presidential primaries in 1916, fifteen on average for the next several decades.[1] Although important in demonstrating popular support to the party bosses that controlled large numbers of convention delegates (John Kennedy, for example, needed to win the West Virginia primary in order to prove his vote-gaining potential among non-Catholic voters), primary wins would do little to guarantee a candidate's eventual nomination. Prior to 1972, primary states never contributed a majority of delegates, and in certain states and times, primary votes were purely advisory in nature. The importance of the presidential primary is only a function of the last quarter of the twentieth century.

The popularity of primaries at the presidential level, however, postdates their continuous use in state and local elections, including contests for the U.S. Congress. By the 1890s, a series of states had enacted mandatory primary election procedures, but, like several registration laws that preceded them, these usually applied only to urban areas, where progressive reformers—and rural legislators—felt the opportunities for corruption were greatest.[2] The 1898 Ohio statute, for example, regulated behavior only in those counties that happened to include the cities of Cincinnati and Cleveland. Similarly, a Massachusetts statute set standards to be applied only in Boston. By 1917, almost every state required primary activity for major party offices and for at least some statewide offices.[3] By the middle of the twentieth century, almost all congressional nominations followed this path.

THE HISTORY OF PRIMARY REFORM—NORTH AND SOUTH

Changes in party nomination procedures developed simultaneously across the nation but advanced for somewhat different reasons in the North and the South. In much of the North, the direct primary was encouraged by the Progressives, who were fighting for a variety of reform policies in the late 1800s and early 1900s that would result in a more open governmental system, one free of party bosses, patronage, and political pressure. The initiation of the Australian ballot in the early twentieth century by several states prompted an increased promotion of primary reform. For some Progressives, freeing the electorate from party-controlled balloting procedures would do little good if the choices were still limited by party organizations.[4] In addition, because the legislation that prompted a shift to a secret ballot often recognized political parties as legal entities, greater control over the internal affairs of the now institutionalized party organizations was deemed necessary. Because states took over creation of the general election ballot, they also had the means and the motive to regulate the rules governing ballot access.[5]

In general, early advocates of nomination reform in the North viewed the direct primary as a method of controlling the corrupting influences of the urban political machine. The Progressives pointed to widespread abuses that took place under the convention system, including bribery, disorder, and manipulation.[6] One reformer contended that removing the nominating decision from a boss-controlled convention would "lead to a better class of public men in office."[7] The New York Citizens Union felt that, among other things, the direct primary would substitute "responsibility to the enrolled voters for responsibility to machine bosses" and would make the "exercise of corrupt influence over the nominating process more difficult."[8]

Robert La Follette perhaps best summed up the Progressive view toward primary reform:

> Put aside the caucus and convention. They have been and will continue to be prostituted to the service of corrupt organizations. They answer no purpose further than to give respectable form to political robbery. Abolish the caucus and the convention. Go back to the first principles of democracy; go back to the people. Substitute for both the caucus and the convention a primary election . . . where the citizen may cast his vote directly to nominate the candidate of the party with which he affiliates.[9]

That a change in the rules of the nomination process might ease the entry of the reformers into positions of power within the very party organizations they were attacking was not entirely an unintended consequence of the legislation. In Idaho, attempts at opening the nominating process were in reality designed to increase the foothold of Progressive elements within the state's Republican apparatus.[10] Similarly, La Follette's espousal of primary reform was perhaps not totally unaffected by his perception of the primary as a vehicle for his own political advancement.[11] Even at the presidential level, Theodore Roosevelt and his supporters worked diligently to have direct primary legislation enacted in as many states as possible in order to wrest control of the Republican Party from William Howard Taft.[12]

While the progressive path to reform proceeded quickly in much of the North and West, it failed to strike as responsive a chord in the South. In the states of the old Confederacy, direct primaries were seen mainly as a device to ensure continued political domination by one party–the Democrats.[13]

Certainly, primary reform in much of the South could be seen as an attempt to restore some form of popular government to individuals in one-party states. Choices made by party elites at Democratic Party conventions were tantamount to general election victory because only one candidate usually had any chance of success. As V. O. Key wrote, "The adoption of the direct primary struck down the intermediate links between the rank and file of the party and the would-be-candidates and permitted a direct expression by the voter of his preferences for party nominations."[14] Yet it was clear that as political battles would be fought in the Democratic primary, the political voice of minority-party voters would be effectively removed. According to partisan advocates in the South, "Deciding party nominations in semipublic primaries rather than in backroom caucuses would legitimate the nominees, settle intraparty differences before the general election, and greatly reduce the power of opposition voters—most often, Negroes—by confronting them with a solid Democratic party."[15] The outcomes of primary contests often differed little from what had existed in the past. In Virginia, for example, the direct primary helped to "forge a new political order for the Commonwealth—which was simply a more firmly entrenched version of the old political order," as anti-organizational candidates proved no match for the established machine politicians.[16]

Interestingly enough, evidence of party organizational support for the direct primary can also be found in the history of reform in the North. Active or tacit support by party regulars may have been an attempt to gain favor with an electorate increasingly suspicious of machine politics. Parties tend to become flexible when their ability to control electoral outcomes is seriously challenged. In several northern states, electoral reform quickly followed a perceived or actual threat to a party's hegemony by third-party or insurgent activity as it had in the South, where primary reform came at the height of Populist and Independent activity that "challenged Democratic hegemony with the specter of a poor white–Negro coalition."[17]

New York's history of early primary reform perhaps best captures the theme of partisan support for direct primary legislation, emanating as it did from a concern about maintaining the electoral viability of the established party organizations. In 1897, just one year after William McKinley headed a ticket that secured Republican victories throughout New York, his party lost its statewide majority and was defeated in almost every urban area. Responsibility for that defeat was due in part to William Jennings Bryan's resounding loss in 1896, after which "it became safe for dissenting Republicans to desert their party in municipal elections without fear of imperiling the gold standard or hurting the national party."[18] The major impetus for desertion, however, was a growing distaste within independent Republican ranks for Thomas Collier Platt's control of the party machinery. Most Republican leaders recognized that without this independent support, recapturing municipal office would be extremely difficult, and so they followed Governor Frank S. Black's advice that "those of us who are pretty strong partisans and sensible at the same time can perform a great service by yielding a little wherever possible."[19] Following extensive and sometimes successful challenges by independent candidates in the spring elections of 1898, the Republican leadership pushed through the legislature the state's first thorough reform of the nomination process.

Belated adoption of primary reform in New York was not limited to the Republican organization, as Democrats discovered a similar need to address Progressive concerns. The additional reforms that Republican Governor Charles Evans Hughes had unsuccessfully promoted were, for the most part, finally carried by the support of the Democratic Tammany machine after it had suffered serious setbacks in the 1909 New York municipal elections. The machine's attentiveness to reform increased "as journals stepped up their attacks on a reactionary Tammany Hall, and as the number of Socialists multiplied on the street corners of New York distributing revolutionary literature among Tammany's constituents."[20] Al Smith perhaps best captured the mood of the New York City Democratic organization when he exclaimed, "Within four hours I've become an advocate of direct primaries. Maybe I did so because I had to. But, never mind, I did so."[21] The 1911 reform bill passed in the Assembly by a vote of 76 to 51, with only six Republicans in favor, and only five New York City Democrats against. Approval in the state Senate was a similar 27 to 19.[22]

The democratization of the nominating process at this stage could have reflected merely an attempt by party leaders to salvage what organizational power they could. Yet the response to these forces of democracy was probably more than just an eleventh hour decision to accommodate reformist impulses. Primary nominations had the potential to bring independent and insurgent candidates and voters back into normal partisan channels where they would be less likely to produce victory by default for the opposition. In return, insurgent forces would be given a chance, however small, to capture the nomination of a major party and, with that nomination, the benefits of major-party candidacy.

While enhancing the attractiveness of a major-party nomination, a democratic primary system also removed a major justification for partisan infidelity. Losses would henceforth be democratically decided defeats; nominations could no longer be viewed as the machinations of backroom politicians, at least not visibly. Vanquished opponents, subsequently, could not as easily justify a decision to embark on an independent or minor-party run for office as they once could. Many states quickly formalized this rule, imposing some sort of "sore loser" provision, which prevented defeated primary contestants from running as independent or third-party candidates in the general election.[23]

In many states, the degree of third-party activity declined dramatically after the introduction of widespread primary reform. In Michigan, for example, "third parties in state and county contests practically disappeared."[24] In Indiana the degree of general election activity in congressional races, measured as both the average number of general election candidacies and the proportion of the vote cast outside the two-party system, declined precipitously after the primary rules were in force and, despite some minor variations, never again reached the levels of the pre-primary era. The return to convention nomination for statewide office after 1929 might have reactivated statewide independent organizations strong enough to field congressional candidacies, but support for those candidacies (proportion of the vote) was minimal.[25]

Of course, party officials might not have been so willing to bargain away control over the nominating process for the advantages of greater democratic legitimacy had they been concerned about losing primary battles to insurgent forces. As with acceptance of the popular election of senators,[26] partisan dedication to the democratization of the nominating process may have been premised on the notion that the established party machinery would seldom lose a contest decided by the counting of votes. Indeed, although most contemporary literature praised primary reform as a method of wrenching political power from the hands of the machine, several politicians, scholars, and journalists attacked the primary for the legitimizing influence it gave to the very machine organizations that they were trying to defeat. The direct primary was viewed as a smoke screen that allowed the party bosses to win through the rallying of their supporters the same offices that they formally controlled without the guise of democratic accountability. Robert Luce, lawyer and opponent of primary reform, noted the supporting aspects of the direct primary when he wrote:

> There can be no factions in a party where noses are counted. The minority must either acquiesce in the result, or by refusing to support the ticket nominated, become bolters. In New York County as a consequence of the official primary there has been no effective anti-Tammany organization, and while the official primary continues there can be none. . . . The opportunity of making the fight inside the primary is afforded the minority, and when the minority loses it is compelled to support the ticket nominated or repudiate the moral obligation assumed by enrolling.[27]

As was the case in much of the South, the candidates selected under new primary rules often differed little from those chosen prior to reform. After New York's primary act of 1898, opponents of the Republican machine found themselves outnumbered in most urban areas during primary balloting.[28] One observer of the aftermath of New Jersey's 1911 Geran Act summed up his bewilderment when he wrote:

> An unbiased consideration of the facts . . . leads one almost inevitably to con-
> clude that either the convention system nominated better men than ardent direct
> primary advocates maintain—men who were acceptable to the members of the
> party, or that if the convention nominees were named at the behest and under the
> domination of cliques, or special interests, as many of the direct primary devo-
> tees and others would declare . . . then the same cliques and special interests are
> largely able to control and do control the nominations at the direct primary.
> Otherwise, why do not the party voters reject the candidates who in time past
> were forced upon them by scheming politicians?[29]

When independent forces (especially those over which the party machinery could exert little control) were able to compete successfully under primary regu- lations, established partisan organizations often met the challenge by weakening or abolishing the reform. Indiana's return to a convention for statewide office was prompted by the successful use of gubernatorial primary access by the Ku Klux Klan. A bipartisan coalition in Idaho enacted a ten-year rescission of its 1910 primary act after the independent Non-Partisan League captured several Demo- cratic nominations.[30] In these instances, democratic legitimacy was not worth the almost complete loss of nomination control.

THE DIRECT PRIMARY IN THE STATES—RULES AND REGULATIONS IN THE TWENTIETH CENTURY

Though primaries in the North and the South may have developed for different combinations of reasons, in both regions primary nomination systems developed rapidly. By 1899, two-thirds of states had enacted some kind of direct primary law. No state, however, had passed a mandatory statewide act. As the nineteenth century drew to a close, the days of optional primary laws were numbered, and states began to establish minimum mandatory regulations over primary elections in exchange for government's recognition of major-party candidates.[31]

Wisconsin, a progressive stronghold, passed the first compulsory, comprehen- sive primary law in 1902 (put into effect in 1903) and was quickly followed by many other states (see table 2.1). By 1917, thirty-two of the forty-four direct primary states had mandatory, legally regulated direct primaries covering all nomi- nations for statewide office.[32] By 1924, all eleven southern states had enacted some form of statewide direct primary laws. Primaries were funded with public money on a fixed date, though the date varied by state.

By the end of World War II, all but three states had incorporated the use of the direct primary. Since World War II, there have been two trends regarding the use of the direct primary. First, there was an expansion of the direct primary to the few remaining holdout states (as well as the new states of Alaska and Hawaii). Second, there was a growing use of preprimary endorsing conventions by parties.[33] Currently primary elections are used in some form by all fifty states to nominate candidates in statewide races and are used in most states (plus the District of Columbia) for presidential nominations.[34]

VARIATION AMONG STATE PRIMARY ELECTION RULES

Although the majority of states instituted their primary systems at approximately the same time, the specifics of primary law differ in many respects. Elections for the House of Representatives are considered federal elections, subject to regulations under federal law. House primaries, however, are predominantly regulated by state law, though federal law continues to regulate primary election campaign

Table 2.1: Development of Statewide Mandatory Primary Election Laws in the United States

Year	State(s)
1903	Wisconsin
1904	Oregon, Alabama
1905	Texas, Montana
1906	Louisiana, Pennsylvania, Mississippi
1907	Iowa, Nebraska, Missouri, North Dakota, South Dakota, Washington
1908	Illinois, Kansas, Oklahoma, Ohio
1909	Arizona, Arkansas, California, Idaho, Michigan, Nevada, New Hampshire, Tennessee
1910	Colorado, Maryland
1911	Maine, Massachusetts, New Jersey, Wyoming
1912	Kentucky, Minnesota, Virginia
1913	Florida, New York, Delaware
1915	Indiana, North Carolina, South Carolina, Vermont, West Virginia
1933	Georgia
1937	Utah
1947	Rhode Island
1953	New Mexico
1955	Connecticut
1960	Alaska
1970	Hawaii

Source: C.E. Merriam and L. Overacker. *Primary Elections* (Chicago: University of Chicago Press, 1928), 61–64 and the election laws of the fifty states.

finance. Legal authority for deciding the type and the date of primary elections, endorsement, and runoff procedures resides with the states and is greatly affected by the strength of political parties in each state.

The structure of an electoral system and the rules that elections must follow dramatically impact election outcomes. Rules influence who participates, when they participate, and how frequently they participate. Primary election rules vary widely among the states. The rest of this chapter discusses the different rules that govern congressional primaries, including endorsement procedures, primary dates, and runoff procedures. Primary types—open, closed, and blanket—are discussed in detail in subsequent chapters.

Endorsement Procedures

Though direct primaries were becoming institutionally entrenched, political party activists did not easily cede their nominating power to the rank and file. In many states, parties attempted to control the nominating process through a system of sometimes formal and sometimes informal endorsement procedures. Party activists preferred to have preprimary endorsing conventions because they enabled the activists to retain more control over which candidates are placed on the ballot. Endorsement systems still exist in many states and can impact a candidate's chance of nomination in some states.

The manner by which candidates get on the primary election ballot has important implications for their chances of winning the primary. If a state has rules that legally allow a political party to endorse candidates, thereby barring nonendorsed candidates or making ballot access for them more difficult, endorsed candidates will have an advantage over and will be challenged less frequently than candidates who do not receive legally binding party endorsements.[35]

Preprimary party-endorsement rules and norms vary greatly from state to state, with some states having no endorsement system at all and others having either legally mandated or informal endorsement procedures. Currently, seventeen states have either legal or informal endorsements at preprimary nominating conventions.[36] Nine states have legal party-endorsement provisions whereby states have party conventions that substantially impact a candidate's ability to get access to the ballot (see table 2.2). If a party formally endorses candidates, they can be given preferences over other candidates in access to and position on the ballot. Those candidates who do not get endorsed or do not meet other requirements can be denied access. With informal endorsements, which occur in eight states, candidates have no advantage in getting on the ballot and improving their ballot position; but they may gain in other ways, such as improving their financial viability. The actions taken by the party in endorsing candidates have no official role in the primary process.

Table 2.2: States with Statutory Party Endorsement Systems

State	*Ballot Provisions*
Colorado	Candidates qualify for the ballot by getting 30 percent of the delegates' votes at the convention. If no candidate receives 30 percent, the top two vote getters advance to the primary election. Candidates can also obtain access by petition. Candidates appear on ballot in order of vote at convention.
Connecticut	Candidates qualify for the ballot only by getting 20 percent on the ballot at the convention. Nonendorsed candidates can only challenge the endorsed candidate if they have received 20 percent of the vote at the convention.
Iowa	A post-primary convention selects the nominee when no candidate receives 35 percent of the vote in the primary.
New Mexico	Candidates qualify for the ballot by getting 20 percent on a single ballot; others qualify by petition but must first seek endorsement.
New York	The candidate who gets a majority of the vote is the party-designated candidate. Other candidates qualify for the ballot by getting 25 percent on any ballot at the convention. Other candidates qualify by petition.
North Dakota	Endorsed candidates at the convention qualify for the ballot. Others qualify by petition.
Rhode Island	The endorsed candidate qualifies for the ballot and is listed first. Other candidates qualify by petition.
Utah	Only endorsed candidates qualify for the ballot. The convention must endorse two candidates, unless one candidate gets 70 percent.
Virginia	The political party's executive committee can substitute a convention for a primary election.

Source: Malcolm Jewell, *Parties and Primaries: Nominating State Governors* (New York: Praeger, 1984); Alexander Bott, *Handbook of United States Election Laws and Practices* (New York: Greenwood, 1990). Petition requirements vary by state.

As shown in table 2.2, there is considerable variance among the eight states that have legal endorsement provisions. Connecticut, the last state to accept the direct primary party and a state with strong political parties and two-party competition, developed a system called the "challenge primary." In Connecticut, endorsed candidates will clearly have a less contentious primary field than candidates from states that give no advantage to party-endorsed candidates. Candidates who fail to receive 20 percent from the party convention are denied access to the ballot. Similarly in Utah, only endorsed candidates can obtain access to the primary ballot, though the party must endorse two candidates unless one obtains 70 percent of the convention vote.

Many of the other states with legal party-endorsement procedures give access to nonendorsed candidates through the use of the petition and are not as strict as either Connecticut or Utah. Endorsed candidates face a variety of advantages, including top positioning on the ballot and the legitimacy of being the official party nominee.

Existing scholarship indicates that endorsements usually reduce primary competition in gubernatorial, Senate, and House contests. In gubernatorial races from 1950 to 1982, endorsements seemed to reduce primary competition.[37] Jewell[38] found that primaries were contested 42.3 percent of the time in races in which one candidate received a legal endorsement from his or her political party. Races were contested 65.7 percent of the time when one candidate received an informal endorsement. In all northern states' primaries, contested races occurred 77.5 percent of the time. Maisel et al. reported similar results for gubernatorial and senatorial contests in 1994 and 1996.[39] For House races, the results vary: formal and informal party endorsements played a significant role in reducing competition for nomination against incumbents but seemed to have had no discernible effect in open-seat races.[40]

Dates of Primaries

States have extremely different practices when it comes to primary election dates. Congressional primaries typically cover a seven-month time span, beginning in early March and ending in early October. The placement of the primary in the election cycle is important to several different aspects of a candidate's campaign. It affects when candidates need to declare their candidacy (as much as four months before the primary) and when the candidate must set up his or her campaign headquarters and begin campaigning. It also affects when the candidate's general election campaign can begin. If the primary date is late and the primaries in a district are very competitive, candidates will be unsure of who their general-election opponent will be.

Rules also vary as to whether the primary takes place on the same day as the presidential primary, dramatically altering turnout expectations, or whether it takes place on a date different from that of the presidential primary. Table 2.3 shows that only twenty states have their congressional and presidential primaries on the same dates. Kenney and Rice have found that when the date of a congressional primary overlaps with the presidential primary, turnout is significantly higher than in states where the congressional and the presidential primaries occur on separate days.[41] They conclude that primary "turnout depends on time, place, and circumstances."[42] It would also be expected that congressional primary turnout should

Table 2.3: Primary Election Dates by State in 2000

State	Congressional Primary Date	Presidential Primary/ Caucus Date
California	March 7	March 7
Maryland	March 7	March 7
Ohio	March 7	March 7
Mississippi	March 14	March 14
Texas	March 14	March 14
Illinois	March 21	March 21
Pennsylvania	April 4	April 4
Indiana	May 2	May 2
North Carolina	May 2	May 2
Nebraska	May 9	May 9
West Virginia	May 9	May 9
Oregon	May 16	May 16
Arkansas	May 23	May 23
Idaho	May 23	May 23
Kentucky	May 23	May 23
Alabama	June 6	June 6
Iowa	June 6	January 24 (caucus)
Montana	June 6	June 6
New Jersey	June 6	June 6
New Mexico	June 6	June 6
South Dakota	June 6	June 6
Maine	June 13	March 7
North Dakota	June 13	February 29-R; March 7-D (caucus)
South Carolina	June 13	February 19-R (primary); March 9-D (caucus)
Virginia	June 13	February 29-R (primary); June 3-D (caucus)
Utah	June 27	March 10
Georgia	July 18	March 7
Kansas	August 1	April 22-D (primary); May 25-R (caucus)
Tennessee	August 3	March 14
Colorado	August 8	March 10
Michigan	August 8	February 22-R (primary); March 11-D (caucus)
Missouri	August 8	March 7
Alaska	August 22	May 19-R; May 20-D (caucus)
Wyoming	August 22	March 10-R; March 25-D (caucus)
Oklahoma	August 22	March 14
Florida	September 5	March 14
Nevada	September 5	May 19 to May 21-D (caucus); May 25-R (caucus)
Delaware	September 9	February 5-D; February 8-R
Arizona	September 12	February 22-R; March 11-D
Connecticut	September 12	March 7

(*continued*)

Table 2.3: Primary Election Dates by State in 2000 (*continued*)

State	Congressional Primary Date	Presidential Primary/ Caucus Date
Minnesota	September 12	March 7 (caucus)
New Hampshire	September 12	February 1
New York	September 12	March 7
Rhode Island	September 12	March 7
Vermont	September 12	March 7
Wisconsin	September 12	April 4
Massachusetts	September 19	March 7
Washington	September 19	February 29
Hawaii	September 23	March 7-D; May 19-R (caucus)
Louisiana	November 7	March 14

Source: Federal Election Commission http://www.fec.gov/pages/2Kdates.htm

be higher in those states with concurrent dates that occur early in the presidential nomination season.

Runoff Elections: The "Second Primary"

Laws regarding whether a runoff election is required also vary by state. Runoff elections have been tried in seventeen states and are presently used in thirteen, mostly southern states (see table 2.4). The theoretical reasoning behind the runoff election is the democratic principle of majoritarianism. In one-party states, many candidates compete in the dominant party's primary election, frequently leading to a winner who has gained only a small fraction of the primary electorate's vote.

Runoffs were instituted for two reasons: First, runoffs became a popular option because they prevented extreme candidates from winning the party's nomination. These extreme candidates had the potential of winning a small portion of the primary vote and could win in a crowded primary field. Second, the runoff system allowed the winner to receive a majority of the dominant party's vote, thus gaining increased party legitimacy.

The potential impact that a runoff election might have on a candidate is not obvious, though it appears that runoffs may potentially harm a candidate. If one party's candidate endures a runoff while the other's does not, the candidate with the runoff will be forced to put off concentration on the general election and will need to expend resources in order to win the runoff. Incumbents rarely face a runoff election unless they are severely in trouble. Challengers who already face a mountain of difficulties in winning elective office may face additional difficulties if they face a runoff because they may emerge from the runoff sapped of resources and with little time to revive their campaign.

Table 2.4: States Using the Runoff System

State	Year of Adoption	Abandoned
Mississippi	1902	
Texas	1903	
North Carolina	1915	
South Carolina	1915	
Georgia	1917	
Louisiana	1922	
Florida	1929	
Maryland	1929	1939
Oklahoma	1929	
South Dakota*	1929	
Alabama	1931	
Arkansas	1933, 1939	1935–1938
Kentucky	1935	1936
Tennessee**	1937	
Utah	1937	1947
Virginia	1952	1969
Arizona***	1988	

Source: Charles S. Bullock III and Loch K. Johnson, *Runoff Elections in the United States* (Chapel Hill: University of North Carolina Press, 1992), 3.
*Rarely used; at times not considered a "runoff state."
**Only in the event of a tie.
***Required in general elections for selected statewide office; not used in primaries.

Bullock and Johnson examine two questions about runoff elections. First, did the candidate who led in the primary win the runoff? Second, what share of the vote did the primary leader get in the runoff? They find that runoffs are more frequent in open-seat races and in races where the status of office is higher, when there has been redistricting, and when there is not two-party competition. They also find that 70 percent of primary leaders won the runoff election. When incumbents were front runners in the primary, they won the runoff 64.7 percent of the time. Only when incumbents trailed in the first primary were they highly likely to lose the runoff. "Once again, a fuller compilation of election results shows that neither competitive runoffs nor first primaries consistently weakened nominees as they entered the general elections."[43]

CONCLUSION

The history of primary reform is as varied as the regions and the states in which it was enacted. In the North, the move from caucuses to direct primaries was an integral part of the progressive attack on machine politics, although the very machines the reforms were meant to weaken often found reason to accommodate the changes. In the South, much of the progressive impulse was subordinated to the need to maintain the hegemony of the Democratic Party. Yet, once developed, primary reform spread rapidly throughout the country. Mandatory statewide primary-election laws were enacted in all but a handful of states within a twelve-year period.

The rules governing primary elections have differed dramatically among states and across time, as have their consequences. One constant, however, remains. The direct primary has been the major path to nomination for congressional, state, and local candidates for most of the twentieth century. It will continue to help determine the course of electoral politics in the new millennium.

NOTES

Interest in primary reform stems from the doctoral research of each contributor, Dr. Galderisi's in the late 1970s, Dr. Ezra's in the mid-1990s.

1. Larry M. Bartels, *Presidential Primaries and the Dynamics of Public Choice* (Princeton, N.J.: Princeton University Press, 1988).

2. Ernst Meyer, *Nominating Systems* (Madison, Wis.: By the author, 1902).

3. Leon Epstein, *Political Parties in the American Mold* (Madison: University of Wisconsin Press, 1986), 169.

4. Meyer, *Nominating Systems.*

5. Epstein, *Political Parties.*

6. V. O. Key, *American State Politics: An Introduction* (New York: Knopf, 1956), 96.

7. Isaac M. Brickner, "Direct Primaries versus Boss Rule" (1909), in *Selected Articles on Direct Primaries*, 3d ed., C. E. Fanning (Minneapolis, Minn.: Wilson, 1911).

8. The New York Citizens Union, *Direct Primary Nominations: Why They Should Be Adopted for New York* (New York: 1909), 23.

9. Ellen Tourelle, ed., *The Political Philosophy of Robert M. La Follette as Revealed in His Speeches and Writings* (Madison, Wis.: Robert M. La Follette, Co.), 1920, 197–98.

10. Boyd A. Martin, *The Direct Primary in Idaho* (Stanford, Calif.: Stanford University Press, 1947).

11. Alan Fraser Lovejoy, *La Follette and the Establishment of the Direct Primary in Wisconsin, 1890–1904* (New Haven, Conn.: Yale University Press, 1941).

12. John Morton Blum, *The Republic Roosevelt* (New York: Atheneum, 1970).

13. Malcolm E. Jewell and David M. Olson, *Political Parties and Elections in American States*, 3d ed. (Chicago: Dorsey, 1988), 87.

14. Key, *American State Politics*, 88.

15. J. Morgan Kousser, *The Shaping of Southern Politics* (New Haven, Conn.: Yale University Press, 1974), 74.

16. Larry Sabato, *The Democratic Party Primary in Virginia* (Charlottesville: University Press of Virginia, 1977), 28.

17. Kousser, *The Shaping of Southern Politics,* 73.

18. Richard L. McCormick, *From Realignment to Reform* (Ithaca, N.Y.: Cornell University Press, 1981), 120.

19. Richard L. McCormick, "Prelude to Progressivism: The Transformation of New York State Politics, 1890–1910," *New York History* (1978): 264.

20. J. Joseph Hutmacher, "Charles Evans Hughes and Charles F. Murphy: The Metamorphosis of Progressivism," *New York History* (1965): 29.

21. Oscar Handlin, *Al Smith and His America* (Boston: Little, Brown, 1958), 45.

22. Figures are taken from the *Journal of the Assembly of the State of New York*, 134th sess., July 19, 1911; and *Journal of the Senate*, October 4, 1911.

23. At last count, almost half of all states have this sort of limitation; see Andrew Appleton and Daniel S. Ward, eds., *State Party Profiles: A 50-State Guide to Development, Organization, and Resources* (Washington, D.C.: Congressional Quarterly Press, 1997).

24. James K. Pollock, *The Direct Primary in Michigan, 1909–1935* (Ann Arbor: University of Michigan Press, 1943), 30–32.

25. Peter F. Galderisi and Benjamin Ginsberg, "Primary Elections and the Evanescence of Third-Party Activity in the United States," in *Do Elections Matter?* ed. Benjamin Ginsberg and Alan Stone (Armonk, N.Y.: M.E. Sharpe, 1986).

26. John D. Buenker, "The Urban Political Machine and the Seventeenth Amendment," *Journal of American History* 56 (1969): 305–22.

27. Robert Luce, "Does Our Ballot Law Fortify the Boss?" *State Service Magazine* (July 1918), 5.

28. McCormick, *From Realignment to Reform*, 128.

29. Ralph Simpson Boots, *The Direct Primary in New Jersey* (Ph.D. diss., Columbia University, 1917).

30. Martin, *The Direct Primary in Idaho*; Merrill D. Beal and Merle W. Wells, *History of Idaho*, vol. II (New York: Lewis, 1959).

31. Charles E. Merriam and Louise Overacker, *Primary Elections* (Chicago: University of Chicago Press, 1928).

32. Merriam and Overacker, *Primary Elections*.

33. Malcolm E. Jewell, *Parties and Primaries: Nominating State Governors* (New York: Praeger, 1984).

34. Three southern states, Alabama, South Carolina, and Virginia, allow parties to choose whether their candidates are nominated by primary or by convention. Only Virginia occasionally exercises this option for congressional nominations; see Alexander J. Bott, *Handbook of United States Election Laws and Practices* (New York: Greenwood, 1990).

35. Jewell, *Parties and Primaries*; Marni Ezra, "The Benefits and Burdens of Congressional Primary Elections" (Ph.D. diss., American University, and paper prepared for presentation at the annual meeting of the Midwest Political Science Association, Chicago, April 18–20, 1996).

36. States with informal endorsement procedures are California, Delaware, Illinois, Louisiana, Massachusetts, Minnesota, Ohio, and Pennsylvania; see L. Sandy Maisel, Cary T. Gibson, and Elizabeth J. Ivry, "The Continuing Importance of the Rules of the Game: Subpresidential Nominations in 1994 and 1996," in *The Parties Respond: Changes in American Parties and Campaigns*, 3d ed., L. Sandy Maisel (Boulder, Colo.: Westview, 1998).

37. Jewell, *Parties and Primaries*.

38. Jewell, *Parties and Primaries*.

39. Maisel, Gibson, and Ivry, "The Continuing Importance of the Rules of the Game."

40. Maisel, Gibson, and Ivry, "The Continuing Importance of the Rules of the Game."

41. It is not clear whether increased turnout in lower-level races results from coordination of primary dates; see Patrick Kenney and T. W. Rice, "The Effect of Contextual Forces on Turnout in Congress and Primaries," *Social Sciences Quarterly* 67 (1986): 335, and Marni Ezra, "A Reexamination of Congressional Primary Turnout," *American Politics Quarterly*, forthcoming.

42. Kenney and Rice, "The Effect of Contextual Forces," 335.

43. Charles S. Bullock III and Loch K. Johnson, *Runoff Elections in the United States* (Chapel Hill: University of North Carolina Press, 1992), 163.

Part II

Nomination Players, Politics, and Outcomes

3

Primary Elections as a Deterrence to Candidacy for the U.S. House of Representatives

L. Sandy Maisel and Walter J. Stone

Democracies, to deserve that designation, must meet certain minimal criteria. For a representative democracy to function effectively, the citizens must be able to participate in choosing who will represent them. Voting must be in secret. Citizens must be given a choice, for they cannot express a preference if only one candidate seeks their support. The election results must make a difference; if an officeholder loses, he must step down and let the winner govern. And there must be freedom of speech, of press, of assembly, and of association, so that the dialogue in a campaign is vigorous and robust.[1]

In the United States, we pride ourselves on the quality of our procedural democracy. The citizenry expresses support or disapproval of those in government and, by extension, of the policies they have adopted through the means of frequent elections. The Founders stressed the need for frequent elections as a way to control the government. The First Amendment was adopted as a guarantee of free and open debate in elections. Secrecy in the voting booth is sacrosanct. The precedent set by John Adams in leaving office after his defeat in 1800 has persisted for two centuries, with losers conceding and allowing their opponents to serve and to govern even when elections were closely contested and controversial.

However, the mere existence of frequent elections does not suffice to serve their intended purpose if those elections are not competitive, that is, unless the citizens are given a viable option to their current elected public officials, they cannot express their opinions about the actions of those who govern them. By design the American system is open enough to permit competitive elections, but the reality of the electoral process in many cases differs from what procedural democracy seems to guarantee.

29

In point of fact, when one examines elections to the U.S. House of Representatives, one concludes that incumbents seeking reelection face very little competition. Incumbent advantage has been discussed frequently in the political science
literature.[2] It is not our intention to repeat those arguments here. But we cannot
resist highlighting that the extent of that advantage, as it was revealed in the 1998
House elections, led to noncompetitive elections: 98.5 percent of the incumbents
seeking reelection did so successfully; only 30 incumbents (out of nearly 400
seeking reelection) polled less that 55 percent of the vote; 39 polled more than 75
percent of the votes cast in their district; and an additional 94 ran without any
major-party competition at all.

The data provided in the previous paragraph refer to the 1998 general election.
But that tells only part of the story. The electoral process in the United States is
a two-step process, with primary elections to determine party nominees preceding the general election. Congressional districts can be arrayed according to how
strongly they lean toward one party or the other. In heavily Democratic or heavily
Republican districts, one would not assume that much competition would be found
in the general election. Republicans generally dominate elections in the conservative rural districts in Kansas or Oklahoma; Democrats rarely lose seats in the
central-city districts of New York or Los Angeles. In those districts, however,
competition might still be found in the primary election. In more competitive
districts—districts in which the partisan balance is more even—the general election should be more hotly contested. But primaries still offer citizens another
opportunity for choice.[3]

In this chapter, we intend to go back a step in the process from the general
elections, which are so often studied, to the primary elections, which are often
ignored by analysts. In an earlier time, political party officials were assigned the
task of ensuring that their party ran candidates for all offices on the ballot. Little
is known about how party officials performed this task, but it is known that rank-
and-file voters had little say. As part of the Progressive era reforms, the direct
primary election was instituted as a means to provide intraparty democracy and
to permit competition. The task of choosing party candidates was removed from
the hands of party officials and was given to party members themselves.[4]

Political party leaders also lost some of their ability to recruit candidates for
office as a result of the institution of direct primary elections. Whereas once a
strong leader could guarantee a prospective candidate a nomination, now party
leaders can only pledge to use the limited resources they have to aid such a candidate in a primary or to discourage others from running. But candidates are aware
that pledges are not guarantees and that party leaders' resources are often minimal. V. O. Key argued more than four decades ago that the direct primary hurt
party officials' ability to perform what had been their most important function in
the electoral process, guaranteeing competition in the general election.[5] In this
chapter, we explore the extent to which parties performed their function in the

1998 congressional elections and the extent to which competition existed at the primary stage in that election. We begin to examine why primary elections deter some strong potential candidates from seeking seats in Congress.

COMPETITION IN THE 1998 PRIMARY ELECTIONS

Table 3.1 shows the extent to which primary elections were contested in the 1994, 1996, and 1998 congressional elections.[6] We examine the data separately according to different levels of competition that were found in the subsequent general election. One could argue that a system produces effective competition and gives the citizenry the opportunity to express policy preferences if those seeking office must face significant opponents in either the primary or the general election or in both. Table 3.1 reveals that such competition existed in only a small percentage of the 435 congressional districts.

We report data from three elections because the contexts of these elections were quite different. In 1994, the Republicans recaptured the House for the first time in four decades. The 1996 congressional elections were held at the same time as a presidential election, and the Democrats made a major push to oust the forty-three Republicans who had first won election two years earlier. Finally in 1998, the Republicans thought that they would take advantage of a Democratic Party weakened by the scandal surrounding President Bill Clinton; but, in fact, the Democrats picked up seats in the midterm election, a rarity for a president's party.

Even though the national-election context was quite different in each case, the general pattern regarding competition is the same. Each of these elections showed relatively little competition. Although the lack of competition is evident in the general-election stage, it is especially evident in the primaries. For illustrative purposes, we discuss only the 1998 experience. First, we begin with the 94 seats in which one major party or the other did not field a candidate. Obviously no primary was held in the party failing to field a candidate. Thus, the party system failed totally in fulfilling its task of guaranteeing competition in the general election.[7]

But one could argue that the electorate had a choice if effective competition occurred in the primary in the incumbent's party. Of the 94 elected without major-party competition, 82 (87.2 percent) faced no competition in the primary either; eleven of the remaining twelve (11.7 percent) faced competition, but no candidate polled even half as many votes as the incumbent; none faced a primary opponent who came within 20 percent of the incumbent's total primary vote. Thus, it seems fair to conclude that effective competition did not exist in 93 of those 94 districts.

Let's then turn to the 304 other districts in which incumbents were seeking reelection, looking first at the ways in which those incumbents were renominated. In nearly 80 percent of those districts the incumbents were nominated without

Table 3.1: Competition in Congressional Primaries, 1994–1998

Primary Results**	Incumbents' General Election Results*		
	No Major-Party Opponent	No Serious Competition	Close Victory or Loss
1998			
Incumbents			
No primary opponent	87.2%	79.6%	76.7%
Very little competition	25.5%	16.1%	13.3%
Some competition	1.1%	3.6%	3.3%
Competitive	0.0%	0.7%	6.7%
$n =$	94	274	30
Challengers to Incumbents			
No primary opponent	0.0%	67.6%	42.9%
Very little competition	0.0%	4.6%	14.3%
Some competition	0.0%	15.1%	26.6%
Competitive	0.0%	12.7%	14.3%
$n =$	0	284	21
1996			
Incumbents			
No primary opponent	46.4%	76.7%	74.0%
Very little competition	21.4%	15.8%	11.0%
Some competition	28.6%	5.4%	12.3%
Competitive	3.6%	2.2%	2.7%
$n =$	28	279	73
Challengers to Incumbents			
No primary opponent	0.0%	61.7%	52.8%
Very little competition	0.0%	8.7%	5.7%
Some competition	0.0%	15.3%	17.0%
Competitive	0.0%	14.3%	24.5%
$n =$	0	300	53
1994			
Incumbents			
No primary opponent	61.7%	68.1%	66.2%
Very little competition	29.8%	20.1%	17.6%
Some competition	6.4%	11.0%	12.2%
Competitive	2.1%	0.8%	4.1%
$n =$	47	254	74
Challengers to Incumbents			
No primary opponent	0.0%	57.8%	26.9%
Very little competition	0.0%	4.2%	10.4%
Some competition	0.0%	20.9%	29.9%
Competitive	0.0%	17.1%	32.8%
$n =$	0	263	67

*Races were characterized as having "no serious opposition" if the incumbent polled more than 55%; challengers were characterized according to whether they polled at least 45%; some *n*s seem inconsistent because of votes for minor-party candidates.

**Candidates were deemed to have "very little competition" if they beat the nearest challenger by more than 50% of the vote; they were deemed to have "some competition" if the nearest opponent was between 20% and 50% behind the winner; they were deemed to be in a "competitive primary" if the nearest opponent came within 20% of their vote total.

primary opposition. Table 3.1 also shows the extent to which those incumbents who did face opposition in the primary were rarely seriously challenged. In fact, only one incumbent, Jay Kim (R-Calif.), lost a primary in 1998. Kim was unable to campaign for reelection because he had been convicted of illegal campaign finance practices and was forced to wear an electronic monitoring device that permitted him to be only in his home and at work in the House.

One could argue that incumbents were challenged by serious competitors but won handily because they simply were more popular than their opponents. However, this does not seem to have been the case in the 1998 primaries. Only 88 of those who challenged incumbents raised enough money to be required to file financial reports with the Federal Election Commission. In beating Kim, Gary Miller (R-Calif.) spent over $600,000 in the primary. On average, the other primary challengers to incumbents spent under $60,000. More than half of the money that these challengers to incumbents spent came from personal contributions or loans to their own campaigns. Thus, it seems clear that they did not put up much competition and that they were unable to garner financial support to carry on their challenges.[8]

What about the challengers in the general election, all but five of whom lost to these incumbents? Most of these candidates, a vast majority of whom turned out to be weak contenders in the general election, won their nominations without serious competition. More than two-thirds won nomination without the necessity of facing any competition in a primary. Another 20 percent won the nomination, without any opponent coming within 20 percent of their vote total. Only 41 of the 304 (less than 15 percent) faced serious primary competition. Again, one is led to the conclusion that competitive primaries are rare.

In fact, only in the 36 open seats in 1998 were competitive primaries even close to the norm (see table 3.2). Of the 72 major-party nominations in those districts, only slightly more than a quarter went by default, that is, without any competition. Most of those were nominations in the party that was at a serious partisan disadvantage in a district with an open seat, and most of those nominees lost badly. In one-third of the nominating contests, at least one contender was within 20 percent of the winner.[9] In these districts intraparty as well as interparty competition was found in 1998. But these certainly represent a minority of the districts in the country. The clear conclusion from tables 3.1 and 3.2 is that true competition, in primaries or in the general election, was the exception, not the rule, in the vast majority of congressional districts.

THE CANDIDATE EMERGENCE STUDY

If a healthy democracy depends on electoral competition, we have cause for concern. In nearly one-fifth of all districts in the country in the 1998 election, either absolutely no competition existed or very little competition was found. Primary elections, put in place to increase democracy and to enhance competition, rarely

Table 3.2: Competition in Congressional Primaries, 1994–1998 (Open Seats)

	1998	1996	1994
No major primary opposition	0.0%	1.9%	0.0%
No primary opponent	26.4%	17.3%	17.0%
Very little primary competition	11.1%	9.6%	4.7%
Some primary competition	29.2%	28.8%	26.4%
Competitive primary	33.3%	42.3%	51.9%
$n =$	72	104	106

have either impact. In a vast majority of the districts, primary elections are non-competitive, both for incumbents seeking reelection and for those seeking to oppose them. It is little wonder that citizen turnout for primary elections is so low. Only in the districts with open seats, and only in some of those districts, is true competition the norm in congressional primaries.

One could argue, we suppose, that no candidates run because citizens are so satisfied with those who currently hold office. But that argument fails on a number of different counts. Theoretically it fails because citizens must have the opportunity to express support for or opposition to those who govern them. Empirically it fails because we know that some incumbents who have been defeated have won previous elections with little or no opposition. In the remainder of this chapter, we explore one aspect of why so little competition exists—the deterrent effect of primary elections on strong potential candidates' decisions about running for the House of Representatives.

The data on which this analysis is based are drawn from the first surveys conducted by the Candidate Emergence Study, a long-term project the goal of which is to understand decision making by those who consider races for the House.

In order to identify a group of potential candidates for the House, we surveyed informants well positioned to provide information about potential candidates in a random sample of two hundred congressional districts. Our goal was to select ten Democrats and ten Republicans in each district. Our sample of informants was composed of delegates to the two parties' 1996 national nominating conventions and of chairs of county political party committees. If we could not reach our goal of ten from each party in a district using those populations, we sampled from the delegates to the 1992 conventions.[10] Our purpose was to use these respondents as informants about their congressional districts. Our reasoning was that convention delegates and county chairs are likely to be knowledgeable about the politics of their districts without themselves being likely candidates. We had tested this technique in an exploratory study with encouraging results.[11]

In this survey, first we asked respondents to answer questions regarding the district and the incumbent in the district. We also asked them to suggest up to four individuals who, in their estimation, would be "potentially strong candidates for the U.S. House," regardless of whether those individuals had ever shown an interest in running and/or had ever been mentioned as possible candidates. We then asked the respondents to answer a battery of questions concerning the characteristics of those whom they considered to be potentially strong candidates. Based on these questions and on the other questions that deal with the characteristics of the district, we can determine the attributes that informants view as important in determining candidate quality.

As a second stage in our research we polled the potential candidates named by our informants and all of the state legislators whose districts overlapped in sum or in part with our sampled congressional districts. We supplemented our informant-identified potential candidates with state legislators for two reasons: (1) more candidates for the House come from state legislatures than from any other single source; (2) most state legislators do not in fact run for the House, and thus we were guaranteed variance on the key dependent variable for our study, the decision to run for the House.[12]

With this survey we asked the respondents to evaluate themselves on the same battery of questions that we had used with the informants. Thus, using the Candidate Emergence Study data, we can get readings on potential candidates from two different perspectives: (1) that of a sample of the political elite in a congressional district and (2) that of those thought to be potential candidates for office themselves. We can also examine how the evaluations of state legislators (and those holding other elective offices) differ from those who were named as potentially strong candidates for office but who did not necessarily hold political office.[13] In this chapter we use data from the Potential Candidate Survey. We draw on the two data subsets that resulted from that survey—one that includes all of the named potential candidates and a second that includes all of the state legislators who responded to our survey, whether their names had been suggested by our informants or not.

The potential candidates identified by our informants scored quite high on measures of both personal characteristics (e.g., integrity, public speaking ability) and strategic characteristics (e.g., name recognition, ability to raise money). Although they did not rate as highly as the incumbents on strategic characteristics, they were consistently ranked higher than the candidates who actually ran against the incumbents in 1996; that is, the informants felt that the potential candidates they identified would have provided more competition than the incumbents actually faced in the general election. Thus, we want to explore why strong potential candidates who chose not to enter races in their districts did not run.

Our particular focus is on why potentially strong challengers did not run in contests for their party's nomination in 1998. Our goal is to understand the extent to which primary elections are a barrier to healthy electoral competition.

THE ABSENT PRIMARY CANDIDATES:
POTENTIAL CANDIDATES WHO OPTED OUT

Those who might be strong candidates for office—those identified by the informants in the Candidate Emergence Study as strong potential candidates—might opt out of running for a variety of reasons.

We theorize that the decision to run for the U.S. House of Representatives is a two-step process.[14] Step one in the process involves a general commitment to run for office; step two involves the commitment to run for a particular office in a particular year.

We analyze two subsets of data from the Potential Candidate Survey. One subset involves only state legislators. By definition, these potential candidates have cleared the first hurdle; that is, they have demonstrated a commitment to seeking elective office, and they have also demonstrated success in so doing. The second subset involves potential candidates who were identified by the Informant Survey. Some of these potential candidates have already run for (and some have won) elective office, and some have not. Of those who have not run, some feel that they might do so in the future, while others express no such interest. These data are presented in table 3.3.

For present purposes we exclude those who have no interest in running for elective office. Clearly the primary is not the only concern that keeps them from entering the fray. But we are interested in knowing more about the decision making of the rest of our respondents. This includes those who currently hold office as well as those who might seek office in the future.

Similarly, our interest in this chapter is not with those who decline to run because they fear they would lose a general election; that is, if a potential candidate thinks he or she would win the nomination easily but then lose the general election and

Table 3.3: Expressions of Interest in Holding Elective Office
(Named Potential Candidates)

	Yes (n = 241)	*No* (n = 191)
No interest		9.4%
Unlikely to seek office	0.4%	12.0%
Open to possibility but no current plans	5.8%	36.1%
Interested in seeking office	3.7%	16.2%
Actively seeking office	1.2%	25.1%
Currently hold office	88.8%	1.0%

if that potential candidate opts out of running, the primary election was not a likely factor in that candidate's decision making. From our perspective what is of interest is that there are certain candidates who have varying degrees of confidence in their ability to win the general election if they were nominated but who believe that they could not win the nomination. Our data (not reported here) show that these potential candidates overwhelmingly report that they are unlikely to run. Our assumption is that the primary is at least one of the factors that serves to deter their candidacies.

Table 3.4 presents data to demonstrate the extent to which the primary acts as a deterrent. The cell entries in the table represent percentages of the total sample. In each case more than one out of six respondents felt that they were either "likely" or "extremely likely" to win the general election if nominated but that they were either "unlikely" or "extremely unlikely" to win their party's nomination. For those potential candidates, the primary election may have had a deterrent effect. The goal then is to understand more about strong potential candidates who opt out of running in their party's primary even though they are interested in seeking elective office *and* think that they have a decent chance of winning the general election. We are assuming that consideration of the primary election was an important step in the decision making of these individuals.

Table 3.4: Potential Candidate's Perceptions of Chances in Primary and General Elections in 1998

	Perceived Chances of Winning General Election in 1998		
Perceived Chances of Winning Party Nomination in 1998	*Extremely Unlikely/ Unlikely*	*Somewhat Unlikely/ Toss-up/Somewhat Likely*	*Extremely Likely/ Likely*
Interested named potential candidates (*n* = 355)			
Extremely unlikely/Unlikely	23.9%	7.9%	16.0%
Somewhat unlikely/Toss-up/			
Somewhat likely	2.5%	7.3%	5.9%
Extremely likely/Likely	13.5%	15.2%	6.8%
State legislators (*n* = 743)			
Extremely unlikely/Unlikely	34.9%	11.5%	18.8%
Somewhat unlikely/Toss-up/			
Somewhat likely	3.2%	10.0%	5.1%
Extremely likely/Likely	4.4%	5.9%	5.8%

ANALYSIS OF THE DETERRENT EFFECT OF PRIMARIES

For this analysis, the dependent variable that concerns us is the perception that potential candidates have that they will win the party nomination if they enter the race. We are interested in understanding the effect of nomination chances because we believe that it sheds light on why primaries are a deterrent to potential candidacies. It is appropriate to summarize our argument to this point.

A number of factors might deter potential candidacies. The logical first factor would be interest in seeking public office. In our analysis, we are examining only those respondents who have an interest in holding public office. Like the lack of interest in holding public office, other factors, either personal or strategic, might deter a potential candidate from running elsewhere.[15] For instance, a potential candidate would not run if he or she felt that the House of Representatives was not the appropriate venue for attacking the problems about which that respondent was most concerned. Or a potential candidate might not run if the cost to his or her family was deemed to be too high. But factors such as these would affect the chances of running independent of whether a primary election were to be held.

Similarly, a potential candidate might opt out of running if winning the general election seemed too improbable. Again, we would argue that, in all likelihood, that conclusion would be reached independent of whether a primary election were to be held and is thus beyond our current scope.[16] Our goal is thus to isolate variables that affect the likelihood of winning the primary under the assumption that if they contributed negatively to that likelihood, they would consequently deter a potential candidate from running.

The variables that meet our criteria for relevance for primary elections are contextual variables, that is, political variables that affect the potential candidacy in a particular district. The presence of an incumbent in the potential candidate's party is an obvious factor to consider when one looks at the impact of primaries; incumbents are notoriously difficult to beat in primaries. Other district factors might also be determinative. For instance, the congruence between a potential candidate's partisanship and that of the voters in the district might help shape chances in a primary. Potential candidates who share the partisanship of the voters in the district might face more competition in a primary because the nomination is seen as being of substantial value. Those whose partisanship contrasts with the district's voters might have an easier time of winning the nomination because fewer others are likely to seek a nomination not seen as valuable.[17]

Strength of party organization in a district could also have an impact. For instance, party organization would contribute negatively were it discouraging the candidate or encouraging some other candidate. Our data set allows us to test both of these relationships.

Similarly the political views of the voters in a district, as they compare to those of the potential candidate, could have an impact. If the potential candidate perceived that his or her views were at odds with those of likely primary voters, candidacy would be discouraged. Alternatively, candidacy would be encouraged were the views seen as congruent.

Tables 3.5, 3.6, and 3.7 show the relationship between the first three of these variables and potential candidates' perceptions of their chances to win a party nomination. In each case the relationship is strong and in the expected direction.

Table 3.5 shows the effect of incumbency. If an incumbent is of the same party as the potential candidate, as is expected, the candidate sees a significantly lower likelihood of winning the party nomination. The normal explanation for this relationship is that incumbents are very strong and difficult to unseat. But table 3.6 leads us to believe that the relationship is more complex than that.

Table 3.6 shows that the more favorable the partisan environment of the district, the *lower* the potential candidate's nomination chances. This suggests that potential candidates in districts where their own party is strong see their chances of gaining the nomination as weak. At the other extreme, those candidates in districts in which the opposite party is very strong see their chances of winning their party's nomination as more likely. The reasoning is simple. If a potential candidate lives in a district that strongly favors his or her party, that party's nomination will be valuable, as it is very likely to lead to election. If the potential

Table 3.5: Potential Candidate's Perceptions of Chances of Winning the Nomination Compared with the Incumbent's Partisanship

Perceived Chances of Winning Party Nomination in 1998	Incumbent's Partisanship Compared with Potential Candidates	
	Same Party	Other Party
Interested Named Potential Candidates		
($p < .001$; Tau $c = -.515$)		
Extremely unlikely/Unlikely	72.5%	28.8%
Somewhat unlikely/Toss-up/Somewhat likely	17.4%	15.2%
Extremely likely/Likely	10.2%	56.1%
$n =$	167	198
State Legislators		
($p < .001$; Tau $c = -.254$)		
Extremely unlikely/Unlikely	75.4%	51.5%
Somewhat unlikely/Toss-up/Somewhat likely	16.3%	21.5%
Extremely likely/Likely	8.3%	27.0%
$n =$	471	307

Table 3.6: Potential Candidate's Perceived Chances of Winning the Nomination Compared with the Partisanship of the District

	Potential Candidate's Partisanship Compared with the Strength of the District's Partisanship		
Perceived Chances of Winning Party Nomination in 1998	*Very Similar*	*Neither Similar nor Dissimilar*	*Very Dissimilar*
Interested Named Potential Candidates			
($p < .001$; Tau $c = -.264$)			
Extremely likely/Unlikely	10.6%	35.4%	64.4%
Somewhat unlikely/Toss-up/			
Somewhat likely	20.0%	15.7%	13.6%
Extremely unlikely/Unlikely	69.4%	48.9%	32.0%
$n =$	85	178	103
State Legislators			
($p < .001$; Tau $c = -.104$)			
Extremely likely/Unlikely	9.4%	15.7%	39.0%
Somewhat unlikely/Toss-up/			
Somewhat likely	17.9%	18.8%	16.9%
Extremely unlikely/Unlikely	72.6%	65.6%	44.1%
$n =$	212	504	59

candidate lives in a district dominated by the other party, his or her party's nomination is much less valuable, as it is most likely to lead to defeat in the general election. The picture becomes complex because there is a high correlation between those districts in which the incumbent is of the same party as the potential candidate and those districts in which the potential candidate's party dominates the partisan scene ($r = .709$, significance $\leq .001$). Because district partisan majorities tend overwhelmingly to elect incumbents in the dominant party, it is difficult to disentangle the effects of district partisanship from incumbency. It is unclear at this point whether shared partisanship with the incumbent or affiliation with the majority party leads a potential candidate to believe that winning a nomination is not likely.

Table 3.7 shows that there is also a strong negative relationship between the strength of the potential candidate's party organization and his or her perceived chances of winning the nomination. In this case, the factor likely to be at work is that the strong party organization is backing another candidate. In many cases, this candidate is the incumbent, as the correlation between strong party organization and the incumbent being of the same party as the potential candidate is also strong ($r = .571$, significance $\leq .001$). Thus, once again the picture as to which factor is at work is less than clear.

Table 3.7: Potential Candidate's Perceived Chances of Winning the Nomination Compared with the Strength of Their Party Organization

	Strength of Potential Candidate's Party Organization		
Perceived Chances of Winning Party Nomination in 1998	*Very Strong/ Strong*	*Neither Strong nor Weak*	*Very Weak/ Weak*
Interested Named Potential Candidates			
($p < .001$; Tau $c = -.199$)			
Extremely likely/Likely	18.4%	40.6%	49.2%
Somewhat unlikely/Toss-up/			
Somewhat likely	16.7%	16.7%	13.6%
Extremely unlikely/Unlikely	64.9%	42.7%	37.3%
$n =$	114	192	59
State Legislators			
($p < .001$; Tau $c = -.097$)			
Extremely likely/Likely	11.5%	16.6%	33.3%
Somewhat unlikely/Toss-up/			
Somewhat likely	17.8%	20.1%	7.7%
Extremely unlikely/Unlikely	70.7%	63.2%	59.0%
$n =$	304	427	39

Before proceeding further, we should note that in each case, the relationships seen are stronger for the Named Potential Candidate sample (from which only those who expressed an interest in holding public office have been chosen) and the State Legislator sample.[18] While we have yet to analyze these differences in detail, it seems likely that they are caused by the greater confidence that state legislators have in their own campaign abilities, compared with those who were named as potential candidates but who do not currently hold seats in the state legislature.

When similar analyses were run to test for the relationship between perceived chances of winning the nomination and the congruence of a respondent's policy views with those of the primary voters in the district, no significant relationship emerged. Two explanations can be offered to help understand this nonfinding. To assess the congruence between a respondent's policy views and those of the primary voters in the district, we used survey items that asked potential candidates to rank themselves and the voters in the district on a seven-point ideological scale. Over 40 percent placed themselves in the identical position as the voters in their party and over 80 percent were within one gradation on the seven-point scale. Thus, to a large extent, the potential candidates thought that this potential problem for their chances of nomination did not exist. However, even those few who saw themselves as ideologically out of step with the voters in their districts did not think their chances of winning the primary were reduced. It is difficult to know whether these perceptions are accurate or not; however, in this case, it does seem that the perception would be the key to understanding behavior.

The second explanation deals with the nonfinding explicitly. There is no statistical difference on the variable measuring perceptions of the likelihood of winning the primary between those who share the ideological position (which in this case is taken as a surrogate for policy preferences) of those in their party and those who do not. Here the explanation relates to how one interprets these differences. On the one hand, a potential candidate could say that because his or her views are different from those of most of the likely primary voters, the chances of winning the primary are reduced. That is the premise with which we began. On the other hand, it is perhaps equally logical to reason that a candidate who is viewed out of the mainstream in his or her party might well be advantaged in a primary— if that candidate can mobilize like-minded extremists and if more than one centrist candidate divides the mainstream vote. At this point we have no way of sorting out the extent to which any or all of these factors were at work. All that we can conclude is that ideological or policy proximity to the primary voters is not a good indicator of the perception of likelihood of winning a nomination.

We return then to sorting out the puzzle of the relationships among sharing partisanship with the incumbent, sharing partisanship with a majority in the district, and strength of party organization and the extent to which these are useful in understanding how a potential candidate perceives chances of winning nomination.

Figure 3.1 is a "path" model that shows the relationships among these variables, as measured by the perceptions of potential candidates in our survey.[19] As we would expect, there is a strong correlation ($r = .78$) between the partisan makeup of districts and the relative strength of party organizations in the district—districts with heavy concentrations of Democrats tend to be districts in which the Democratic Party's organization is much stronger than Republican organizational strength, and vice versa. Together, these two variables capture what we mean by district partisanship because they reflect the partisan proclivities of the average voter in the district and the organizational strength and capability of the parties in the district.

Both of the indicators of district partisanship help explain whether the incumbent and the potential candidate are in the same party, that is, as a district becomes more strongly Republican, it has a tendency to select Republicans. Therefore, the more strongly the district partisanship favors the Republicans, the more likely the incumbent is to be a Republican, and vice versa for Democratic incumbents. The reason this produces a tendency for incumbents and potential candidates to be in the same party is because we have recorded the information about the district partisanship as it relates to the partisanship of the potential candidate. Rather than recording it as "Democratic" or "Republican," we record it on a scale

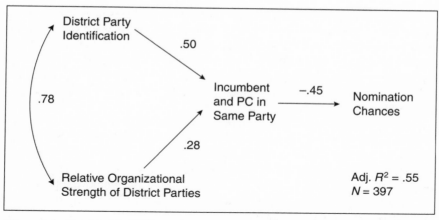

Figure 3.1: Path Model of Effects of District Partisanship on Nomination Chances of Potential Candidates (PC) (multiple regression standardized coefficients).

ranging from "strongly opposed to the party of the potential candidate" through "strongly in favor of the party of the potential candidate." Thus, as the district partisanship becomes more strongly consistent with that of the potential candidate, it tends to have elected incumbents in the same party as the incumbent.

The point of the figure is that the potential candidates' chances of winning their party's nomination depends heavily on whether the incumbent is in the same party. If the incumbent and the potential candidate are in the same party, the potential candidate's chances are very much lower than if they are in opposite parties. And whether the potential candidate and the incumbent are in the same party depends heavily on the partisanship of the district. Indeed, all of the effect of district partisanship is mediated by whether the incumbent and the potential candidate are in the same party. The conclusion we draw is that the partisan context of the district has a lot to do with why potential candidates are deterred from running in primaries. Potential candidates' chances of winning their party's primary are weakest in districts where their party is most strongly favored. Why? One big reason is that there is likely to be an incumbent in the same party seeking reelection. And incumbents are notoriously difficult to beat in primaries.

CONCLUSIONS

A number of conclusions follow from this analysis. First, it is clear that primary elections do not serve to stimulate more competition, and, to the extent that competition is an essential ingredient of democracy, it is not clear that they accomplish their intended purpose of enhancing U.S. democracy. Merely holding elections does not meet the principle criteria of an effective democracy. Holding elections in which the populace is given a real opportunity to voice their views is what is necessary. If holding primary elections serves to restrict effective choice more than to enhance it, they stand as a far too infrequently criticized step in the wrong direction. They appear to be a reform the consequence of which approximately a century after their invention may well be the opposite of what was intended.[20]

Second, it seems clear that the existence of a two-step process serves to discourage some potential candidates from running. It is also evident that the primary election itself is seen as an impediment to winning office by a substantial number of potential candidates who are then discouraged from running because of this impediment. It also seems evident that the partisan context in the district is strongly and negatively related to that potential candidate's perception of his or her chances to win the nomination.

From here the conclusions are less certain. When we examined the potential candidates' perceptions of their chances to win the nomination at some time in the foreseeable future, as opposed to in 1998 (in analysis not shown), we found the same negative relationships that were seen for 1998. These relationships, while highly significant, are not as strong as were those for the perceived chances of winning the nomination in 1998. Yet they were strong enough to lead us to conclude that these potential candidates view these factors as immutable impediments, not as temporary factors. Certainly the incumbent may no longer be on the scene, but competition in a highly partisan district will always be intense and thus chances of winning diminished.

To the extent that such an interpretation is accurate, the potential candidates see the presence of the incumbent as a deterrent, but they also feel that another strong candidate (or a pool of strong candidates) would emerge if the incumbent were not present and that the chance of winning the nomination would still be relatively low. Constituent partisanship leads to the conclusion that one party or the other is likely to maintain control over many districts. Whether the potential candidates' assessments are accurate depends on whether running against other strong potential candidates in a primary would be as daunting as running against a sitting incumbent.

Although potential candidates cannot change the partisan context of a district, they can change how those in a district relate to them. By influencing some of the strategic or personal factors, such as name recognition or the perception of their ability to work with other leaders, potential candidates can in fact also influence how they will fare in a contest among the substantial number of candidates who would run for a valued nomination.

The nomination of the dominant party in single-party districts will always be highly prized because winning that nomination is often viewed as tantamount to winning the general election. That would be as true in a system such as ours based on primaries as in the elite-driven system the primaries sought to replace. When no incumbent is involved, these primary elections are highly competitive, even though potential candidates understand that other strong potential candidates will also be running.

The remaining question, in our view, is whether primaries give an unfair advantage to incumbents and as a result reduce competition for these valued prizes when incumbents are running. The incumbent advantage in the case of primary elections for dominant-party nominations results from two factors. First, party leaders in the district will not intervene to unseat an incumbent, either because they are prohibited from taking sides in intraparty contests or because they do not choose to oppose a co-partisan who holds office. Second, no other possible candidate can match the incumbent's resources and visibility among the primary electorate, and therefore other strong potential candidates opt not to run. To the extent that these factors deter challengers to incumbents, primary elections may actually depress competition in contrast to the hopes of the reformers who viewed them as a means to extend competition and to enhance intraparty democracy.

NOTES

1. G. Bingham Powell Jr., *Contemporary Democracies* (Cambridge, Mass: Harvard University Press, 1982), 3.

2. See the following examples, Gary C. Jacobson and Samuel Kernell, *Strategy and Choice in Congressional Elections* (New Haven, Conn.: Yale University Press, 1981). Gary C. Cox and Jonathan N. Katz, "Why Did the Incumbency Advantage in U.S. House Elections Grow?" *American Journal of Political Science* 40 (1996): 478–97. Gary C. Jacobson, *The Politics of Congressional Elections,* 4th ed. (Boston: Allyn and Bacon, 1996). Paul S. Herrnson, *Congressional Elections: Campaigning at Home and in Washington* (Washington, D.C.: Congressional Quarterly Press, 1998).

3. Walter J. Stone and L. Sandy Maisel, "The Not-So-Simple Calculus of Winning: Potential House Candidates' Nomination and General Election Chances" (paper presented at the annual meeting of the American Political Science Association, Atlanta, September 1999).

4. Direct primary elections were put into place on a state-by-state basis, beginning in the first decade of the twentieth century. Some states still permit party caucuses or conventions to nominate candidates for some offices. States also differ as to who may qualify as a candidate in a primary, who may vote in a primary, what role (if any) party officials may or must play in the nominating process, and what percentage of the votes are needed to gain a party's nomination. For a complete discussion of the nominating process as it has evolved in the various states, see L. Sandy Maisel, *Parties and Election in America: The Electoral Process,* 3d ed. (Lanham, Md.: Rowman & Littlefield, 1999), chap. 7, as well as chapter 2 in this book.

5. V. O. Key, *American State Politics: An Introduction* (New York: Knopf, 1956).

6. For the purpose of this chapter, we consider only major-party primary elections. In point of fact, most state laws permit parties other than the major parties (often generically referred to as "third" parties, even though more than one such party may exist in some

states) to nominate in a variety of ways other than through primary elections. We concentrate on the major party candidates because they provide most of the competition in congressional elections. Only one member of the 106th Congress, Bernie Sanders (I-Vt.) was not elected as a Democrat or a Republican. Only a very few other non-major-party candidates in 1998 gained enough votes so that if all of their supporters had voted for the candidate finishing second, he or she would have won the election. See John Bibby and L. Sandy Maisel, *Two Parties—or More? The American Party System* (Boulder, Colo.: Westview, 1999); Theodore J. Low and Joseph Romance, *A Republic of Parties? Debating the Two-Party System* (Lanham, Md.: Rowman & Littlefield, 1998).

7. To be fair, we should note that some of these incumbents did face one or more minor-party candidates in the general election. However, few of the minor-party candidates polled even half as many votes as the incumbent.

8. We are indebted to Jennifer Steen for providing this analysis of Federal Election Commission data for us.

9. The level of competition in primaries was characterized by the closeness of the nearest challenger to the winning candidate. Thus, in multicandidate primary races, more than one candidate might well have been within 20 percent of the winner's vote total.

10. Our total pool of usable informants was 3,573. We mailed to each informant up to three times. Our total response rate for the survey was 43 percent. See J. Walter Stone, L. Sandy Maisel, and Cherie Maestas, "Candidate Emergence in U.S. House Elections" (paper presented at the annual meeting of the American Political Science Association, Boston, 1998), footnotes 9 and 10.

11. L. Sandy Maisel and Walter J. Stone, "Determinants of Candidate Emergence in U.S. House Elections: An Exploratory Study," *Legislative Studies Quarterly* 22 (1997): 79–96.

12. We mailed 3,640 surveys—1,399 to potential candidates named in our Informant survey and 2,241 to state legislators whose districts overlapped the sampled congressional districts but who were not named in our Informant survey. Our response rate for this survey, again with reminder mailings sent and those responses included, was 33 percent. The response rate was approximately the same for named potential candidates as it was for state legislators who had not been named by our informants.

For analytical purposes, we have created two data sets from this survey. The first is a data set that includes the answers from all of the named potential candidates. We have merged these data with responses from the informants who named each individual as a potential candidate. The second data set includes the responses from all of the state legislators, whether they were named potential candidates or not. One advantage of our design is that, although we polled all state legislators whose districts overlapped with the two hundred congressional districts in our sample, we were able to distinguish among the respondents by whether our informants had identified them as strong potential candidates. Thus, we expected a good deal of variance in terms of candidate strength among this group.

In the analysis and discussion in this chapter, these data sets will be referred to as the Named Potential Candidates and the State Legislators, respectively. Note that named state legislators are included in both data sets. Because of the difference in the two ways in which we identified our potential candidate pool, the entire data set is never treated as a single unit.

13. We also had a built-in check on the validity and the reliability of our survey results, because we could test intersample correlations as well as respondent answers against objectively obtained data (Stone and Maisel, "The Not-So-Simple Calculus of Winning").

14. Maisel and Stone, "Determinants of Candidate Emergence." Walter J. Stone, L. Sandy Maisel, Cherie Maestas, and Sean Evans, "A New Perspective on Candidate Quality in U.S. House Elections" (paper presented at the annual meeting of the Midwest Political Science Association, Chicago, April 1998).

15. Stone and Maisel, "The Not-So-Simple Calculus of Winning." Maisel and Stone, "Determinants of Candidate Emergence."

16. We recognize that one could claim that the likelihood of winning the general election itself might be dependent on having or not having a primary. In fact the professional literature on this point (i.e., the impact of divisive primaries) is extensive. One could also argue that the existence of a primary might have a beneficial impact on a general election campaign, allowing a candidate to increase name recognition and to "field test" a campaign organization.

17. This argument is developed at length in Stone and Maisel, "The Not-So-Simple Calculus of Winning."

18. It should be recalled that some state legislators are in both samples because they were named by one or more of the informants and also hold a state legislative office.

19. We asked respondents to score the partisanship of their districts on a seven-point scale, ranging from "Strongly Democratic" through "Strongly Republican." We also asked them to score the strength of the Republican and Democratic party organizations in their districts. The relative party-organizational-strength measure in the figure is simply a comparison of the separate party-strength ratings. Nomination chances were determined by asking respondents to estimate their chances of winning their party's nomination in 1998 if they were to decide to run.

20. Of course, we cannot make the claim that parties would perform the function of nominating competitive candidates better in the absence of primaries. Parties are, in fact, quite weak in many areas. Nomination by party organization would not necessarily result in more competitive general elections. However, recalling Key (*American State Politics*), we wonder whether stripping parties of the raison d'être led to weak institutions that now cannot perform what was once their most important function for democratic purposes.

4

The Benefits and Burdens of Congressional Primary Elections

Marni Ezra

Primaries suck up and waste large sums of money from contributors who might better be tapped for the November finals; the charges and countercharges of primary civil war provide the enemy party with ammunition it can later use with blast effect against whichever primary contender emerges victorious; primary campaigns exhaust the candidate, use up his speech material, drain his vital energy, leave him limp before he clashes with the major enemy.[1]

Anyone familiar with American primaries in recent years would recognize that there are certain kinds of primaries which, in producing a close result, will lead to a loss of resources for the winner. . . . When the general election follows soon after the primary, and the winning candidate has to use virtually all his funds in a close primary, there will be insufficient time to raise adequate funds before the general election.[2]

The preceding quotations represent the views of many candidates, campaign professionals, political scientists, and journalists. These individuals consider primary elections unfortunate hoops through which candidates must successfully jump in order to make it to the general election.[3] When faced with a primary challenge, candidates do not forecast all of the potential benefits they might receive. Instead, campaigns devise strategies that minimize the primary's damage.

Campaigns, the media, and much previous scholarship have improperly portrayed the impact of primary elections on candidacies for the U.S. House of Representatives as purely negative. In an attempt to condense the primary's effects into a simple statement of help or harm, there has been little effort to explore the different ways that campaigns are influenced by primary elections.[4] For campaigns, understanding the ways that a primary helps or harms their cause is crucial in planning their overall strategy. It is important for political scientists and election analysts to know how primaries affect campaigns because primaries can change the outcomes of elections and, in turn, the policies that our government produces.

Primary elections are complex events that can both shower a campaign with benefits in one area and wreak havoc in another. The following example illustrates the good and the bad that can come with a contested nomination. An unknown, inexperienced candidate received substantial media attention in his hotly contested primary, increasing his name recognition and legitimacy in the district. However, as a result of the hard-fought primary, the candidate had had to spend a substantial portion of his war chest fending off his opponent's attacks. The candidate then had to spend much of his time during the general election raising money instead of campaigning against his opponent. Analyses that attempt to reduce the primary's impact to a single number ignore the intricate dynamics of nomination politics.

There are many ways that primary elections can assist House candidates. They can help increase a candidate's media coverage, leading to higher name recognition, and they can boost the winning candidate's legitimacy. Also, a competitive primary election can provide an inexperienced candidate with an opportunity to fine-tune her or his skills before facing the general election opponent. None of these potential benefits has been systematically explored by political scientists.

Primaries can also serve to burden candidates. A divisive primary election is both cash and labor intensive. By draining a campaign's treasury, a divisive primary can leave a campaign fewer resources with which to fight the general election, and it forces a campaign to spend more time raising money. Depending on the date on which the primary occurs, the campaign may have little time to replenish its resources before the final weeks of the general election.

A competitive primary can also create partisan rifts that continue into the general election, resulting in disgruntled activists who choose not to campaign for the nominee[5] and voters who either abstain from voting or crossover and vote for the opposite party's nominee.[6] Further, divisive primary elections typically produce negative publicity for all candidates contesting the nomination and can leave the party's nominee exhausted and drained going into the general election.

In this chapter, we explore the potential benefits and burdens created by primary elections by using in-depth interviews with congressional candidates and campaign managers from the 1994 election cycle. Exploratory questions are used to pinpoint the array of benefits and burdens that candidates face during the primary. In addition, we observe the ways in which candidates, with different levels of political experience and resources, are affected by primary competition.

LITERATURE REVIEW

Several interesting studies examine how presidential, senatorial, gubernatorial, and House aspirants are affected by primary competition. This body of research uses both individual and aggregate data to study the impact of primary competition on the results of the general election. Several conclusions can be drawn from these works. The impact that intraparty competition has on a campaign differs depending on both the type of candidate and the level of office being sought. The higher the office and the more experienced the candidate, the fewer benefits the primary will provide. Conversely, the lower the office and the less experienced the candidate, the more the primary may help.

Being challenged for the presidential nomination is rarely considered helpful in the long term.[7] Studies that use aggregate data suggest that candidates vying for the presidential nomination fare worse in the general election than do their unchallenged counterparts. Because most presidential aspirants are seasoned candidates, they receive little benefit from a nomination contest.

Using individual-level data, several studies indicate why challenged presidential candidates fare worse. First, there are negative carryover effects among voters in presidential elections. Voters who support a candidate who loses the nomination are more likely to abstain from voting or to crossover and vote for the opposite party than voters who voted for the party's nominee.[8] Second, competition may negatively impact party activists who withdraw their support for presidential[9] nominees after their candidate is defeated. The party's nominee does not benefit from this pool of campaign support in the general election.

As one moves down the ladder of prestige to lower-level offices, the impact of primary competition is less clear. Some find that senatorial[10] and Democratic gubernatorial candidates[11] are negatively affected, whereas others find little or no affect for these types of races.[12]

Descending still further to the House of Representatives, the evidence is even less conclusive. What we do know from the small body of research on House primaries is that not all House candidates will be similarly affected by primary elections. Studies using aggregate data show the inconsistent impact that primaries have on the general election percentages won by incumbents and challengers.[13] When individual-level data are used to explore the impact that primaries have on voters and activists, scholars find that activists are less likely to campaign for and to vote for their party's nominee after supporting a losing candidate in the primary.[14] The aforementioned studies focus almost completely on general election totals using aggregate data and omit open-seat races; only a single study utilizes individual data to investigate the specific ways that primaries affect these candidates.

While it is important to understand whether a primary challenge helps or prevents a candidate from prevailing in the general election, it is not as important as knowing the specific ways that primaries help or harm candidates. Knowing the specific ways that candidates are helped or harmed allows them to anticipate and plan accordingly. The general election must be examined as part of a larger election cycle; candidates do not enter the general election with a clean slate. Knowing how events in the primary carry over into the general election is crucial to understanding why certain candidates win and others lose elective office.

THE RESEARCH DESIGN

Unlike most prior studies that use aggregate data, this research relies on individual-level, interview data with candidates and campaign managers to determine the ways that congressional primary elections affect campaigns for the U.S. House of Representatives. These data permit two areas of inquiry: (1) In what ways do primary elections benefit or burden campaigns? More specifically, do candidates report being helped or harmed by their primary elections? (2) How does the distribution of benefits and burdens from a primary differ for incumbent, challenger, and open-seat candidates? Which types of candidates receive the most benefits or burdens from primary elections?

To examine the ways in which primary elections can assist or can hinder House campaigns, campaign managers and candidates from the 1994 congressional elections were interviewed between November 30, 1995, and January 12, 1996.[15] Participants were selected using a proportional, stratified random sample, choosing every fifth person. The sample was stratified by the competitiveness of the primary (both competitive, one competitive, or neither competitive), the type of race (incumbent/challenger or open-seat), and the date of the primary (early to late). The goal was to obtain a sample with respondents in each stratified category that matched their proportions in the population.

In semistructured interviews, respondents were asked to describe the ways in which their campaigns were helped or harmed by their primary election.[16] Participants were also asked whether they strongly disagreed, disagreed, neither agreed nor disagreed, agreed, or strongly agreed with five statements about their primary elections (statements used in the interview can be found in Appendix 4-A).

Candidates were then classified based on their level of political capital. *Political capital* is defined as the candidate's combined level of "quality" score and campaign expenditures. *Candidate quality* is defined using a scale from 0 to 8— candidates receive points for such items as holding elective office, running for office, and celebrity status.[17] Based on candidate expenditure data obtained from the Federal Election Commission, a candidate is given one point for each $100,000 spent on the election, the total expenditures rounded up or down to the nearest hundred thousand. The two scores are added together for a possible 18 points. The capital variable is then categorized as low (1–6), medium (7–12), or high (13–18), and the responses of the three groups are compared.[18]

Using these data, two specific hypotheses are examined. First, candidates with low levels of political capital will be more likely to report primary benefits than candidates with high levels of political capital. Second, candidates with high levels of political capital will be more likely to report primary burdens than candidates with low levels of political capital.

The sample breaks down in the following manner (shown in table 4.1): 56 percent of the individuals interviewed are from incumbent/challenger districts, and 44 percent are from open districts.[19] Open districts are represented in the sample in greater numbers than in the population for two reasons: (1) they constitute a larger portion of competitive primary races than their percentage in the population; and (2) they had a lower rejection rate than either incumbents or challengers.[20]

The sample is a good representation of the population from which it was drawn—50 percent of the respondents are Democrats, and 50 percent are Republicans; approximately 50 percent are winners and 50 percent losers, the same proportions as the population. The sample also perfectly matches the population in the numbers of competitive and noncompetitive primaries.

Although the characteristics of participants and nonparticipants are similar, one apparent difference exists between the two groups. Participants faced more competitive primaries than nonparticipants did.[21] Seventy percent of the respondents had competitive primary elections, whereas only 35 percent of the nonparticipants had competitive primaries. This difference should not lead to systematic bias in any particular responses. It will be necessary, however, to compare the responses of campaigns with competitive primaries and those with noncompetitive primaries to determine if competition has different effects on campaigns.

Table 4.1: Description of Participants by Type of Election, Party, and Electoral Success

	Lose		Win		Total	
Incumbent ($n = 7$)						
Democrat	0	(0)	3	(9)	3	(9)
Republican	0	(0)	4	(13)	4	(13)
Challenger ($n = 11$)						
Democrat	6	(19)	0	(0)	6	(19)
Republican	3	(9)	2	(6)	5	(15)
Open Seat ($n = 14$)						
Democrat	6	(19)	1	(3)	7	(22)
Republican	1	(3)	6	(19)	7	(22)
TOTAL	16	(50)	16	(50)	32	(100)

Note: Figures are frequencies, with percentages in parentheses.

THE FINDINGS

The interview data both confirm and contradict previous research about primary elections. Primaries clearly affect campaigns in many complex and at times conflicting ways. Table 4.2 describes the aggregate responses that are discussed in the following sections.

Primary Election Benefits

In response to two open-ended questions, participants describe five ways that primaries helped their campaigns: (1) increased publicity, (2) better organization, (3) heightened legitimacy, (4) ability to practice their message, and (5) the opportunity to contact their base supporters. First, respondents report that the primary allowed candidates to be introduced to the media and to get "free" media coverage that was crucial to boosting candidates' name identification in the district. Of the respondents, 44 percent volunteered that the primary helped their campaigns by increasing the attention that their candidate received. One respondent describes this benefit as follows: "The primary helped because it allowed us to get through

Table 4.2: Aggregate Responses to Open-Ended Questions, "How Did the Primary Help/Harm Your Campaign?"

	Total (n = 32)	
Harm (n = 19)		
Resources	16	(50)
Negative publicity	6	(19)
Party rifts	4	(13)
Exhaustion	3	(9)
Didn't harm	13	(34)
Help (n = 25)		
Publicity	14	(44)
Organization	9	(28)
Legitimacy	6	(19)
Practice	4	(13)
Base	3	(9)
Didn't help	7	(22)

Notes: Figures are frequencies with percentages in parenthesis. Percentages are based on the number of respondents answering this question, not on total interviews. The numbers for help and harm do not add up to the total because they are multiple response questions.

the district and get our name out. We began with zero name I.D. and the primary enabled us to boost our I.D."

Candidates who ran against incumbents in the general election especially appreciated the primary because it was the only time that the press paid attention to them. Once they were up against an incumbent, the press ignored them. Another challenger discusses her experience with the media: "If the primary wasn't contested, I would have gotten no coverage. It got us some media coverage. It was the only time to get attention in the press." Especially for candidates opposing incumbents in the hope that they will get their name known for a future run, media coverage in the primary is crucial. Had this candidate not had primary competition, she would have had little chance to get any publicity, as she was ignored once she faced the incumbent.

Second, primary elections force campaigns to organize early and to put their people on the ground. Early organization was cited as a benefit by 28 percent of the participants, especially when they ran against a candidate who did not have a primary. They reported that their opponents tended to wait for the primary to end, losing important campaigning time.

Third, primaries assist candidates by increasing their legitimacy. After winning the primary, one-fifth of the respondents offered that their candidates were perceived to be more credible: "The primary helped to establish [my candidate] as a credible candidate because he beat the Speaker of the House."

Fourth, participants reported that the primary provided them an opportunity to practice their message prior to the general election and to learn how to effectively respond to attacks. The candidates who appreciated the practice were typically those who had never run for elective office or had limited political experience. One inexperienced candidate explains: "First-time candidates benefit from primaries in that it prepares you well for the general election in terms of driving your message and organization."

Finally, primaries can help campaigns by giving them time to solidify their partisan base. A few campaigns appreciated the primary because it gave them extra time to inform and to persuade their base voters. Campaigns were especially able to do this when they had a low-quality primary challenger and were sure that they would win the primary. Since campaigns must typically concentrate on wooing swing voters during the general election, it is beneficial to court the party's base during the primary election.

Primary Election Burdens

Although primaries can clearly assist campaigns, respondents offered four ways in which they believe their campaigns were harmed by primaries: (1) resource drain, (2) negative publicity, (3) division of party, and (4) exhaustion of the candidate and campaign staff.

First, of the ways in which primaries harm campaigns, the most substantial is through a reduction of a candidate's resources: 50 percent of the participants volunteered that the primary harmed their campaigns by draining their resource base. Respondents were very clear in their descriptions of how the primary sapped their funds. Many said that they had to spend all of their money to win the nomination, necessitating that they raise money all over again for the general election. Three respondents clearly describe this dynamic.

- "The way it harms you is with resources. Money is always a scarce resource, and when you have to exhaust it, which we did—every dime that we raised—in a sense you are starting from scratch."
- "We spent $350,000 in the primary, and if we had not had a primary, we would have had $350,000 more to spend in the general election."
- "Even when you win a primary, these bills come from all over. In August we spent so much time paying off bills from the primary. You stagger with that right through Labor Day."

Second, candidates are harmed by the negative publicity they receive from their primary opponents. Some primaries are very combative, and many negative attacks are exchanged, harming the candidate's image. One-fifth of the respondents expressed that negative publicity in the primary had a negative influence on their campaigns. These negative attacks provided ammunition for the general election opponent.

- "One opponent ran a nasty personal campaign against [my candidate] and dropped personal attacks three or four days before the primary."
- "We were harmed by negative campaigning that was very personal."

Third, the primary harmed some campaigns by causing rifts in the party. Candidates reported that they had to spend time attempting to win back the part of their base that they lost during the nomination phase. One candidate stated that "it was a primary based on the NAFTA (North American Free Trade Agreement) vote, so there was a division in [my candidate's] base. A labor candidate ran against [my candidate], and there was a division in the base in the district." Candidates that experience intraparty rifts during the primary must spend a substantial portion of their general election campaign winning back their base. Candidates could have better spent their time focusing on swing voters, and not those who are already most likely to vote for them.

Finally, primaries harmed campaigns by exhausting the candidates and their staffs. By the time the primary was over, candidates and their staffs were simply worn out and lacked the stamina to put forth a similar effort in the general election.

IMPACT OF PRIMARIES ON CANDIDATES WITH
DIFFERING LEVELS OF CAPITAL

Primary elections appear to influence candidates with different levels of political capital in very different ways. Candidates with high levels of political capital, usually incumbents and select open-seat candidates, report being harmed by the primary election. The potential benefits of the primary for these candidates are slim while its burdens are very high. Candidates with political experience, name recognition, and resources do not need the primary election to help them communicate with, and woo, potential voters. The primary forces them to expend their resources without assisting them in the way that it would candidates with little experience and name identification.

In contrast, the primary election is a benefit to candidates with little political capital, usually challengers. These candidates lack experience, legitimacy, and name identification as well as the money to help improve their position. The primary helps these candidates to increase their standing through free publicity. It also gives them an opportunity to practice their message before the general election, helping them to become stronger candidates. These results largely support Herrnson's[22] and Alvarez, Canon, and Seller's[23] studies of the 1992 congressional elections and Ezra's[24] aggregate analysis of the 1994 elections.

As shown in table 4.3, all 10 candidates with low capital said that they were helped by having a primary, 4 said that they were both harmed and helped, and

Table 4.3: Responses to Open-Ended Questions, "How Did the Primary Help/Harm Your Campaign?" by Level of Capital

	Low (n = 10)		Medium (n = 15)		High (n = 7)	
Harm						
Resources	3	(30)	8	(53)	5	(71)
Party rifts	1	(10)	0	(0)	3	(43)
Exhaustion	0	(0)	3	(20)	0	(0)
Negative publicity	1	(10)	3	(20)	2	(29)
Didn't harm	6	(60)	6	(40)	1	(14)
Help						
Organization	2	(20)	6	(40)	2	(29)
Legitimacy	3	(30)	1	(6)	2	(29)
Base	0	(0)	1	(6)	2	(29)
Publicity	9	(90)	5	(33)	0	(0)
Practice	2	(20)	2	(13)	0	(0)
Didn't help	0	(0)	4	(27)	3	(43)

Note: Figures are frequencies, with percentages in parenthesis. Percentages are based on the number of respondents answering this question, not on total interviews.

not a single candidate reported only negative effects. Approximately 30 percent of these candidates found that having a primary drained their resources.

In contrast, 71 percent of candidates with high capital said that the primary harmed them by absorbing their resources. The high group was also the most likely to report that the primary did not help them at all, and only one member of this group said that the primary exclusively helped their campaign.

For candidates with medium levels of capital, the primary clearly served as a trade-off between the benefits of increased publicity and legitimacy and the burdens of resource depletion. Of candidates with medium capital, 53 percent volunteered that they were harmed because their resources were drained by the primary. When asked whether they agreed or disagreed that their resources were exhausted, 60 percent agreed (table 4.4). In contrast, approximately one-third of these candidates said that the primary increased both their publicity and their legitimacy.

Table 4.4: Responses to Closed-Ended Questions by Level of Political Capital*

	*Agree***		*Disagree****	
Low (*n* = 10)				
Media	7	(70)	2	(20)
Legitimacy	8	(80)	2	(20)
Resources	6	(60)	4	(40)
Time	6	(60)	3	(30)
Negative publicity	0	(0)	10	(100)
Medium (*n* = 15)				
Media	13	(87)	2	(13)
Legitimacy	12	(80)	3	(20)
Resources	9	(60)	4	(27)
Time	8	(53)	7	(47)
Negative publicity	8	(53)	6	(40)
High (*n* = 15)				
Media	3	(43)	4	(57)
Legitimacy	3	(43)	4	(57)
Resources	6	(86)	2	(29)
Time	7	(100)	0	(0)
Negative publicity	6	(86)	1	(14)

Notes: Figures are frequencies with percentages in parenthesis. Percentages are based on the number of respondents answering this question, not on total interviews. Numbers of responses do not always add up to one hundred because individuals responding in the neutral category were omitted.
*Actual question wording can be found in Appendix 4–A.
**Agree* is the combination of respondents who said Agree or Strongly Agree.
***Disagree* is the combination of respondents who said Disagree or Strongly Disagree.

CONCLUSIONS

Two themes emerge from this study. The most important and most prevalent theme is that a candidate's level of political capital plays a role in whether the primary serves as a help or a hindrance to winning the general election. Candidates who begin the election cycle with substantial political experience, whether they are an incumbent or hold another elected office, are generally harmed by a primary election. In contrast, candidates who bring little to the primary in the way of experience, recognition, and resources find the primary extremely helpful.

The second theme that can be gleaned from these data is that for many campaigns, the primary was not purely helpful or purely harmful; it was usually some combination of the two. Primary elections tend to harm candidates by draining their resources but to help them organizationally by forcing them to "get their troops on the ground" and begin campaigning early. Many campaigns viewed the primary as a trade-off between early exposure and the expenditure of funds.

The final theme is that the results of this study provide insights into why previous studies on divisive primaries have come up with such inconclusive results. The majority of prior studies of congressional primaries use aggregate data to determine whether having a divisive primary harms a candidate's vote share in the general election. The reasons that primaries help and harm campaigns have been more complex than previous data have measured.

Using the percentage of the vote won by a candidate in the primary election masks what the researchers are attempting to study in two ways: First, the actual percentage of the vote in the primary election does not necessarily indicate whether the candidate was helped or harmed by that primary. A candidate who wins a primary with 65 percent of the vote may still spend a lot of money fending off his or her challenger. Second, the ways that a primary can hurt a campaign may be counterbalanced by the ways that a primary can help a campaign; the results then show that primary elections have little impact on the outcome of the general election. Again, looking only at the percentage primary vote hides the situation's complex dynamic.

The results of this study do not preclude the use of aggregate data. They do, however, recommend that aggregate analyses use measures that go beyond simply looking at the percentage vote won in the primary. Through a more detailed use of aggregate data analysis, it will be possible to produce more conclusive results about the interaction between primary and general elections.

NOTES

I would like to acknowledge first, the National Science Foundation for partial support of this project through its Doctoral Dissertation Support Grant #SBR-9528841 and, second, the candidates and the campaign managers who graciously shared their stories with me.
   1. Theodore White, *Making of the President 1960* (New York: Atheneum, 1961), 78.

2. Alan Ware, "Divisive Primaries: The Important Questions," *British Journal of Political Science* 9 (1979): 381–84.

3. R. Michael Alvarez, David T. Canon, and Patrick Sellers, "The Impact of Primaries on General Election Outcomes in the U.S. House and Senate," Social Science Working Paper 932, California Institute of Technology, 1995. Jennifer Babson, "Explosive Infighting Takes Toll," *Congressional Quarterly Weekly Reports* 52 (1994): 2541.

4. Several studies examine the ways in which divisive primaries harm campaigns. Most look at the impact that the divisive nomination has on party activists and voters in presidential elections. See the following examples: Walter J. Stone, "On Party Switching among Presidential Activists: What Do We Know?" *American Journal of Political Science* 35, no. 3 (1991): 598–607. Walter J. Stone, "The Carryover Effect in Presidential Elections," *American Political Science Review* 80, no. 1 (1986): 271–8; E. H. Buell Jr., "Divisive Primaries and Participation in Fall Presidential Campaigns: A Study of the 1984 New Hampshire Primary Activists," *American Politics Quarterly* 14 (1986): 376–90. Walter J. Stone, Lonna Rae Atkeson, and Ronald B. Rapoport, "Turning On or Turning Off? Mobilization and Demobilization Effects of Participation in Presidential Nomination Campaigns," *American Journal of Political Science* 36, no. 3 (1992): 665–91. James I. Lengle, "Divisive Presidential Primaries and Party Electoral Prospects, 1932–1976," *American Politics Quarterly* 8, no. 3 (1980): 26–77. Priscilla L. Southwell, "Prenomination Preferences and General Election Voting Behavior," *Social Science Journal* 31, no. 1 (1994): 69–77.

Few examine the specific ways that primaries impact congressional races. See the following examples: John Comer, "Another Look at the Effects of the Divisive Primary," *American Politics Quarterly* 4, no. 1 (1976): 121–28. Donald Bruce Johnson and James R. Gibson, "The Divisive Primary Revisited: Party Activists in Iowa," *American Political Science Review* 68 (1974): 67–77.

5. Walter J. Stone, "Prenomination Candidate Choice and General Election Behavior: Iowa Presidential Activists in 1980," *American Journal of Political Science* 28 (1984): 361–78. Stone, "The Carryover Effect." Stone, "On Party Switching." Buell, "Divisive Primaries," Penny M. Miller, Malcolm E. Jewell, and Lee Sigelman, "Divisive Primaries and Party Activists: Kentucky, 1979 and 1983," *Journal of Politics* 50, no. 2 (1988): 459–70. Johnson and Gibson, "The Divisive Primary Revisited." Comer, "Another Look at the Effects."

6. Stone, Atkeson, and Rapoport, "Turning On or Turning Off?" Lengle, "Divisive Presidential Primaries." Priscilla L. Southwell, "The Politics of Disgruntlement: Nonvoting and Defection among Supporters of Nomination Losers, 1968–1984," *Social Science Journal* 8, no. 1 (1986): 81–95. Southwell, "Prenomination Preferences."

With the exception of Johnson and Gibson's "The Divisive Primary Revisited" and Comer's "Another Look at the Effects," these studies examine presidential primaries. Little research explores the effects of primary competition on congressional candidates.

7. Patrick Kenney and T. W. Rice, "The Relationship between Divisive Primaries and General Election Outcomes," *American Journal of Political Science* 31 (1987): 31–44. Patrick Kenney and T. W. Rice, "Presidential Prenomination Preferences and Candidate Evaluations," *American Political Science Review* 82, no. 4 (1988): 1309–19. James I. Lengle, Diana Owen, and Molly W. Sonner, "Divisive Nomination Mechanisms and Democratic Party Electoral Prospects," *Journal of Politics* 57, no. 2 (1995): 370–83. Buell, "Divisive Primaries." Southwell, "Prenomination Preferences." Lengle, "Divisive Presidential Primaries."

8. Lengle, "Divisive Presidential Primaries." Southwell, "Prenomination Preferences." Southwell, "The Politics of Disgruntlement."

9. Stone, "Prenomination Candidate Choice." Stone, "The Carryover Effect." Stone, "On Party Switching." Buell, "Divisive Primaries." Miller, Jewell, and Sigelman, "Divisive Primaries and Party Activists."

10. Alan Abramowitz, "Explaining Senate Election Outcomes," *American Political Science Review* 82 (1988): 385–403. Patrick Kenney and T. W. Rice, "The Effect of Primary Divisiveness in Gubernatorial and Senatorial Elections," *Journal of Politics* 46 (1984): 904–15. Robert A. Bernstein, "Divisive Primaries Do Hurt: U.S. Senate Races, 1956–1972," *American Political Science Review* 71 (1977): 540–55.

11. Kenney and Rice, "The Effect of Primary Divisiveness."

12. Patrick Kenney, "Sorting Out the Effects of Primary Divisiveness in Congressional and Senatorial Elections," *Western Political Quarterly* 41 (1988): 765–77. James E. Pierson and Terry B. Smith, "Primary Divisiveness and General Election Success: A Re-examination," *Journal of Politics* 37 (1975): 555–62.

13. Paul S. Herrnson, *Congressional Elections: Campaigning at Home and in Washington* (Washington, D.C.: Congressional Quarterly Press, 1995). Alvarez, Canon, and Sellers, "The Impact of Primaries." Marni Ezra, "The Benefits and Burdens of Congressional Primary Elections" (Ph.D. diss. American University, 1996). Richard Born, "The Influence of House Primary Election Divisiveness on General Election Margins, 1962–1976," *Journal of Politics* 43 (1981): 640–61.

Two studies, Kenney "Sorting Out the Effects" and Mark C. Westlye ("The Effects of Primary Divisiveness on Incumbent Senators, 1968–1984" [paper presented at the annual meeting of the American Political Science Association, New Orleans, 1985]), find that neither candidate's general election total is affected by primary election competition.

14. Johnson and Gibson, "The Divisive Primary Revisited."

15. If the candidate had a campaign manager who managed the campaign throughout both the primary and the general election, the campaign manager was interviewed. If the campaign had no campaign manager, if the candidate ran his or her own campaign, or if the campaign manager came on board only after the primary election, the candidate was interviewed in place of the campaign manager. In the sample, 85% of the respondents are campaign managers, and 15% are candidates.

16. The interviews were conducted either in person or on the telephone, depending on whether the respondent resided in the Washington, D.C., metropolitan area. The 32 completed interviews averaged 32 minutes in length and ranged from 15 minutes to 105 minutes.

17. Jonathan S. Krasno and Donald Phillip Green, "Preempting Quality Challengers in House Elections," *Journal of Politics* 50, no. 4 (1988): 920–36.

18. It is more appropriate to categorize candidates based on their level of capital rather than on their type of candidacy (incumbent, challenger, open seat) because of the variation within groups. The type of candidate is not as important as the capital that the candidate brings to the election. The groups, however, are highly correlated with their expected levels of capital (correlation of .62). Seven of the 10 individuals with low capital are challengers and the rest are open seats. Of the 15 campaigns with moderate levels of capital, 8 are open seats, 4 are challengers, and 3 are incumbents. In the high group, 4 are incumbents, and 3 are open seats. There are no challengers.

19. Open districts constitute approximately one-eighth of the total number of districts in 1994; however, they represent one-quarter of the competitive primary elections.

20. A rejection means that the individual either could not be located or was located and refused to be interviewed. Of the 16 potential open-seat interviews in the sample, 14 were interviewed, an acceptance rate of 88%. Of the 51 potential incumbent and challenger interviews in the sample, 18 interviews were conducted, a 35% response rate. The response rate is lower among incumbent/challenger races than open-seat races for two reasons. First, and most important, challengers were extremely difficult to locate because the large majority of them lost their elections. Second, the refusal rate among incumbents was higher than any other group.

21. *Competitive primaries* are defined as primaries in which the winner won less than 60% of the vote.

22. Herrnson, *Congressional Elections*.

23. Alvarez, Canon, and Sellers, "The Impact of Primaries."

24. Ezra, "The Benefits and Burdens."

APPENDIX 4–A: INTERVIEW QUESTIONS

Candidates and campaign managers with primary elections were asked these two questions:

1. "Can you think of any ways in which your campaign was harmed by having a primary election?"

2. "Can you think of any ways in which your campaign was helped by having a primary election?"

In addition, interviewees were asked whether they strongly disagree, disagree, neither agree nor disagree, agree, or strongly agree with the following five statements:

1. The primary election helped my candidate by generating media coverage.

2. The primary election helped to legitimize my candidate among campaign contributors.

3. The primary election absorbed many of our campaign's resources.

4. After we won the primary election, we had enough time to raise money before the general election.

5. My candidate received negative publicity in the primary.

5

Campaign Finance in U.S. House Primary and General Elections

Jay Goodliffe and David B. Magleby

This chapter explores the relationship between U.S. House primary and general elections, focusing specifically on campaign finance. We assess how competitiveness in primaries may correspond to competitiveness in general elections and investigate the sources of campaign funding for these races. We find similarities in primary- and general-election funding patterns and a broad association between electoral competitiveness and candidate spending. We also find that nonincumbents in primary elections receive little political action committee (PAC) funding and that they rely on personal funds far more than incumbents do.

To guide our analysis, we first consider contrasting perspectives on the expected patterns of competitiveness and funding in congressional primaries. We find one such perspective in the goals of the reform movements that led to the creation of congressional primaries. Most basically, the goal of these reform movements was to reduce the power of political machines. A second goal was to increase accountability to the voters.[1] One indication of whether congressional primaries serve this purpose would be relatively high levels of congressional primary competitiveness. In our campaign finance data, we interpret approximate equality in candidate spending as an indication of competitiveness, with a lopsided funding ratio being suggestive of noncompetitiveness.

The need to establish primaries as an avenue of accountability was most acute in districts where there was little interparty competition, as normally was the case in the many large, eastern cities and in the Deep South early in the twentieth century. In such districts, primary elections afforded the only realistic opportunity to displace an ineffective, unresponsive, or corrupt incumbent. A finding of relatively high levels of congressional primary competitiveness in districts where general elections are the *least* competitive, with lower levels of primary competitiveness in districts where a healthy measure of two-party competition does exist, would suggest that primaries are serving this specific purpose.

For a contrasting perspective on what might turn up in our data, we draw on the modern scholarly literature on congressional elections, specifically on the concept of "candidate quality" and the "strategic politicians" theory of congressional candidacy developed by Jacobson and Kernell.[2] A *quality candidate* is one who has political experience or other credentials that should enable him or her to attract substantial voter support. Elections involving incumbents are almost never competitive unless a quality challenger enters the contest.

Being politically savvy and understanding the sacrifices involved in seeking election to Congress, quality candidates make strategic choices about when and where to run.[3] They base these choices largely on their prospects for success. Given the low probability of defeating an incumbent in a general election and the even lower probability of beating one in a primary, quality candidates will often wait for opportunities to run for open seats, challenging incumbents in general elections selectively and rarely challenging them in primaries. Thus, the strategic politicians theory predicts that primaries involving incumbents will seldom be competitive and that opposition-party primaries in districts where an incumbent seeks reelection will less often be competitive than open-seat primaries. The exceptions are most likely to occur when an incumbent appears to be highly vulnerable. These highly vulnerable incumbents are likely to attract quality general-election challengers as well as quality primary challengers. The strategic politicians theory suggests, then, that when competitive primaries involving incumbents do occur, they will often be associated with competitive general elections. This is quite the opposite of the reformers expectation that competitive primaries would offer a recourse to voters in districts with noncompetitive general elections.

STUDY DESIGN AND METHODOLOGY

We examine campaign spending and election results in primary and general elections for the U.S. House during the 1992–98 election cycles. Using data from Federal Election Commission (FEC) detailed candidate report files, we merged primary vote data from the published editions of *America Votes*.[4]

One of the difficulties in studying primary-election finance is that the FEC does not require candidates to report complete receipts and expenditures for the primary phase. Rather, candidates are required to report twelve days prior to the primary.[5] To derive an estimate of primary spending, we first calculated the number of days between the preprimary report and the next FEC report submitted. We then computed the average expenditure per day for that period, and added the product of the average expenditure per day and the number of days to the preprimary expenditures. Although still an estimate, this computation is superior to relying on the preprimary report or on the next regular submission to the FEC.[6]

We excluded Louisiana from our analysis because of its unusual system in which the primary often functions as a general election as well.[7] We also excluded several 1996 Texas primaries,[8] special primaries, third-party primaries, and a few other oddities.[9] This left us with 3,142 cases.

FINDINGS

We first investigate the general relationship between primaries and the corresponding general elections. In table 5.1, we list the numbers of primary-election defeats and general-election defeats for the U.S. House from 1946 to 1998. Since 1946,

Table 5.1: U.S. House Incumbents Retired or Defeated, 1946–1998

Year	Retired	Primary Defeat	General Defeat
1946	32	18	52
1948	29	15	68
1950	29	6	32
1952	42	9	26
1954	24	6	22
1956	21	6	16
1958	33	3	37
1960	26	5	25
1962	24	12	22
1964	33	8	45
1966	22	8	41
1968	23	4	9
1970	29	10	12
1972	40	11	13
1974	43	8	40
1976	47	3	13
1978	49	5	19
1980	34	6	31
1982	40	10	29
1984	22	3	16
1986	40	3	6
1988	23	1	6
1990	27	1	15
1992	65	19	24
1994	48	4	34
1996	49	2	21
1998	33	1	6

Source: Norman Ornstein, Thomas Mann, and Michael J. Malbin. *Vital Statistics on Congress 1999– 2000* (Washington, D.C.: American Enterprise Institute for Public Policy Research, 2000), Table 2–7, 57.

an average of 6.9 incumbents have been denied renomination in primaries, with wide variability over time. A spike in the data appears in each election immediately following redistricting, when incumbents sometimes ran in radically reconfigured districts and were occasionally forced to run against each other because two districts were consolidated into one.

Gradually over the past four decades, incumbents have become less likely to lose in a primary. In the 1960s, with pervasive redistricting resulting from Supreme Court malapportionment decisions, the average number of incumbents defeated was 7.4. In the 1970s, the average was 7.6. It dropped to 4.6 in the 1980s, and was 5.4 in the 1990s. We consider this 5.4 mean for the 1990s to be misleading. Nineteen of those who failed to win renomination in the 1990s did so in 1992, after redistricting and the House banking scandal.[10] When this unusual year is removed, the average number of incumbents suffering defeat in a primary was 2.0.

We see a somewhat different trend in general elections. The number of incumbents losing in general elections declined from an average of 28.4 in the 1960s, to less than 20 per election in the 1970s, to 17.6 in the 1980s. In the 1990s, the average rose again to 20 per election.

We next consider how a competitive primary election appears to affect the competitiveness of the general election. We define a *competitive* primary as one in which the difference in vote percentage between the first- and second-place candidates was *less* than 20 percent.[11] This gives us a measure of competitiveness that applies in two-candidate and multicandidate elections.[12] We classify contested primaries where the difference between the top two vote getters was *more* than 20 percent as *weakly competitive*.

In table 5.2, we present a candidate's average two-party vote share according to the competitiveness of the primary election and the type of candidate who won

Table 5.2: Average U.S. House General-Election Percentage by Primary Competitiveness and Candidate Type, 1992–1998

Primary Competitiveness	Incumbent (N)	Open Seat (N)	Out-party Challenger (N)
Unopposed	69.3	44.3	31.7
	(1030)	(70)	(692)
Weakly competitive	67.3	49.5	37.0
	(383)	(130)	(337)
Competitive (within 20%)	56.4	52.3	37.4
	(51)	(192)	(253)

Source: Compiled from *America Votes.*

Notes: General election percentage is percent of two-party vote. Data include candidates who won the primary election and did not drop out of the race before the general election and exclude incumbents who ran against other incumbents.

the primary.[13] The findings are fully consistent with the strategic politicians theory. Open-seat primaries were the most likely to be competitive, with 49 percent (192 of 392) meeting this standard. Only 18 percent of the open-seat winners ran unopposed. In contrast, over 70 percent of the incumbents ran unopposed, and only 51 of 1,464 (3 percent) of the primaries involving incumbents were competitive. Fifty-four percent of the out-party primaries were uncontested; 20 percent were competitive.

We also find predictable associations between the competitiveness of primaries and the competitiveness of the corresponding general elections in table 5.2. The winners of competitive open-seat primaries fared better in general elections than did unopposed or weakly opposed winners, possibly suggesting that open-seat primaries are most likely to become competitive when candidates perceive that a primary winner will have good prospects in the general election. Incumbents who won competitive primaries averaged only about 56 percent in the general election. In comparison, those who won weakly competitive or unopposed primaries averaged 67 percent and 69 percent, respectively. Out-party challengers who won competitive primaries averaged about 37 percent in general elections, as did those who won weakly competitive primaries. Unopposed out-party challengers averaged only about 32 percent.

Thus, in the districts where incumbents sought reelection, competitive primaries portended competitive general elections. This is what should occur if challengers respond strategically to perceptions of incumbent vulnerability, entering primaries only when they consider incumbents to be weak.

We regard one other finding involving a very small number of cases as noteworthy. Of the 22 challengers who did beat an incumbent in a primary, 18 went on to win the general election.[14] One would not expect so much general-election success for these primary winners in a representative cross section of districts. Almost certainly, many of these must have been one-party-dominated districts in which the general election provided little opportunity to displace the incumbent and the primary served the reformers purpose.

HOW CANDIDATES FUND THEIR RACES

We now assess primary-election funding, comparing it with funding for general elections. In table 5.3, we present the total funding and the percentage of funding from various sources in both primary and general elections.[15] Among the primary winners, incumbents raised twice as much money as open-seat candidates, five times as much as out-party challengers, and about ten times as much as out-party challengers who went on to lose in the general election. In-party challengers who defeated incumbents collected nearly as much as the incumbents. This finding suggests that when an incumbent runs for reelection, seriously contested primaries in either party are uncommon. To the extent that funding is appropriate as a

Table 5.3: Sources of Campaign Receipts in U.S. House Primary and General Elections

Candidate	Election Status	Average	Percentage of Contributions from:					N
			PAC	Individual	Candidate	Party		
Incumbent	Primary losers	$411,879	30%	58%	4%	1%		22
	Primary winner	410,873	42	52	1	1		1442
	General	259,912	46	48	1	3		1442
Open-seat	Primary losers	112,126	63	53	39	0		784
	Primary winner	215,536	17	63	18	1		392
	General	392,434	32	48	15	8		392
Out-party challenger	Primary losers	46,779	5	53	39	0		811
	Primary winner	81,607	13	64	20	1		1282
	General	145,939	21	55	18	10		1282
In-party challenger	Primary losers	41,784	6	64	36	0		476
	Primary winner	328,347	7	39	53	0		22
	General	474,370	24	39	34	5		22

Source: Federal Election Commission data.

Notes: All figures adjusted for inflation (1998 dollars). General-election spending is money raised after the primary election. Candidate contributions include loans candidates made to their own campaigns. Primary-winner and general-election data include candidates who won the primary election and did not drop out of the race before the general election and exclude incumbents who ran against other incumbents.

measure of competitiveness, this finding conforms with the strategic politicians theory.

With respect to sources of funding, we note that most incumbents keep a fundraising operation in place at all times,[16] and as a result, we expect incumbent primary- and general-election funding patterns to be similar, with the overall total amount raised increasing over the election cycle. We anticipate that open-seat candidates and challengers will collect less (PAC) funding than incumbents will and that they have to wait until after the primary to receive much of this funding, especially if their primary is contested. We base this prediction on existing studies of PACs' funding strategies.[17] PACs that follow an access strategy generally contribute to incumbents. They will also contribute to open-seat contests but usually stay out of primary contests. In contrast, other PACs will implement ideological strategies. Herrnson[18] notes: "Ideological PACs spend more time searching for promising challengers to support than do PACs that use access-seeking or mixed strategies. Ideological committees are also more likely than other PACs to support nonincumbents in congressional primaries." The willingness of ideological PACs to fund challengers is, however, conditional. They give money where they think it will make a difference—in competitive elections. Thus, we assume that ideological PACs will normally reserve their contributions to challengers and open-seat candidates until after these candidates have emerged from primaries as nominees.

The data pertaining to funding sources are consistent with these expectations. Candidates in every category depended most heavily on individual contributions, with these contributions typically accounting for slightly more than half of the total funding. Incumbents collected a larger percentage of their funds from PACs than any category of nonincumbent candidates—42 percent. Open-seat candidates and out-party and in-party challengers received 17 percent, 13 percent, and 7 percent, respectively. After winning the primary election, open-seat candidates and both types of challengers collected a much higher percentage from PACs than they did prior to their primaries. For example, open-seat primary winners got 17 percent of their primary funding from PACs, but after the primary, their PAC funding increased to 32 percent of their total.

The greatest differences between categories of candidates appeared in the self-financing of campaigns[19]—"In primaries and the general elections for the House in 1994, some 163 candidates contributed $50,000 or more to their own campaigns."[20] Self-financing accounted for only 1 percent of all spending by incumbents, which makes sense given that incumbents have ready access to many other sources of money. In contrast, open-seat primary winners contributed 18 percent of their campaign funds, and out-party primary winners, 20 percent. Self-financing accounted for 39 percent of the funding for primary losers. We find it particularly significant that challengers who *defeated* incumbents provided 53 percent of their own campaign funds.[21] These data indicate that without self-financing, challengers would have had even less money in comparison to incumbents and that on the average, congressional primaries probably would have been even less competitive than they were.

Maisel characterizes self-financing as somewhat of a last resort for candidates unable to find money elsewhere. He notes that the "more that is spent on a campaign, the lower the percentage of that expenditure that comes from the candidate."[22] In table 5.4, we plot candidate self-financing as a percentage of total primary spending for each type of primary. We find a result consistent with Maisel's—a negative correlation between self-financing percentage and total spending for the top two vote getters in all races: $r = -.13$ ($p < .001$). But this correlation does not control for the type of primary and candidate. We expect candidates to spend more of their own money if the race is close. When we recalculate candidate self-financing as a percentage of total primary spending, controlling for types of races and candidates, the correlation is positive, meaning that the percentage of self-financing increased as races became more competitive.[23] The relationship was strongest for open-seat and in-party challengers.

SPENDING AND COMPETITIVENESS

Anticipating a replication of the patterns found in general elections, we expect to find a close association between competitiveness and funding levels in primary elections. Recognizing that competitive elections attract money and that money makes elections competitive, we do not attempt to disentangle the causal relationship between money and competitiveness. Following Herrnson's study of spending and competitive races in the 1996 general election, we define *competitive elections* to be "contests that were decided by margins of 20 percent of the vote or less."[24]

In table 5.5, we first calculate the total amount of money spent in a general election (by the two major-party candidates) according to the type of candidate

Table 5.4: Correlation between Percent Self-Funding and Total Spending in U.S. House Primary Elections, 1992–1998

	Correlation (r)	*N*
All candidates	−.13	4522
Incumbents	.07	1462
Open-seat candidates	.13	717
Out-party challengers	.05	1907
In-party challengers	.16	436

Source: Federal Election Commission data.

Notes: All correlations significant at $p < .05$ (two-tailed). All figures adjusted for inflation (1998 dollars). Data include top two vote getters and exclude incumbents who ran against other incumbents.

Table 5.5: Average General Election Spending and Competitiveness, U.S. House, 1992–1998

Candidate Type	Competitiveness (Two-Party Vote)	Average Spent	N
Incumbent	Unopposed (100%)	$344,513	164
	Weakly competitive (60-99%)	517,517	842
	Competitive (< 60%)	902,821	440
Open-seat	Uncompetitive (< 40%)	277,791	88
	Competitive (> 40%)	670,674	304
Challenger	Uncompetitive (< 40%)	111,935	932
	Competitive (> 40%)	518,792	372

Source: Federal Election Commission data.
Notes: All figures adjusted for inflation (1998 dollars). Data include top two vote getters and exclude incumbents who ran against other incumbents.

and his or her level of competitiveness.[25] Unopposed incumbents spent about $345,000, compared to about $518,000 for those that drew weak competition and $903,000 for those with strong competition. Uncompetitive open-seat candidates spent about $278,000, compared to $671,000 for candidates in competitive open-seat races. For challengers who were uncompetitive, the average was about $112,000, with $519,000 being the average for competitive challengers.

In table 5.6, we next present the comparable results for primary elections. We use only the primary winner in our calculations. Overall, incumbent spending dwarfed challenger spending. Even incumbents unopposed in the primary spent more than the average competitive open-seat candidate or (out-party) challengers. On average, incumbents spent $265,000 before the primary election, open-seat candidates spent $161,000, and (out-party) challengers spent $57,000.

As we expected, we find that candidates spend more money when primaries are competitive. For example, candidates unopposed in an open-seat primaries averaged about $106,000 in expenditures before their primaries. In comparison, weakly opposed open-seat candidates averaged about $167,000, and strongly opposed open-seat candidates averaged $117,000. The only anomaly in these data is for out-party challengers. They spent more in weakly competitive elections than in competitive ones.[26]

THE RELATIONSHIP BETWEEN PRIMARY SPENDING AND VOTE PERCENTAGES

Finally, we examine the relationship between primary spending and primary vote percentages. We anticipate that the patterns will be similar to those found in gen-

Table 5.6: Average Primary Election Spending and Competitiveness

Candidate Type	Competitiveness (Difference)	Average Spent	N
Incumbent	Unopposed	$252,116	1030
	Weakly competitive	283,274	383
	Competitive (within 20%)	517,117	29
Open-seat	Unopposed	105,632	70
	Weakly competitive	166,926	130
	Competitive (within 20%)	117,373	192
Out-party challenger	Unopposed	39,185	692
	Weakly competitive	83,050	337
	Competitive (within 20%)	71,421	253
In-party challenger	Weakly competitive	201,389	7
	Competitive (within 20%)	342,239	15

Source: Federal Election Commission data and *American Votes*.

Notes: All figures adjusted for inflation (1998 dollars). Data include candidates who won the primary election and did not drop out of the race before the general election, and they exclude incumbents who ran against other incumbents.

eral elections, with more spending corresponding to a larger vote share for open-seat candidates and challengers, but with the reciprocal for incumbents.[27] The major constraint on open-seat and challenger spending is the candidate's ability to raise money; and the stronger that a candidate appears to be, the more readily the money flows into his or her campaign treasury. In contrast, incumbents can almost always raise substantial sums if they perceive the need to do so. When incumbents spend less, it is usually by choice and usually because they face either no opposition or token opposition. When seriously challenged, they normally spend more.

In table 5.7, we present the data on spending and percentages of vote for the different types of candidates. For the primary election, we use the spending of the top two finishers and the percentage of the total vote. For the general election, we use the spending of the primary winner and the percentage of the two-party vote.

We find the anticipated negative correlation between spending and vote percentage for incumbents, in both primaries and general elections. The negative relationship is somewhat stronger in the general election ($r = -.40$) than in the primary ($r = -.26$). The probable explanation for this is that competitive general elections are more common than competitive primaries.

Also as anticipated, we find that open-seat candidates and challengers got more votes as they spent more in both primary and general elections. For open-seat candidates, the coefficient is about the same in primaries ($r = .19$) as it is in general elections ($r = .22$). For challengers, however, the correlation is much stronger in general elections ($r = .51$) than in primaries ($r = .17$). We note, however, that for open-seat and challenger primary *winners*, the relationship between spending

**Table 5.7: Correlation between Spending and Vote for U.S. House Primary
and General Elections, 1992–1998**

Candidate Type	Primary (N)	General (N)
Incumbent	−.13	−0.40
	(432)	(1282)
Open-seat	.19	.22
	(644)	(392)
Challenger	.17	.51
	(1634)	(1304)

Source: Federal Election Commission data and *American Votes.*
Notes: All correlations in this section are statistically significant at $p < .001$ (two-tailed). Data
exclude unopposed candidates. For the primary election, data include spending of the top two
finishers and the percentage of the primary vote. For the general election, data include the total
spending of the primary winner and the percentage of the two-party vote.

and vote percentage was *negative* (as it was for incumbents). This suggests that
the open-seat and challenger primary *winners* implemented primary spending
strategy much as the incumbents did. It appears that when they did not face serious competition in primaries, they reserved their resources for the general election; they spent more only when they perceived a need to do so. The positive overall
correlation between primary spending and vote percentage among open-seat candidates and challengers was entirely an artifact of spending by the second-place
candidates, who won significantly more votes as they spent more.

CONCLUSION

Our data indicate that House primaries resemble House general elections in several important respects. We found that about half of all open-seat primaries were
competitive but that competitive primaries in districts where incumbents sought
reelection were uncommon. Incumbents usually ran unopposed in primaries, and
when opposed, they almost always won. Normally outspending their in-party
opponents and candidates in the opposition party primary by wide margins, incumbents collected far more money from PACs and relied much less on self-financing in their campaigns. Close primary elections involving incumbents usually seemed to result from a combination of two circumstances: (1) the incumbent
appeared to be vulnerable; and (2) a challenger was able to provide significant
funding for his or her own campaign.

The data are consistent with the prediction that quality candidates will be strategically reluctant to challenge incumbents. Generally speaking, the data do not
support the proposition that primary elections increase the accountability of the

House. Few incumbents face primary challengers, and the vast majority of those challengers are not visible.[28] Incumbents are less threatened by primaries than by general elections, and that threat is infrequent.

But as David Mayhew argued, incumbents worry about reelection even though the odds are heavily in their favor in general elections.[29] For this reason, primaries need not necessarily be competitive to encourage responsiveness to constituents. The possibility that a serious primary challenger might come along may enhance incumbent accountability to in-party activists and important allied interest groups.

Campaign spending since 1984 demonstrates that when incumbents encounter strong in-party challenges, they are more likely to find themselves in competitive general elections. This reality is more an artifact of a weak incumbent attracting competition in and out of the party than evidence that primaries enhance accountability. Indeed, party machines were more likely to engender loyalty to party leaders than direct primaries are.

An additional limitation of primaries is that they add substantially to the overall costs and sacrifices associated with seeking election to Congress, and as a result, they may create a general disincentive for candidates to run. In this regard, we encourage further investigation of how primaries may affect the recruitment of out-party candidates. As general election underdogs who must scramble for every dollar and contend with every advantage that incumbency bestows, out-party challengers must feel especially burdened by primaries. Primaries may help them to hone their campaigning skills, but primaries can also wear candidates down, drain their resources, reduce their position-taking flexibility, and tarnish their personal images. We can readily envision situations in which possible out-party candidates weigh the low probability of defeating an incumbent against the difficulty of first running in a primary and *then* running in a general election, only to decide to wait for an open seat or to seek a different office. If this is occurring with any regularity, then primaries are constricting the out-party candidate field, potentially reducing the incentive for U.S. incumbents to be accountable.

NOTES

We thank the research assistants who helped us build the data set used for this chapter: Brant Avondet, Damon Cann, Nathan Cherpeski, Hannah Michaelsen, Jay Shafer, Kim Spears, Peter Stone, Jon Tanner, and Amanda Telford. Michael Lyons provided valuable comments and suggestions for this chapter. We appreciate the research funds provided by the College of Family Home and Social Sciences at Brigham Young University. Bob Biersack of the Federal Election Commission assisted with the 1998 data, and Rhodes Cook graciously provided data for 1998 primary election voting.

1. V. O. Key, *American State Politics: An Introduction* (New York: Knopf, 1956). Also see chapter two in this volume.

2. Gary C. Jacobson and Samuel Kernell, *Strategy and Choice in Congressional Elections,* 2d ed. (New Haven, Conn.: Yale University Press, 1983), 13–34.

3. For further discussion on this theme, see chapter three in this volume.

4. Richard M. Scammon and Alice V. McGillivray, *America Votes* 20 (1992) (Washington, D.C.: Congressional Quarterly Press, 1993). Richard M. Scammon and Alice V. McGillivray, *America Votes* 21 (1994) (Washington, D.C.: Congressional Quarterly Press, 1995). Richard M. Scammon and Alice V. McGillivray, *America Votes* 22 (1996) (Washington, D.C.: Congressional Quarterly Press, 1997). Richard M. Scammon, Alice V. McGillivray, and Rhodes Cook, *America Votes* 23 (1998) (Washington, D.C.: Congressional Quarterly Press, 1999). (We are grateful to Rhodes Cook for providing information before the 1998 edition was published.)

5. Candidates may also file a report 30 days after the primary. Few, if any, do so. Marni Ezra ("The Benefits and Burdens of Congressional Primary Elections" [paper prepared for presentation at the annual meeting of the Midwest Political Science Association, Chicago, April 18–20, 1996]) explains both the theoretical and the practical difficulties of estimating primary expenditures. She uses an alternative method to the one we use here, isolating money on primary election voter contact.

6. To compare across years, we adjust the financial data for inflation; all figures are in 1998 dollars.

7. We include Alaska and Washington (and California in 1998) since the top vote getter in each party advances to the general election. Even though it is a blanket primary, we have divided the votes into the two parties to get the percentage received by each candidate within his or her party.

8. "In August 1996, the U.S. District Court for the Southern District of Texas, in *Vera et al. v. Bush et al.*, redrew district boundaries, invalidated the results of the primary and runoff elections, and ordered new elections in 13 congressional districts. In those districts, candidates participated in a special general election on November 5, 1996. Where no candidate received a majority of the vote cast, a runoff election was held on December 10, 1996, between the top two vote getters, regardless of party." (Federal Election Commission, *Federal Elections 96: Election Results for the U.S. President, the U.S. Senate, and the U.S. House of Representatives,* Washington, D.C.: Federal Election Commission, 1997.) The districts were 3, 5, 6, 7, 8, 9, 18, 22, 24, 25, 26, 29, and 30.

9. In two cases, the incumbent representative runs for senator. When comparing primary and general elections, we exclude cases where the primary winner drops out of the race. Whenever there was a special election in a district during an election cycle, we also exclude the subsequent (regular) primary election, for we have not yet been able to separate the spending in the special and the general (primary or general) elections, as a result of inconsistencies in FEC coding. Finally, we generally omit the four primary elections in which two incumbents ran against each other.

10. While certain elections are thought to be bad for Democrats or Republicans, some elections will be hard on incumbents generally. The most recent example of this was in 1992, which was a bad year for incumbents for two reasons: First, the reapportionment forced five incumbents to run against five other incumbents (in four primary elections, and one general election). Other redistricting changes forced incumbents to adjust to a new constituency. Second, in 1991, the public learned that many House members had bounced checks at the House Bank. In response to this scandal, voters could vote against the incum-

bent in the general election *and* the primary election. Additionally in 1992, because of redistricting, four incumbents defeated other incumbents in the primary (and another incumbent was defeated by an incumbent in the general). With such an unusual circumstance and so few cases, we usually do not include it in the analyses that follow.

11. Robert A. Bernstein ("Divisive Primaries Do Hurt: U.S. Senate Races, 1956–1972," *American Political Science Review* 71 [1977]: 540–55) and Paul S. Herrnson (*Congressional Elections: Campaigning at Home and in Washington,* 2d ed. [Washington, D.C.: Congressional Quarterly Press, 1998]) use the 20 percent margin to define a competitive general election.

12. Andrew Hacker ("Does a 'Divisive' Primary Harm a Candidate's Election Chances?" *American Political Science Review* 59 [1965]: 105–10) defines a divisive primary as one in which the winning candidate receives less than 65 percent. If one measures by absolute vote percentage, one cannot distinguish between a candidate who defeats one candidate 55 to 45 from a candidate who wins 55 percent of the vote while three other candidates split 45 percent evenly. Paul S. Herrnson and James G. Gimpel ("District Conditions and Primary Divisiveness in Congressional Elections," *Political Research Quarterly* 48, 1 [1995]: 117–34) devise a more complex, linear measure that takes into account the primary vote proportion for all candidates. Since we treat these data as a simple dichotomy, we use the simpler 20 percent margin.

13. We exclude those cases in which the incumbent lost in the primary election (or primary runoff) to a challenger ($N = 22$) and cases where the incumbent ran against another incumbent in the primary ($N = 4$). We also drop candidates such as Dean Gallo of New Jersey's 11th district in 1994; after he won the primary election, he withdrew from the general.

14. All seven challengers who defeated the incumbent by a margin exceeding 20 percent won the general election. This does not include incumbents who faced other incumbents in primaries, nor the challengers who ran against two incumbents in a primary.

15. Herrnson (*Congressional Elections*) presents figures for the 1996 general election (figures 6.4, 6.5, and 6.6). His data are consistent with the results presented here, as are Ezra's ("The Benefits and Burdens of Congressional Primary Elections") for the 1994 election. Herrnson's data are also consistent with data in Norman J. Ornstein, Thomas E. Mann, and Michael I. Malbin (*Vital Statistics on Congress, 1999–2000* [Washington, D.C.: American Enterprise Institute, 2000] table 3.8). In general, all financial data are right-skewed. However, all of our conclusions hold when using the median as a basis for comparison. For ease of exposition, we use the mean (average).

16. Gary C. Jacobson, *The Politics of Congressional Elections*, 4th ed. (Boston: Allyn and Bacon, 1996).

17. John R. Wright, *Interest Groups and Congress: Lobbying, Contributions, and Influence* (Boston: Allyn and Bacon, 1996).

18. Herrnson, *Congressional Elections*, 112.

19. Following Herrnson, "candidate contributions include loans candidates made to their own campaigns" (Herrnson, *Congressional Elections*, 113).

20. Theodore J. Eismeier and Philip H. Pollock III, "Money in the 1994 Elections and Beyond," in *Midterm: Elections of 1994 in Context*, ed. Philip A. Kinkler (Boulder, Colo.: Westview, 1996), 86.

21. The eight incumbents who faced other incumbents in the primary election (not

included in the table) are qualitatively similar to other incumbents, except that the four incumbents that lost relied more heavily on PACs (56 percent) and less heavily on individuals (34 percent).

22. L. Sandy Maisel, *From Obscurity to Oblivion; Running in the Congressional Primary*, rev. ed. (Knoxville: University of Tennessee Press, 1982), 68.

23. The same results hold when examining only the winner in each primary.

24. Herrnson, *Congressional Elections.*

25. For this section, general-election spending includes spending that occurred before the primary election. The spending that took place before the primary election likely was affected by (and affected) the competitiveness of the general election race. As Edie N. Goldenberg and Michael W. Traugott note, "Incumbents who were vulnerable spent a great deal of money both before and during the general-election campaign" (*Campaigning for Congress* [Washington, D.C.: Congressional Quarterly Press, 1984], 83). We expect viable challengers and open-seat candidates to do the same.

26. This anomaly disappears when considering the top two finishers in the primary.

27. In this section, we exclude unopposed primaries since, by definition, spending cannot affect the vote percentage.

28. David B. Magleby and Candice J. Nelson, *The Money Chase: Congressional Campaign Finance Reform* (Washington, D.C.: Brookings Institution, 1990).

29. David R. Mayhew, *Congress: The Electoral Connection* (New Haven, Conn.: Yale University Press, 1974).

6

Elections and Amateurs: The Christian Right in the 1998 Congressional Campaigns

John C. Green

In a closely watched prelude to the 1998 congressional campaign, a special election was held to fill the seat vacated by the death of California Democrat Walter Capps.[1] The Democratic nomination was straightforward: Lois Capps, the widow of the late congressman, was the presumptive nominee. In contrast, the Republican nomination was contested. Hoping to pick up the seat for the GOP (Grand Old Party) in a swing district, party professionals recruited a state legislator, Brooks Firestone. A successful vintner and an heir to the Firestone tire fortune, his moderate views on abortion and related issues resembled those of Michael Huffington, who had represented the district prior to 1994. At the same time, amateur activists, especially from the Christian Right, hoped to expand the ranks of cultural conservatives in Congress by taking advantage of this opportunity. They recruited another state legislator, Tom Bordonaro. Confined to a wheelchair and of a blue-collar background, Bordonaro's conservative views on abortion and related issues resembled those of Andrea Seastrand, who won the seat in 1994.

The Republican nomination was hard fought. The GOP establishment rallied to Firestone with endorsements and money, while the Christian Right aided Bordonaro with voter guides in churches and issue advertisements on television, including extensive independent spending by the Campaign for Working Families, headed by soon-to-be GOP presidential candidate Gary Bauer. Bordonaro won a narrow victory over Firestone in the primary but then lost an equally contentious and close general-election contest to Democrat Capps a few weeks later.[2]

Bitter recriminations followed Bordonaro's defeat. Party professionals blamed the Christian Right for missing an opportunity to take a seat from the Democrats and expand the slim GOP majority in Congress—a view shared even by former Christian Coalition leader Ralph Reed.[3] From this point of view, the Bordonaro campaign was too culturally conservative for the district. However, Gary Bauer and other Christian Right amateurs were unrepentant, arguing that the narrow loss resulted from poor execution, not poor strategy or message. From their point of view, nominating candidates like Tom Bordonaro was essential to furthering the goals of the Christian Right because more moderate Republicans, like Brooks Firestone, typically failed to support a culturally conservative agenda once in Congress.

The controversy surrounding the Bordonaro campaign raises important questions: What kind of impact can amateur activists have via the nomination process? Are they doomed to disappointment because their candidates are too extreme for the electorate? Or can amateurs use primaries as vehicles for electing candidates who will advance their agenda once in office?

Using a unique data set, this chapter explores the involvement and the impact of the Christian Right in the 1998 primary and general elections, identifying factors associated with both success and failure at the ballot box. We find that success was most likely when a combination of grievances, resources, and opportunities allowed the Christian Right to affect the composition of the vote on election day. Overall, the Christian Right's efforts were about as likely to help as to hurt Republican fortunes in 1998, which was a bad year for the GOP.[4] This evidence suggests that amateur activists can make some modest headway on behalf of their agenda via the nomination process, although their efforts are risky and often fail.

ELECTIONS AND AMATEURS

Even casual observers of American politics will recognize the Bordonaro-Firestone contest as a classic confrontation between party "professionals" and "amateur" activists over a nomination.[5] This kind of conflict is best known from presidential primaries, where negative outcomes are legendary. For instance, the success of conservative amateurs in nominating Republican Barry Goldwater in 1964 led to a landslide defeat in the general election, and similar results were obtained when liberal amateurs helped nominate Democrat George McGovern in 1972. The Christian Right is just the latest group of amateur activists to contest primary elections in this fashion.[6] And like other amateurs, they are best known for their nomination successes and general-election failures, as in the Bordonaro campaigns. Of course, amateurs of all sorts as well as some scholars read the electoral record quite differently, noting successes as well as failures.[7]

The spatial or Downsian model of elections offers a baseline against which to assess the influence of amateur activists via elections. The simplest version of this model assumes a two-candidate race in which citizen preferences are normally distributed from "right" to "left" along a single continuum and in which all citizens vote. Under such circumstances, the desire to win leads both candidates to take positions close to the preferences of the median voter, thus converging toward the proverbial "center" of the electorate.[8] Candidates positioned away from the center lose votes to their more centrally located opponents.

While this simple formulation captures an important reality of electoral competition, it also ignores other aspects of elections, and for this reason, scholars have produced numerous elaborations of this simple model,[9] two of which are especially useful here. First, scholars have assumed a sequence of two contests, a primary and a general election.[10] It is generally assumed that primary voters have more "extreme" preferences than the median voter in the electorate as a whole.[11] This pattern can occur simply because the primary electorates represent the "right" and the "left" tails of the distribution of preferences, but it could also reflect other factors, such as intensity of opinion.[12]

In a two-contest model, the desire to win leads candidates first to take positions near the median primary voter and away from the center of opinion (to secure a nomination), but then to change positions to be closer to the median general-election voter (to win the general election). In this formulation, the more extreme primary voters stick with the respective nominees in the general election, despite their move toward the center, because such voters "have no place to go," that is, no other candidate for whom to vote. Thus, candidates converge toward the center of the electorate after diverging in the primaries.[13]

Much criticism of the Bordonaro campaign assumed something like this simple two-contest model. By this logic, Bordonaro won the GOP primary by seeking out the median voter in the GOP nomination contest, who was more conservative than the median general-election voter, but then did not—or could not—move far enough to the center, losing potential voters and the election to Democrat Capps. Echoing common complaints about amateur activists,[14] some critics accused the campaign and its Christian Right allies of "ignorance" (basically, not understanding the spatial model of elections) and "irrationality" (for, in effect, backing a candidate who guaranteed the victory of a Democrat who strongly opposed their agenda). To these critics, Christian Rightists were amateurs in all senses of the word.

Christian conservatives saw the situation quite differently, however. They argued that conservative voters did indeed have "somewhere to go" and that was to stay home.[15] Conservative citizens needed a good reason to vote in the primary and general elections, one that could only be supplied by a conservative candidate, campaign, and message.[16] They believed Bordonaro won the nomination by encouraging turnout among conservative citizens and was nearly elected to Congress by the same means. Rather than based on ignorance or irrationality, this strategy was a sophisticated, if risky, approach to pursuing a culturally conservative agenda.

Second, scholars have adapted the simple spatial model to allow citizen turnout to vary. Here the relevant distribution of voter preferences is the one that materializes on election day, and campaigns can alter this structure by bringing new groups of citizens to the polls.[17] Under such circumstances, the candidates still converge toward the median voter on election day, but the median preference would be more "extreme" (that is, farther from median preference of the citizenry at large) than in the absence of the campaign. Put another way, the Bordonaro campaign was directed at changing the distribution of voter preferences on election day rather than responding to the distribution presumed by past elections or polling. Of course, failure to achieve this change would leave the nominee badly "out of position" on election day, that is, too far from the actual median voter preference. Fear of taking this kind of risk, in the opinion of the Christian Right, makes party leaders all too professional.

In the final analysis, party professionals and Christian Right amateurs had quite different goals in the California special election. Most of the party professionals actually preferred Brooks Firestone's moderate positions on cultural issues and were fairly content with current public policy on these matters. Thus, they were quite comfortable accepting what appeared to be the existing distribution of voter preferences as the basis of their strategy and pursuing an additional Republican seat in Congress—an outcome likely to solidify the policy status quo. Of course, if the median voter had been sufficiently conservative on cultural issues, Christian conservatives might well have followed suit.[18] However, since these activists were unhappy with the policy status quo, they predicated their strategy on altering the distribution of voter preferences on election day—and potentially increasing the number of cultural conservatives in Congress.

THE CHRISTIAN RIGHT AND ELECTORAL POLITICS

The Christian Right is a social movement among religious conservatives, especially evangelical Protestants, dedicated to restoring traditional morality in public policy.[19] Like other social movements, the Christian Right seeks to implement its agenda by challenging existing institutions and policies and by changing the structure of preferences that support them.[20] This movement arose in the late 1970s and first attracted attention when Jerry Falwell and the Moral Majority supported Ronald Reagan for president in 1980. Since then, the movement has been very active in politics, including Pat Robertson's efforts to obtain the Republican presidential nomination in 1988. Most of the original movement organizations have faded (the Moral Majority was disbanded in 1989) and have been replaced by a second generation of groups, of which the Christian Coalition is best known (it was founded by Pat Robertson in 1989). Other prominent movement groups include a network of organizations revolving around James Dobson and Gary Bauer, such as Focus on the Family, the Family Research Council, and the Campaign for Working Families. By 1998, this network had become especially aggressive in congressional campaigns as a prelude to Bauer's bid for the 2000 Republican nomination. The Bordonaro special-election campaign was part of these efforts.

Christian Right political activity arises from the movement's grievances, resources, and opportunities.[21] Grievances lie at the root of all social movements and can be used to mobilize members to political action. The Christian Right's grievances are focused on cultural issues, such as opposition to abortion and gay rights. However, aggrieved citizens cannot be mobilized into politics without tangible resources, such as money, personnel, and leadership, including sympathetic candidates and officeholders. Movements typically secure such resources from preexisting nonpolitical groups associated with the aggrieved population. For the Christian Right, these resources were found principally in the membership, churches, and parachurch organizations of evangelical Protestantism. Finally, to be effective, such resources must be deployed where they have the greatest likelihood of addressing the motivating grievances. Movement leaders thus seek out the best opportunities to successfully challenge existing institutions to effect changes in policy.

From the beginning, congressional elections presented the Christian Right with valuable opportunities.[22] First, the aggrieved religious population that the movement sought to mobilize, evangelical Protestants and other religious conservatives, was quite numerous in many places. Second, this population had not been very active in elections prior to 1980 and thus represented a potential addition to the active electorate. And third, this geographical constituency was concentrated in areas experiencing rapid social and political change, where new votes could be moved from one party to another. All these factors were especially relevant in competitive campaigns, where mobilizing even a small number of voters could alter the distribution of voter preferences on election day and in contests with the Republican Party, which was most receptive to cultural conservatism.

Overall, the Christian Right has been the most active and most successful in elections where the movement's grievances, resources, and opportunities occurred together: in districts with large populations of evangelical Protestants, where movement activists and sympathetic candidates were common, and when primary and general elections were competitive.[23] Put in the terms just discussed, these were contests in which the movement could alter the distribution of voter preferences on election day by using its resources to bring its aggrieved constituents to the polls.

Given these circumstances, the Christian Right has been most active in stimulating turnout in general elections.[24] The tactic of choice was the distribution of "nonpartisan" voter guides in churches just prior to an election, providing evangelical voters with relevant information on the candidates. Movement activists have also used door-to-door canvassing, telephone banks, direct mail, and even television advertising to reach their prime constituency. These efforts have helped numerous Republican candidates, including many that were not strong supporters of the movement's agenda.[25]

In fact, the unresponsiveness of many GOP officeholders to the movement's agenda has been a principal motivation for the Christian Right's involvement in primaries and other nomination contests. There was an additional reason for this involvement, however: the movement's turnout strategy was much easier to implement when candidates reflected the movement's goals and stressed the grievances of the movement's constituency. For these reasons, the Christian Right quickly became involved in all stages of the nomination process, from recruiting candidates and organizing campaigns to mobilizing voters. The Bordonaro campaign was a prime example.

This background suggest some clear expectations regarding the involvement and the impact of the Christian Right in the 1998 primary and general elections. First, we would expect involvement and impact to occur in races in which the movement's aggrieved constituency is concentrated, movement resources are common, and elections are competitive. Armed with these expectations, we can turn to describing the involvement of the Christian Right in the 1998 elections, its impact on the outcomes, and the factors that influenced success and failure. Was the Bordonaro campaign typical of movement activism in 1998?

DATA AND METHODS

This chapter is based on a list of congressional races in which the Christian Right was involved in 1998. This list was developed from a variety of sources, including interviews with Christian Right activists and opponents, news reports, and documentary sources. Christian Right involvement was defined by evidence of substantial campaign activity on behalf of a candidate. These races included three kinds of candidates: (1) candidates who arose from within the movement itself, having been members of Christian Right groups or associated religious organizations; (2) candidates who were closely associated with the movement, through a history of support from the movement or strong support for issues central to the movement, but who were not members of the movement per se; and (3) candidates who were not closely associated with the movement but who were supported nonetheless in 1998. This list of races will serve as the basis for describing the involvement of the Christian Right in the 1998 campaign (see table 6.1).

In order to assess the factors associated with the involvement and the impact of the Christian Right in primary and general elections in 1998, we turn to statistical analysis. Unfortunately, our measure of movement involvement is not of even quality, so it must be treated as nominal data for statistical purposes. For example, when we investigate movement involvement in primary campaigns, the dependent variable is coded "1" if the Christian Right was involved and "0" if not (see the first column of table 6.2). Likewise, when we investigate the success of Christian Right impact in primaries or general elections (see the second and third columns of table 6.2), the dependent variable is coded "1" for a victory of a movement-backed candidate and "0" for a loss. All the analyses in table 6.2 employ

Table 6.1: The Christian Right and House Campaigns, 1998

Movement-Supported Candidates with:	Percent	n =
Contested Primary		
Primary and general-election winners	15.9	22
Primary winners	16.6	23
Primary losers	10.8	15
No Contested Primary		
General-election winners	44.9	62
General-election losers	11.6	16
Totals	100.0	138

logistic regression because the dependent variables were dichotomous. The independent variables used in these analyses are rough measures of (1) grievances, (2) resources, and (3) opportunities associated with the Christian Right.[26]

Because of the lack of district-level public opinion data, movement *grievances* are difficult to measure directly, and we use three indirect measures for the cultural conservatism of the district. The first of these proxies is the most straightforward: the percentage of district population belonging to evangelical Protestant denominations, the key constituency of the Christian Right. These figures were estimated for congressional elections by aggregating county-level church membership data.[27] The second variable is also straightforward: the 1996 district vote for the Republican presidential candidate, Bob Dole. The Republican presidential vote is often used as a rough proxy for district conservatism.[28] The third measure is the Christian Coalition score of the incumbent member of Congress, based on roll call votes. Such measures have been associated with the underlying opinion of the district.[29]

The second set of variables in table 6.2 represents movement *resources*. The first is the most direct: an estimate of the number of movement activists in the district, derived from mailing lists of movement organizations.[30] The next two measures refer to the resources bound up in candidates, an important factor in candidate-centered politics. One is a dummy variable for incumbent supporters of movement (measured by 80 or higher on Christian Coalition score); these candidates represent the movements past "investment" in congressional supporters. The second variable is a dummy variable for viable nonincumbent candidates (measured as nonincumbents that raised either the most funds in the race or more than 75 percent of the winner's funds); these are the kind of candidates that allow the Christian Right to increase its level of congressional support.[31]

The third set of variables assesses electoral *opportunities*. The first two are simple measures of electoral competition: the winner's margin of victory in the

Table 6.2: Involvement and Impact of the Christian Right in House Campaigns, 1998

Logistic Regression	Primary Election Involvement	Primary Election Victory	General Election Victory
Grievances			
Percent evangelical Protestants	NS	.17**	.11**
Vote for Dole, 1996	.09*	.20***	.07*
Christian Coalition scores	.06*	NS	NS
Resources			
Number of movement activists	.07*	.17**	.29***
Incumbent supporters	NS	.21***	.11**
Viable challengers	NS	.15**	.10
Opportunities			
Electoral competitiveness	−.25***	NS	−.22***
Primary competitiveness	−.21***	−.11**	NS
Open-seat	.13**	.10*	NS
Contested primary	—	—	NS
Percent predicted correctly	60	64	69

*Significant at the .10 level.
**Significant at the .05 level.
***Significant at the .01 level.
All dependent variables are scored "1" or "0"—"1" for primary involvement by the Christian Right (first column); primary victory of Christian Right–supported candidate (second column); general election victory by Christian Right–supported candidate (third column).

primary and general elections in 1998. Here the smaller the margin of victory, the more competitive the election. Using the actual election results to judge competitiveness is problematic, of course, because political decisions are made in anticipation of competitiveness, but scholars have judged the two things to be highly correlated.[32] We also include a dummy variable for open seats in 1998, and for the final analysis, we include a dummy variable for primaries contested by the Christian Right.

THE CHRISTIAN RIGHT AND THE 1998 ELECTIONS

The 1998 congressional election was a major disappointment for the Christian Right.[33] Several movement supporters were defeated and many promising candidates failed to win primaries or general elections. Of course, 1998 was a bad year for the GOP and all its allies—the Democrats, the party holding the White House, picked up seats in midterm election for the first time in 64 years. In contrast, the 1994 election was a very positive experience for the movement and for the GOP in general—the Republicans took control of Congress for the first time in 40 years.[34]

Our task here is to investigate the factors associated with Christian Right activity, success, and failure in 1998. We begin with a profile of Christian Right activity in the 1998 campaign. Table 6.1 describes the House races in which the Christian Right was involved, categorized by electoral context.

Overall, the Christian Right was involved in 138 races, a little more than one-third of all congressional districts. These figures are typical of the level and the range of movement activity in the 1990s and are somewhat larger than in the 1980s. Approximately three-quarters of the candidates listed in table 6.1 had strong and clear connections to the Christian Right. Very few originated from within the movement itself, and as in the past, most of these did very poorly. Most such candidates were recruited through normal political channels, either having been supported by the Christian Right for lower offices or having championed issues of concern to the movement. As in the Bordonaro case, movement activists were often aggressive in recruiting and supporting these candidates in nomination contests.

However, roughly one-quarter of the candidates backed were not closely associated with the Christian Right. These were a diverse lot: some were legislative leaders in safe seats, others were imperiled Republican incumbents, and still others were weak opponents of Democratic candidates especially disliked by movement leaders. Two were conservative Democrats, backed at least in part to demonstrate the movement's "bipartisanship." Thus, the Christian Right revealed some pragmatism in 1998, as well as strong commitment to furthering its agenda.

The first major category in table 6.1 reports Christian Right involvement in contested primary elections. These races accounted for better than two-fifths of the cases. These candidates secured the nomination three-fourths of the time (or some 33 percent of all such cases) and failed to win in the remaining one-quarter of the cases (11 percent of the total). It is interesting that about one-half of the movement-supported nominees went on to win the general election (16 percent of the total) and that almost the same number failed to do so (17 percent). On the face of it, these data suggest that movement-supported candidates were as likely to help as to hurt Republican fortunes in 1998.

It is worth noting that the power of incumbency was at work in these numbers: some three-quarters of the primary victors were movement-backed incumbents who faced challenges from within the GOP. Nearly all of these candidates were also reelected. Many of these candidates first entered Congress in the 1990s, often beginning their congressional careers with help from the Christian Right in primaries. In contrast, only one-fifth of nonincumbent primary candidates backed by the movement prevailed in the general election.

Incumbency was even more of a factor in the second major category in table 6.1, races with no contested primary. Some four-fifths of these candidates (or about 45 percent of the total) won reelection, and most were incumbents. Some of these candidates were in safe seats, but others faced significant general-election opposition or the potential for a serious challenge early in the 1998 election cycle. Many were long-time supporters of the Christian Right, also the fruit of past movement recruitment and primary battles.

The remaining one-fifth of these candidates (some 12 percent of the total) lost the general election. However, only one-quarter of these candidates were closely connected to the Christian Right, the remaining being threatened incumbents and competitive open-seat races in which the GOP had a good prospect of prevailing but ended up losing. As much as anything, it was these races that produced the historic Democratic midterm election gains in 1998. Had these candidates prevailed, as similarly situated candidates did in 1994, the Republicans—and the Christian Right—would have been able to claim considerable success. But here the movement also batted .500: just one of the defeated Republican incumbents was closely associated with the Christian Right, and the only Republican to defeat a Democratic incumbent was as well.[35]

ELECTORAL INVOLVEMENT AND IMPACT

What factors accounted for the involvement of the Christian Right in primary elections? And what factors were associated with winning nominations and then general elections? Table 6.2 offers answers with three analyses using logistic regression (dependent and independent variables are described earlier). These analyses do not offer a full explanation of the election results, which is far beyond the scope of this chapter. Instead, we seek simply to understand the involvement and the potential influence of the Christian Right by comparing races in which the movement was active and its candidates successful to other races in which the movement was not active or was unsuccessful.

The first column in table 6.2 investigates the Christian Right's involvement in primary campaigns and shows an immediate surprise: the percentage of evangelical Protestants in the district was not statistically significant. This figure suggests that the movement was as likely to be active in primary campaigns in which their prime constituency was more numerous as in campaigns in which it was less so. This finding may reflect the fact that districts with large numbers of evangelicals have become heavily Republican—at least for the purposes of GOP primaries. The other grievance factors perform more as expected: the movement was most likely to be active in districts that voted for Dole in 1996 and in which the incumbent is not rated highly by the Christian Coalition. Taken together, these last two variables suggest that the movement activity was motivated in part by the conservatism of the district.[36]

The resource variables in the first column reveal similar surprises: the presence of neither incumbents who strongly favored the movement nor viable challengers was statistically significant. This finding suggests that candidate status was not by itself a factor in primary involvement. The number of movement activists was modestly associated with primary involvement. However, by far the largest coefficients were for the electoral opportunity variables. The Christian Right was most likely to be involved in competitive elections (where the margins of victory of general election and primary winners were small), and in open-seat races.

A very different pattern held for primary victories by candidates backed by the Christian Right. First, unlike involvement in primary campaigns, the percentage of evangelical Protestants was positively associated with securing nominations. This finding is consistent with the strategy of changing the distribution of voter preferences in an election. Similarly, the success was associated with the Republican vote, and presumably conservatism, of the district, although the Christian Coalition score of the incumbent member of Congress was not significant. Movement resources were also associated with primary victories. Note that the number of Christian Right activists was positively associated with success, as was the presence of both supportive incumbents and viable challengers. Electoral opportunity factors were statistically significant as well, especially the competitiveness of the primary and the presence of open seats.

A comparison of the first and second columns of table 6.2 suggests that the Christian Right was involved in primary races primarily because of electoral opportunities, but that movement-based candidates were successful when such opportunities were coupled with an aggrieved population (evangelical Protestants, conservatives) and the resources to mobilize it (movement activists and good candidates).

This pattern is even stronger in the third column of table 6.2, which considers general-election victories by movement-backed candidates. The percentage of evangelical Protestants is especially important here, followed by the 1996 Republican vote in the district. Movement resources also mattered, especially the number of movement activists. Once again, both incumbent supporters and viable challengers are associated with success. General-election competitiveness was statistically significant, once again pointing to the importance of electoral opportunities.

It is interesting that the presence of a primary contested by the movement-backed candidates was not statistically significant. If movement involvement in primaries consistently helped candidates win elections, we would expect this coefficient to be positive and significant. In contrast, if movement activists consistently hurt movement-backed candidates, we would expect this coefficient to be negative and significant. The fact that the coefficient is neither suggests that movement involvement in primaries, of itself, neither hurt nor helped Republican fortunes. Or, put another way, sometimes movement-backed candidates cost the GOP at the ballot box, and sometimes the party benefited from them, depending on the combination of grievances, resources, and opportunities in the district. Taken as a whole, the patterns in table 6.2 suggest that the Christian Right had some modest success in advancing its agenda via nomination contests in 1998.

CONCLUSIONS

The Bordonaro special-election campaign was in some important respects typical of Christian Right involvement in the 1998 campaign. The movement helped recruit a culturally conservative candidate and then lavishly supported him in nomination and general election campaigns, deploying its resources to mobilize an aggrieved population in a contest in which such efforts had a good opportunity to succeed. Such mobilization was predicated on a strategy of changing the structure of voter preferences on election day.

However, in other respects the Bordonaro campaign was atypical of Christian Right involvement in the 1998 campaign: movement-backed primary winners were not uniformly defeated in the general election. In fact, the Christian Right involvement was as likely to help as to hurt Republican fortunes at the polls. To be sure, incumbency played a major role in these results, with movement-backed incumbents more likely to win and movement-backed challengers more likely to lose. But the impact of incumbency is hardly unique to candidates backed by the Christian Right. Just as important to movement-backed candidates' success was the ability to bring their constituency to the polls.

The Bordonaro campaign was certainly a major disappointment to Christian conservatives. It could well be, as movement operatives argued, that the failure of the campaign resulted from poor execution, not poor strategy. Such a failure in execution would have left Bordonaro out of position on election day, too far to the right of the median voter on cultural issues. And it is also possible that Bordonaro and his allies misjudged the population of the district, and the campaign would have been too conservative in any event. As we have seen, the Christian Right was involved in a number of primary races in 1998 where the district was not especially conservative in cultural terms. Of course, in close elections, it is quite difficult to determine for certain the relative impact of any one factor.[37]

However, the narrow defeat of the Bordonaro campaign and the broader pattern of Christian Right activity in 1998 suggest that primary elections are vehicles by which amateur activists can advance their agenda. It is this possibility that has motivated generations of amateur activists to contest nominations, from advocates of civil, women's, and gay rights to the Christian Right. Such a strategy can be successful but it is risky: it first requires that aggrieved populations exist in the right numbers and in the right places, and then it requires that these populations be brought to the polls in a fashion that changes the distribution of preferences on election day. The distribution of voter preferences may not be set in stone, but neither is it infinitely malleable.

These findings also suggest that scholars and politicians should apply simple spatial models of elections to real contests with some caution. Indeed, it is the uncritical application of such models that has made the failures of amateur activists in primary elections legendary, while their successes—and the failures of party professionals—attract less attention. For example, Barry Goldwater's defeat in 1964 is laid at the feet of amateur activists, but such activists rarely receive credit for Ronald Reagan's victory in 1980, and party professionalism is rarely blamed for Bob Dole's defeat in 1996. A similar situation routinely obtains with regard to the Christian Right, as demonstrated by the Bordonaro campaign. A more complete understanding of elections and amateurs would assign both blame and credit where they are due.

NOTES

1. Norah M. O'Donnell, "Capps 53 Percent Win Cheers Democrats, Restores Old Record of 53 Women in House," *Roll Call* 43, no. 65 (1998): 1, 28. J. Christopher Soper and Joel Fetzer, "The Christian Right and the Republican Party in California: Necessarily Yoked," in *Prayers in the Precincts*, ed. John C. Green, Mark J. Rozell, and Clyde Wilcox (Washington, D.C.: Georgetown University Press, 2000).

2. The special election was held in the 22nd Congressional district in California. The contest was a blanket primary, where Capps, Bordonaro, and Firestone all ran on the same ballot; Capps received 46%, Bordonaro 30%, and Firestone 24% of the two-party vote. In a runoff election between Capps and Bordonaro, Capps received 54% and Bordonaro received 46% of the two-party vote.

The events of the spring special election were replayed in the regular fall contests: Capps and Bordonaro once again won their party's nominations, and Capps won the election with 56% of the two-party vote (Michael Barone and Grant Ujifusa, *The Almanac of American Politics* [Washington, D.C.: National Journal, 1999]).

3. Rachel Van Dongen, "Even His Allies Question Use of 'Partial Birth' Ads," *Roll Call* 43, no. 76 (1998): 15, 18.

4. Barone and Ujifusa, *The Almanac of American Politics*.

5. Jeffrey Berry and Deborah Schildkraut, "Citizen Groups, Political Parties, and Electoral Coalitions," in *Social Movements and American Political Institutions*, ed. Anne Costain and Andrew S. McFarland (Lanham, Md.: Rowman & Littlefield, 1998). James Q. Wilson, *The Amateur Democrat* (Chicago: University of Chicago Press, 1962).

6. Duane Oldfield, *The Right and the Righteous: The Christian Right Confronts the Republican Party* (Lanham, Md.: Rowman & Littlefield, 1996). Allen D. Hertzke, *Echoes of Discontent* (Washington, D.C.: Congressional Quarterly Press, 1993).

7. Denise L. Baer and David A. Bositis, *Elite Cadres and Party Coalitions* (New York: Greenwood, 1988).

8. Anthony Downs, *An Economic Theory of Democracy* (New York: Harper and Row, 1957).

9. See James M. Enelow and Melvin J. Hinich, eds., *Advances in the Spatial Theory of Voting* (New York: Cambridge University Press, 1984).

10. Peter Aranson and Peter C. Ordeshook, "Spatial Strategy for Sequential Elections," in *Probability Models of Collective Decision Making*, ed. R. Niemi and H. Weisberg (Columbus, Ohio: Merrill, 1972).

11. See Barbara Norrander, "Ideological Representativeness of Presidential Primary Voters," *American Journal of Political Science* 33 (1989): 570–87. For activists, see John S. Jackson III and Nancy L. Clayton, "Leaders and Followers: Major Party Elites, Identifiers, and Issues, 1980–92," in *The State of the Parties*, ed. John C. Green and Daniel M. Shea (Lanham, Md.: Rowman & Littlefield, 1996).

12. John H. Aldrich, "A Downsian Spatial Model with Party Activism," *American Political Science Review* 77 (1983): 974–90.

13. There is considerable debate over whether the convergence assumed by spatial models produces policy moderation or polarization (Gary W. Cox, "Centripetal and Centrifugal Incentives in Electoral Systems," *American Journal of Political Science* 34 [1990]: 903–35). Both outcomes are possible; the activities of amateur activists probably contribute to policy polarization.

14. Nelson Polsby, *The Consequences of Party Reform* (Oxford: Oxford University Press, 1983).

15. Another place for voters to go is to minor parties. In 1998, a Christian Right minor party contributed directly to the defeat of Republican incumbent Rick White (Wash.-1) (Andrew M. Appleton and Michael Buckley, "Washington: Christian Right Setbacks Abound," in *Prayers in the Precincts*, ed. John C. Green, Mark J. Rozell, and Clyde Wilcox [Washington, D.C.: Georgetown University Press, 2000]).

16. Van Dongen: "Even His Allies Question."

17. Another alternative is to allow voters to change their preferences based on appeals from candidates. The Christian Right makes relatively little effort to change the preferences of citizens in campaigns.

Ingemar Hansson and Charles Stuart, "Voting Competitions with Interested Politicians: Platforms Do Not Converge to the Preferences of the Median Voter," *Public Choice* 44 (1984): 431–41. Donald A. Wittman, "Candidate Motivations: A Synthesis of Alternatives." *American Political Science Review* 77 (1983): 142–57.

18. But perhaps not: Christian Rightists might well have bypassed the election and worked in other races where they could have changed the structure of opinion.

19. Clyde Wilcox, *Onward Christian Soldiers* (Boulder, Colo.: Westview, 1996).

20. Robert H. Salisbury, "Political Movements in American Politics," *National Journal of Political Science* 1 (1989): 15–30.

21. John C. Green, James L. Guth, and Kevin Hill, "Faith and Election: The Christian Right in Congressional Campaigns 1978–1988." *Journal of Politics* 55 (1993): 80–91.

22. John C. Green, Mark J. Rozell, and Clyde Wilcox, eds., *Prayers in the Precincts: The Christian Right in the 1998 Elections* (Washington, D.C.: Georgetown University Press, 2000).

23. Green, Guth, and Hill, "Faith and Election." James L. Guth and John C. Green, "Politics in the Promised Land: The Christian Right at the Grassroots," in *Research in the Social Science Study of Religion*, ed. Monty L. Lynn and David O. Moberg (Greenwich, Conn.: JAI Press, 1993), 219–34.

24. Mark J. Rozell and Clyde Wilcox, *Interest Groups in American Campaigns* (Washington, D.C.: Congressional Quarterly Press, 1999).

25. John C. Green, James L. Guth, Corwin E. Smidt, and Lyman A. Kellstedt, *Religion and the Culture Wars* (Lanham, Md.: Rowman & Littlefield, 1996). Mark J. Rozell and Clyde Wilcox, eds., *God at the Grass Roots* (Lanham, Md.: Rowman & Littlefield, 1995). Mark J. Rozell and Clyde Wilcox, eds., *God at the Grass Roots 1996* (Lanham, Md.: Rowman & Littlefield, 1997).

26. John C. Green, James L. Guth, and Clyde Wilcox, "Less than Conquerors: The Christian Right in State Republican Parties," in *Social Movements and American Political Institutions*, ed. Anne N. Costain and Andrew S. McFarland (Lanham, Md.: Rowman & Littlefield, 1998). Green, Guth, and Hill, "Faith and Election."

27. The proportion of evangelical Protestants at the district level and the number of evangelical churches were estimated from the county-level data on religious group membership supplied by the Glenmary Research Center (Martin B. Bradley, et al., *Churches and Church Membership in the United States 1990* [Atlanta, Ga.: Glenmary Research Center, 1992]. For coding, see Green, Guth, Smidt, and Kellstedt, *Religion and the Culture Wars*. Religious population could also be considered a resource (see Green, Guth, and Hill, "Faith and Election"), but since we have a more direct measure of movement resources, we consider it as a measure of cultural conservatism.

28. John C. McAdams and John R. Johannes, "Determinants of Spending by House Challengers 1974–84," *American Journal of Political Science* 31 (1987): 457–83.

29. Robert S. Erickson, "Roll Calls, Reputations, and Representation in the U.S. Senate," *Legislative Studies Quarterly* 25 (1990): 623–43.

30. The number of movement activists was estimated by aggregating the zip codes of names of membership and fundraising lists of Christian Right organizations by congressional district. Districts with large numbers of activists are not necessarily culturally conservative. The movement is well organized in many suburban districts, which are culturally moderate (Guth and Green, "Politics in the Promised Land").

31. Green, Guth, and Hill, "Faith and Election." Candidate status can be considered an opportunity variable as well. However, when looking at primaries from the point of view of social movements, candidates are also potent resources for mobilizing voters.

32. Gary C. Jacobson, *Money in Congressional Elections* (New Haven, Conn.: Yale University Press, 1980).

33. Green, Guth, and Wilcox, "Less than Conquerors." Green, Rozell, and Wilcox, eds., *Prayers in the Precincts*.

34. John C. Green, James L. Guth, Lyman A. Kellstedt, and Corwin E. Smidt, "Evangelical Realignment: The Political Power of the Christian Right," *Christian Century* 112, no. 21 (1995): 676–79. Rozell and Wilcox, eds., *God at the Grass Roots* (1995).

35. The former was Vince Snowbarger (Kans.-3) and the latter Mark Green (Wis.-8).

36. In previous work, we have found that ideological mismatch between incumbents and their districts invited Christian Right activity. Similar measures of mismatch in 1998 were not statistically significant (Green, Guth, and Hill, "Faith and Election").

37. There were other factors at work in the special election as well. For example, Capps agreed to term limits and Bordonaro did not, resulting in issue advertisements against Bordonaro by advocates of term limits.

Part III

The Politics of Representation—Primaries and Polarization

7

The Polarizing Effects of Congressional Primaries

Barry C. Burden

Even more than in earlier periods in American history, Congress has recently become a highly polarized institution. Interparty differences on policy matters have grown so that there is little middle ground left, especially in the House of Representatives. One indicator of the growing polarization is the rise in "party votes" on the floor of the House. Such votes occur when a majority of Democrats vote against a majority of Republicans. In the 1950s and early 1960s, about half of roll calls could be labeled party votes. The percentages fell to the 30 percent range in the 1970s but began rising again in the 1980s. By the early 1990s, almost two out of every three roll calls were party votes. Following the 1994 takeover of the House by Republicans, party voting reached a modern high of 73 percent. Despite this clear rise in partisanship, polarization in Congress is not altogether new. Democrats and Republicans have always differed with one another, though more sharply in some eras and in some areas than in others. The degree of polarization depends on many things: the tactics of leaders, preferences of members, Congress's relationship with the president, the nature of legislation being considered, and electoral forces of all kinds. These factors all deserve study to determine what separates the congressional parties.

In this chapter, I analyze the role that primary elections play in maintaining congressional polarization. Rather than study institutional, historical, or personal factors that affect ideological positions, I am focusing on the *electoral* motivations that drive legislators to do what they do. This approach links the campaign promises made by congressional candidates to the policies they support once elected to office. Rather than study change over time, I seek to explain how primaries contribute to general interparty differences in the House within any given election cycle. These differences are important because they contradict respected theories of electoral politics that predict that candidates and parties in the United States will adopt similar policy positions.

Cox[1] makes a useful distinction between *centripetal* and *centrifugal* forces in election systems. Just as in the physical world, centripetal incentives draw candidates inward—they lead to moderate and similar platforms. As I document in the following section, political scientists have traditionally viewed centripetal forces as the dominant ones in American campaigns. Centrifugal forces, on the other hand, lead candidates outward to more extreme positions. I will make the simple argument that primary elections are important centrifugal forces that work against the powerful incentives for candidates to moderate their positions. In short, the continuing polarization witnessed in the U.S. Congress is partly a result of primary election dynamics. Primaries, especially at the subpresidential level, have been underappreciated as sources for the differences between Democratic and Republican candidates and representatives in government. Primaries are surely not the only centrifugal forces at work on members of Congress, but they play an important role that ought to be assessed in its own right.[2]

It is appropriate at this point to raise briefly the "so what?" question. Why should one care about ideological polarization? Though the reasons are many, I suggest at least two normative concerns about polarization. First, general-election voters must choose from among candidates, usually a Democrat and a Republican in each district. To the degree that candidates are offering a clear "choice" rather than an "echo," the electorate can see starker differences between them and can choose the one who best represents their interests. Thus, candidates who offer different positions make it easier for voters to steer government policy after the election. So issue voting should rise as candidates' positions are made more salient. At the same time, this may not be satisfactory to the large portion of Americans who consider themselves moderates. A voter who sees himself as "middle-of-the-road" might not want either candidate to win because of the extreme policies that might result from a candidate's victory. So polarization is important because it determines the nature of alternatives that are available to voters. It might be that neither alternative represents the "average" voter at all.

Second, voters should care about candidate positions because the promises that candidates make on the campaign trail translate into policies once in office. Though many citizens prefer candidates whom they can distinguish from one another, the stalemate and gridlock in Congress that result from such differences are uniformly disliked by the public. Polarization can lower levels of trust in government.[3] Consequently, there is a tension that arises from disliking campaigns in which "there's not a dime's worth of difference" between the candidates and yet criticizing government when members from opposing parties disagree with one another. Further, there is a link between divided government and party polarization. Most empirical studies find that candidate polarization discourages split-ticket voting because the differences between the parties are clear to voters and thus provide a handy voting cue.[4] So the degree to which candidates are polarized is important because of its wider implications for representation and responsiveness by elected officials.

This chapter examines the role that primaries play in polarizing candidates for Congress. After reviewing well-known theories that favor centripetal forces and thus expect little polarization, I explain why primaries encourage candidate separation. Using estimates of ideological positions based on roll call voting records, I examine position taking by incumbent members of Congress during primary and general elections. The data are drawn from the 1992 House elections. Though shifting between primary and general election campaigns is neither dramatic nor widespread, I find that incumbents do indeed adopt extreme positions during primary campaigns and then slightly moderate them during general election campaigns. In the end, however, primary voters' preferences are weighed more heavily than are general-election voters' preferences, which has the net effect of prohibiting candidate convergence and limiting the total amount of candidate movement. I also identify some conditions that foster polarization during primaries. I find that primary extremism is more likely as real-world elections begin to resemble their formal theoretic abstractions. Above other variables, competition is the driving force behind congressional polarization in primary elections.

CENTRIPETAL FORCES AND CANDIDATE CONVERGENCE

The overwhelming conclusion coming from models of two-party elections is that rational candidates will move to the center to win. The result began with Hotelling's[5] model of businesses adopting locations, but it is grounded in political science by Black's[6] Median Voter Theorem. The theorem states that when alternatives are being considered by voters as locations in a unidimensional space, the alternative that wins under plurality rule will be located at the median voter's position.[7] So the power of the median as a kind of "average" or "centrist" position has been given great importance in studies dealing with ideology in elections.

This simple, seemingly innocuous result has had a profound impact on our view of ideology in elections. Despite being an abstract model, the description sounds a lot like the U.S. political system. The "unidimensional space" could represent the left–right ideological continuum, and most American elections use the plurality rule system by choosing as the winner the candidate who received the most votes. So when the theory is applied to real campaigns, it suggests that a candidate should adopt a moderate—the median voter's—position to maximize his or her chances of winning. This implies that candidates' positions will be indistinguishable by election day since everyone will want to obey the centripetal pull of the median voter.

Downs similarly argued in *An Economic Theory of Democracy* that, in a two-party system with a unimodal distribution of voters, candidates "rapidly converge" on the center of the ideological spectrum "so that parties closely resemble one another."[8] This general finding from both Black and Downs (that candidates move toward one another as election day approaches) may be called the *convergence prediction*—a term I use broadly to summarize the many results that predict that centrist positions are dominant. Though a few models have produced candidate divergence by allowing for uncertainty or for policy-motivated candidates,[9] the basic convergence prediction dominates.[10] Indeed, several decades after Black and Downs introduced the models to political science, a well-known textbook summarized that "the candidate who is closest to the center . . . stands the best chance of winning" and that "the closer the candidate is to the center, the better."[11] Though not stated in Cox's terminology, it is clear that centripetal forces have been seen as the sole motivating factor behind candidate behavior.

POSITION TAKING BY MEMBERS OF CONGRESS

One area to which the convergence prediction has been applied is legislative roll call voting. Members of Congress adopt positions all of the time in the form of votes on bills and resolutions. These votes often have an ideological interpretation. Interest groups even rate members' liberalism according to the kinds of votes they take. It is commonplace for reporters to say things like "Congressman A has a liberal voting record" or "Senator B's votes became more moderate over his career." Because these votes are taken sequentially, they allow researchers to examine how legislators alter their public positions over time. Though the types of votes offered affect the positions available for the taking to some extent, the convergence prediction offers a clear expectation: members running for reelection ought to moderate their positions to approach the median voter's ideal point as election day approaches. Let us label this expectation the *vote moderation hypothesis*. It is probably best thought of as a corollary to the convergence prediction. Just as the convergence prediction says that candidates ought to moderate their campaign positions, the vote moderation hypothesis says that incumbent legislators ought to moderate their roll call positions.

Most election models find that candidates should be motivated by centripetal forces to move to the middle, yet observation suggests that few members actually adopt centrist positions. To take but a few easy examples, who would argue that presidential candidates Ronald Reagan and Walter Mondale had similar platforms in 1984 or that California senatorial candidates Barbara Boxer and Matt Fong made identical promises to voters in 1998? Empirical studies confirm that candidates routinely offer distinct positions to voters during campaigns.[12] And Poole and

Rosenthal[13] have shown that members of Congress reflect these positions in office. Though U.S. candidates and parties are probably more centrist than those in other democratic nations, the fact remains that convergence is far from complete.

This leaves a contradiction between theory and evidence. I argue that position-taking theories have ignored primary elections, which are important but not exclusive forces that foster candidate polarization. During primary election campaigns, extremism is better than moderation because primary voters are located near the ends of the ideological spectrum. Only after primary nominations are settled is moderation toward the center a reasonable strategy. Of course, this only works for incumbents if they adopt positions in order to win elections and not the other way around.[14]

So we must assume that reelection is an important goal that motivates representatives' behavior in office. Mayhew stated most clearly that "United States congressmen . . . are interested in nothing else" but reelection.[15] Though incumbents (and challengers) have other goals, including personal recognition and good policy,[16] election is, in Mayhew's words, "proximate," as it is necessary to achieve the others. Other goals may have to be compromised (if temporarily) to be elected. Fiorina adeptly notes that legislators' "goals are numerous" but that "reelection is the primary goal that the constituency controls: the district gives and the district can take away. . . . Realistically or cynically as the case may be, we believe that constituents' preferences are reflected in a representative's voting (if at all) through his concern for electoral survival."[17]

Though candidates will adopt positions to make general-election voters happy, exactly *when* this moderation should begin has not been made clear. A common assumption is that positions taken during the second (election) year of a representative's term will be more moderate than those taken in the first (nonelection) year. This assumption rests on the belief that incumbents are concerned enough about the *general election* to strategically modify their policy positions during the entire year in which it is held. But this view neglects an important prerequisite for incumbents to run for reelection: nomination by their political parties in primary elections. In contemporary congressional elections most candidates must pass at least two hurdles to take office. The primary election requires fellow partisans to compete for the right to run in the general election. The key difference between them is that primaries are *intraparty* competitions, whereas generals are *interparty* competitions. As such, primary and general elections bring different sets of voters to the polls and different motives for candidates as a result. Though legislators are rational to move toward the median voter in the general election, it may be a losing strategy in a primary.

Much research has been concerned with the "representativeness" of primary voters. The conventional wisdom holds that primary voters are not a microcosm of the entire electorate nor of their parties' followings. These voters are more partisan and ideological. For example, Republican primary voters are more knowledgeable and conservative than the average general-election voter and even more than the typical person who votes Republican in the general election. Likewise, participants in Democratic primaries are somewhat more liberal and knowledgeable than other Democratic identifiers and much more liberal and knowledgeable than general-election voters. Studies of presidential primary voters confirmed this notion.[18] In general, the median Democratic primary voter's ideal point is to the left of that of the general-election voter's.

To make clear how the gaps between primary and general election median voters contribute to polarization, consider the model in figure 7.1. When Democrats are competing for their party's nomination, it is this left-of-center position they wish to approach. Though moderation may improve their chances in November, it can actually cost them votes in the primary if the median *primary* voter is significantly to the left of the general-election median. As a result, polarization is rational during primary campaigns.[19] If one supposes that most Democratic candidates' preelection positions are between the primary and general-electorate medians, then the candidates should move leftward to capture the nomination and then moderate before November.

We do not have to assume that primary voters' positions are the *only* centrifugal forces at work on candidates. Among other things, candidates have values of their own, which tend to be noncentrist.[20] Because most candidates will not completely "sell out" their own preferences to win office, they adopt different positions. Another group with strong preferences is party activists. *Activists* are a subset of the primary electorate who contribute money, run campaigns, and support candidates beyond simple voting.[21] Ideological interest groups and party organizations play a similar role by supporting candidates who endorse their relatively polarized views. If evidence is found for the effects of voters' positions alone, their total influence is probably underestimated because of the great pull of these other factors.

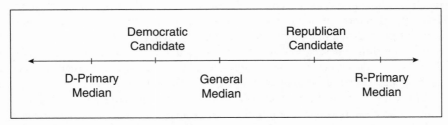

Figure 7.1: Unidimensional Spatial Model with Primaries.

WHY CANDIDATES CARE ABOUT IDEOLOGY IF VOTERS DON'T

Satisfying both primary and general-election voters can be a difficult task for candidates. The problem for the representative is a trade-off between pleasing what Fenno[22] called the "primary constituency" and the "reelection constituency." This is difficult because primary and general-election supporters often have different preferences.[23] But at this point, one might object that the relationship between candidates is not so clear or direct in the real world. After all, spatial models are exaggerated abstractions of the real world.[24] Many citizens, even voters, it might be argued, do not have firm ideological preferences and do not choose candidates on the basis of issue positions. Members of Congress probably do not bother shifting their public positions in order to appease an electorate that is so inattentive.[25]

But this is the story taken from the voter's point of view. Election surveys routinely find, based on self-reports, that citizens are not aware of their representatives' actions. But we should not forget that voter attention is not a necessary condition for candidate concern. Consider how a candidate views the situation. Because incumbents believe that they are or may be watched, a member tries to "avoid giving opponents in his own party or outside of it material they can use against him."[26] Though the "electorate's sanctions are potential rather than actual," candidates and incumbents behave as if their positions matter. Because they fear that a misstep may cost them the election, they end up running scared most of the time. And *"less important than whether constituents actually care is whether the representative thinks they can be made to care."*[27] Using an analogy from physics, it is potential rather than kinetic energy to which legislators and their challengers are attentive. It is more about what might happen than what is happening now.

Studies of representatives show that they believe that the positions they adopt on legislation and issues of the day affect their chances of reelection. And reelection is an important if not dominant goal, so positions are taken carefully. A common conclusion is that members (and challengers) feel *as if* their policy positions matter even if they are safe electorally.[28] For instance, Arnold, in developing a theory to explain congressional policy making, argues that "legislators believe that issues matter and that they act in accordance with this belief."[29] Fenno states that reelection is "fraught with *uncertainty*."[30] And as long as legislators think that positions matter, then researchers should treat them as if they do.

It is commonly noted that members of Congress run scared despite objective evidence that they are electorally safe.[31] Though some voters may punish representatives for taking unpopular positions on the most important roll call votes, many constituents do not pay attention to the details of Washington activity. It is ironic that legislators act as if voters are paying attention to their position when they seem not to be. Miller and Stokes[32] point out this "notable contradiction: Congressmen think that their legislative actions have considerable impact on the electorate but some simple facts about the Representative's salience to his constituents imply that this could hardly be true." Thus, *actual* electoral penalties need not be realized for members to be concerned about the issues that they take; their *potential* effects, however unlikely, are usually enough. Strategic position taking, particularly in the form of moderation, is a reasonable way for members to ward off these potential penalties.

But we should not expect candidates to shift their positions around wildly to satisfy the median voter. Too much position shifting allows opponents or the media to label it "inconsistent" or better yet "flip-flopping," which can damage one's public reputation. Simple complaints such as these resonate with voters because reputations matter to them.[33] A consistent reputation builds trust and leeway among constituents.[34] As I further argue later, electoral sanctions do not need to occur for strategic position taking to take place, but they make it more likely. Thus, the probability that voters are paying attention to one's positions is related to the range of positions available for the taking. A competitive race that features a strong challenger is likely to make voters more attentive and thus to make incumbents care more about the positions they adopt.

DATA AND METHOD

Though the theory of candidate position taking in primaries and generals offers several intriguing hypotheses to be tested, finding adequate data is difficult. What is minimally required are estimates of where members of Congress position themselves during their primary and general elections, two observations for each member. Many general ideological indicators, such as interest-group ratings, are available; but they aggregate data by session or Congress, which makes them unsuitable here. I have chosen to modify a commonly used measure of ideology based on roll call voting records by dividing votes into two different campaign periods: primary and general.

Data used to estimate legislators' positions are drawn from congressional voting records of members of the U.S. House of Representatives in 1992. The 1992 contests allow further insights into the relationship between members' career decisions and the roll call positions they take.[35] A hefty 53 members retired in 1992, and 20 were defeated in primaries. The retirees are particularly important here because their behavior should not be driven by their own electoral concerns, a fact that allows them to play the role of a "control group" in some of the analysis. All of the votes taken in 1992 have been recoded as "yea," "nay," or something else (e.g., present or abstain).[36] This system essentially dichotomizes member behavior to make estimation practical. The technique used to identify members' positions from the data is the well-known NOMINATE, developed by Poole and

Rosenthal.[37] NOMINATE recovers point estimates of each legislator's position in a multidimensional space. For each member, the technique generates a score between −1 and +1. Lower scores are more liberal, and higher scores are more conservative. While a large number of dimensions are possible, just one accounts for more than 85 percent of the variance in recent congressional votes. Accordingly, Poole and Rosenthal have given the first dimension an ideological interpretation of a "liberal-conservative continuum." It is these scores that I use.

NOMINATE scores are an improvement over more common interest-group ratings of members for at least two reasons. First, they are more externally valid because they are based on (nearly) every roll call taken, rather than on a nonrandom sample of "important" votes. Second, they are based on a theoretical understanding of spatial roll call behavior in contrast to group ratings, which are used mostly to identify allies and enemies in Congress.[38]

Though roll call data are not ideal for estimating legislators' *personal* ideologies, they are nearly ideal for estimating legislators' *positions*. Rohde[39] makes a useful distinction between the *personal* and *operative* preferences of legislators: *Personal preferences* are a legislator's own ideology, free of other influences; *operative preferences* include other influences as well as one's personal views and are reflected in roll call votes. Though the two types of preferences are probably interrelated, it is reasonable to assume that voters care more about operative than about personal ideologies. Recall Mayhew's definition of position taking as "the public enunciation of a judgmental statement on anything likely to be of interest to political actors" that "may take the form of a roll call vote."[40] In fact, casting a roll call vote is probably the single best way for a House member to take a position on an issue. It is concrete, public, and durable. When the same issue arises for a second time, the member may vote as he or she did in the past, maintaining the earlier position, or vote differently, if "electoral danger" leads to "innovation," in Mayhew's words. The moderate preferences of a looming general electorate or even the extreme preferences of primary activists may be enough to persuade members to alter their positions. In addition, personal and operative preferences probably overlap substantially.[41] Regardless, to the degree that roll call scores do not match campaign positions, my results will be weakened. Thus, the results I present probably underestimate the influence of electoral forces on campaign positions.

One way to test for strategic position taking is to examine how members' adopted positions change with time. I have chosen to examine NOMINATE scores from two periods within the election year: (1) the primary election campaign period, from January 1, 1992, until the date of each candidate's primary; (2) the general election campaign period (after nomination), from the day after the primary until November 3. Primary dates vary across states, so representatives' two roll call records are of different lengths. The two data sets were stacked on one another, and NOMINATE coordinates were generated for each of the periods.[42]

If position taking occurs on a large scale, then incumbents ought to take more

extreme positions during the primary season and to moderate afterward in anticipation of the general election in November. Scores run from −1 to +1, so Democrats ought to earn lower scores during primary campaigns and higher scores
afterward. Republicans should have higher scores before the primary and lower
scores after getting their party's nomination. Further, I expect that these relationships will be stronger for some members than for others, but that movement will
be modest overall. The closer that real-world election campaigns come to resem-
bling their theoretical counterparts—particularly in terms of competition—the more
clearly will primaries induce centrifugal behavior and general elections centripetal behavior.

COMPETITION AND PRIMARY POLARIZATION

We begin with simple comparisons between primary and general-election campaign positions. Table 7.1 presents the median primary election and general election positions for House members in 1992.[43] The data are presented separately
for those who faced primary election opponents and those who did not, under the
expectation that having an opponent would foster polarization.

There are several conclusions that may be drawn from these data: First, members of all stripes adopted more extreme positions in primaries than in general
elections. Democrats were farther to the left and Republicans farther to the right
during primary campaigns than during the later general-election campaigns. Second, the amount of post-primary moderation is slight. Representatives of both
parties edged only about .03 back to the center on average. This indicates a great
deal of sluggishness or immobility inherent in candidates' ideological reputations.
Third, members who faced primary opposition were more polarized than those

Table 7.1: Positions in the 1992 Primary and General Election Campaigns

	Democrats			Republicans		
	Primary Election Position	*General Election Position*	*Change*	*Primary Election Position*	*General Election Position*	*Change*
Primary opponent	−.533	−.506	−.027	.842	.813	+.029
	(82)	(82)		(42)	(42)	
No primary opponent	−.524	−.491	−.033	.797	.771	+.026
	(114)	(114)		(.83)	(83)	
Retiring member	−.532	−.514	−.018	.765	.759	+.006
	(33)	(33)		(21)	(21)	

Note: Cell entries are median NOMINATE scores for members in each category.

who did not. This effect is greater for Republicans than for Democrats, though still modest. Because representatives with primary opponents started their general-election campaigns farther away from the median voter, they also finished the general-election campaigns with more polarized positions. All running candidates moderated about the same (small) amount, but the starting and ending points were more extreme for members who had to tangle with primary challengers. Though the data confirm that competition is an important factor behind candidate position taking, it is remarkable that even incumbents who had no primary competition apparently felt it necessary to polarize.

Included in the final row of the table are comparable data for retirees. Recall that 1992 was selected for analysis because there were enough retiring members of the House to make comparisons fruitful. Because retirees are "lame ducks" (they will not be facing the voters again), they are free from the "electoral connection" to pursue policies for reasons other than voter satisfaction. They should feel no major centripetal or centrifugal pressures other than their own policy preferences. It is surprising, then, that retirees are also more moderate during general-election campaigns. This counterintuitive result may be an artifact of the methodology used because different types of roll call votes are not likely to be distributed uniformly throughout the year. However, the most important features of retirees' positions are that (1) they are generally *less* polarized during primaries than running members, especially those facing opponents, and (2) their total amount of moderation is *less* than that of their campaigning colleagues. Relative to members who are running for reelection, retirees feel less centrifugal pull and less centripetal push. So though the agenda or some other factor tends to make later votes more moderate, running incumbents moderated even more following their primaries.

A theme running throughout this chapter is that the spatial model best describes elections that approach its assumptions. Most important among them is the presence of two viable candidates whose positions are known to all voters. At a minimum, this requires that the incumbent face a challenger. In primaries, having an opponent of any kind (but particularly a strong one) is likely to push representatives toward the primary electorate's median, which is a relatively extreme position. Thus, primary competition enhances the centrifugal nature of those elections. Table 7.1 demonstrated that this is the case by comparing "average" positions for both Democrats and Republicans who do and who do not face primary challengers, but these summary statistics cannot reveal the diversity of positions taken by members. An alternative way to examine this relationship, a way that presents the full range of data, is to plot the distributions for each of these candidate types.

To provide an example of the kind of plots that will be presented, figure 7.2 shows the distribution of Democrats' 1992 primary positions. This graph—known as a kernel density plot—is just a "smoothed" version of a histogram so that peculiarities of some observations are subordinated to the more general pattern.

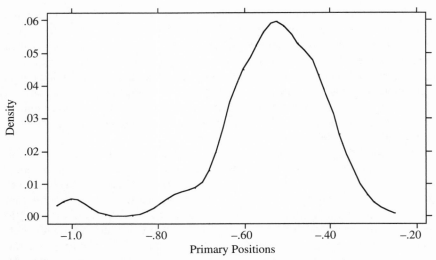

Figure 7.2: Democratic Primary Positions

Like a histogram (bar graph), higher points on the curve indicate that more cases are located there. The figure shows that most Democrats were left of center, averaging around −.5 or so (see also table 7.1). The distribution is also asymmetric—the left end extends farther out than the right one does. Some of this heterogeneity represents differences in primary voters' positions across districts, but it also captures variation in members' ideological preferences, party loyalties, lobbying influence, and the like. We will not attempt to distill all of these influences here.

Our purpose is to determine how primary competition alone moves the distribution. This issue is addressed in figure 7.3, which shows separate graphs for Democrats with and without primary opponents. The differences between the distributions are slight. In accord with expectations, however, primary competition did move Democrats a bit to the left. The fact that the effect is small may indicate several things. First, not all challengers are equal. Perhaps a more subtle measure of primary challenger quality, such as Jacobson's[44] "experience" indicator or Green and Krasno's[45] additive index for general election challengers, would reveal larger effects. Such a measure might be problematic, however, in that primary challengers are usually political amateurs[46] and background data on these candidates are sometimes difficult to find. Second, perhaps it is the mere presence of a primary more than the nature of one's opposition in the election that shapes polarization. This would fit with the "potential" versus "actual" distinction made earlier. Third, maybe other factors, such as the locations of primary voters, donors, and the gen-

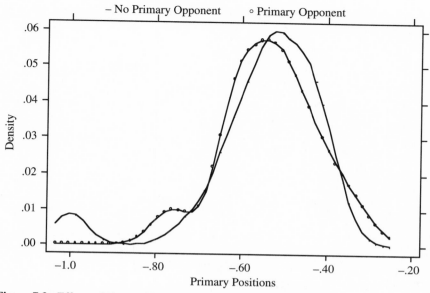

Figure 7.3: Effects of Competition on Democratic Primary Positions

eral electorate, are much more important than whether a Democrat faces a primary opponent.

Figure 7.4 presents the basic distribution of primary campaign positions for all running Republican members in 1992. It is centered around .8, as we saw in table 7.1, and is flatter than the Democratic distribution, suggesting greater Republican heterogeneity for some reason. Figure 7.5 then separates Republicans into those who did and those who did not have primary challenges. Here the differences are clear. Republicans who had primary opponents were more extreme than those who did not. Candidates without opponents have an average primary position around .77 or so, while candidates with opponents are farther to right, centered around .85. Thus, some of the greater Republican dispersion in figure 7.4 is the result of combining rather different distributions for Republicans who did or did not have to run against another candidate in their primary elections.

This leaves the question of why the effect is observed so clearly for Republicans but only marginally for Democrats. Because the data are only drawn from one election cycle—one in which Democrats retained their control of the House—I can only speculate about why Republicans' positions react more acutely to competition. First, it is possible that this is not a real result, but merely an artifact of the roll call data used. Because Democrats were the majority party in 1992 and

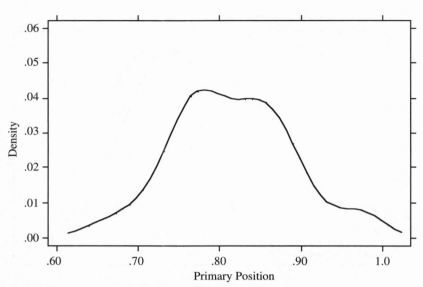

Figure 7.4: Republican Primary Positions

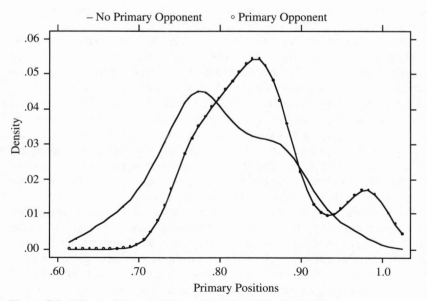

Figure 7.5: Effects of Competition on Republican Primary Positions

largely determined the nature of the floor votes, they may have allowed themselves greater latitude and forced Republicans into a kind of ideological corner. There is also a plausible political explanation for the effect. It is often assumed that the Republicans are the more homogenous party, at least in terms of ideology. If this is true, then Republican candidates would feel compelled to take more specific and more extreme positions to win their contested primary battles. Because Democrats, even the activists, are a more diverse lot, their heterogeneity does not allow us to observe the effects of primary competition on the left end of the spectrum.

THE CAUSES OF POST-PRIMARY MODERATION

We also wonder about the amount of movement that takes place between primary and general-election campaigns. Because of reputations and the potential for voter backlash, I argued that members should not change their positions much. When they do, it will be in response to two factors: (1) the amount of time between the elections and (2) their chances of winning.

Consider first how the chances of winning the general election affect position taking. Incumbents who believe that they are in electoral jeopardy are likely to engage in a host of activities aimed at salvaging their flagging campaigns. One of these activities may be moderating their post-primary positions to satisfy general-election voters. Thus, we should expect that the likelihood of winning will be negatively associated with ideological movement. Row 1 of table 7.2 presents some evidence to this effect by correlating the amount of movement between elections (primary position—general position) with the closeness of the election as predicted by a *Congressional Quarterly* scale published a few weeks before the election.[47] Because high values of the prediction variable indicate greater likelihoods of Democratic victories, the correlations should be negative for Democrats (as positive movement is associated with negative predictions) and likewise positive for Republicans. This is precisely what happens, about equally for Democratic and Republican members.

With regard to the timing of elections, I hypothesize that pre- and post-primary positions will differ more because the primary is held earlier in the year. Primaries occur any time from March to October across the states, though general elections must take place in November. Movement is slow, and candidates prefer not to move because it draws attention to their ideological locations. Row 2 presents the correlations of the amount of moderation and the number of days between primary and general elections. The modestly sized coefficients indicate that the more days there are between a state's congressional primary and its general elections, the more candidates moderate their post-primary locations. However, the relationship is only statistically meaningful for Democrats, who seem to

Table 7.2: The Effects of Closeness and Timing on Moderation

Correlation between Amount of Moderation and:	*Democrats*	*Republicans*
Predicted closeness of general election	−.17*	+.21*
Days between primary and general elections	−.26*	+.09

Note: Entries are Pearson *r* correlation coefficients.
*$p < .05$, two-tailed test.

take greater advantage of the time provided between elections. This could be because Democrats were the majority party in 1992 and held some "marginal" seats where members had to be more strategic.

The degree of polarization between and moderation among candidates also depends heavily on the partisan and ideological makeup of the district. For simplicity, let us consider two rather different congressional districts. One is a competitive (or marginal) district where Republicans and Democrats have similar chances of winning, as long as they field candidates of equal quality. The other district is more liberal than most and almost always votes overwhelmingly for the Democrat. As a result, Republicans seldom field a strong general election candidate, and he or she is usually beaten soundly even if they do. Any competition that does exist in the district is likely to occur in the Democratic primary; the candidate who gets the Democratic nomination is almost surely going to win the general election.[48] It is in districts like these where a candidate is pulled by centrifugal forces because of the critical importance of primary voters. This is not to say that competitive districts will not produce polarized candidates,[49] but a vigorous primary, often found in districts that lean to one end of the spectrum, routinely contributes to polarization as well.

DISCUSSION

In the context of the classic spatial model that has dominated studies of ideology in elections for so long, it is surprising that candidates do not completely converge after winning their respective primaries. Regardless of where they start from, the centripetal incentives that general electorates offer should dominate in the post-primary season. Thus, the traditional Downsian spatial model ignored two-stage elections, not because primaries do not affect what candidates do but because the first election does not matter in the long run since it will not effect where candidates finish in November. But such a purist argument neglects two facts about the real world that could easily be included in a formal election model.

First, movement is not costless. The classic spatial model assumes that candidates may shift their positions without penalty, so it is wise for them to move to the center. As I have argued elsewhere,[50] there are several reasons to believe that changing one's position, even toward the median voter, might cost, not earn, votes. Candidates, especially incumbents, have political reputations. Adopting positions that are at odds with one's reputation might lead an interest group, the media, or even an opposing candidate to point out the inconsistencies. This could lead to charges of "waffling" or "flip-flopping" on the issues, which many voters would dislike if true. Voters might decide against a candidate because his or her change in position suggests a lack of integrity or core values. A side effect is that a candidate's credibility with voters is lowered.[51] Voters may also be apt to avoid candidates who frequently change positions because the changing raises uncertainty about them.[52] In Downs's words, "Ideological *immobility* is characteristic of every responsible party, because it cannot repudiate its past actions unless some radical change in conditions justifies this."[53] So there is some "stickiness" in candidates' positions because voters may penalize those whose ideological locations shift too far or too quickly. Candidates face a trade-off between the centripetal logic of the spatial model and the real possibility that moving to the center might lose votes.

Second, primary voters care more than general-election voters do about candidates' positions. These activists are more informed, see greater ideological differences among candidates, and probably weigh candidates' positions more heavily when reaching vote decisions. General-election voters, who are less ideological and less partisan, value nonpolicy factors such as candidate characteristics and performance in office more highly. For primary voters, ideology is often the candidate's litmus test; for general-election voters, ideology is one criterion among many. Thus, if the resultant positions that candidates adopt are to be some weighted combination of the median primary and general-election voters,[54] the former ought to outweigh the latter. This leads to candidates who are closer to primary activists than to general election participants and hence fosters the polarization of Democrats and Republicans.

The fact that primary elections contribute to candidate polarization is ironic if put in the larger context of representation in American politics. Primaries developed as a means for selecting party nominees in the early 1900s because the Progressive reformers believed that the direct primary would open up the electoral process, allowing for more citizen control over candidate selection. The primary did indeed take nominating power away from parties. At the same time, the primary did not correct what many citizens believe to be flaws in the electoral system. Because primary voters are an unrepresentative subset of the full electorate, primaries might actually choose candidates who are less appealing to the electorate than traditional party conventions would have. Parties at least weighed electability in their calculations, whereas primary activists are more concerned about the ideological genuineness of the positions that candidates adopt.

NOTES

I thank Tom Rice for comments, Keith Poole for technical assistance, and the National Science Foundation for financial support (grant number SBR-9618079).

1. Gary W. Cox, "Centripetal and Centrifugal Incentives in Electoral Systems," *American Journal of Political Science* 34 (1990): 903–35.

2. Elisabeth R. Gerber and Rebecca B. Morton, "Primary Election Systems and Representation," *Journal of Law, Economics, and Organization* 14, no. 2 (1998): 304–24.

3. David C. King, "The Polarization of American Parties and Mistrust of Government," in *Why People Don't Trust Government*, ed. Joseph S. Nye Jr., Philip D. Zelikow, and David C. King (Cambridge, Mass.: Harvard University Press, 1997).

4. Barry C. Burden and David C. Kimball, "A New Approach to the Study of Ticket Splitting," *American Political Science Review* 92 (1998): 533–44. John R. Petrocik and Joseph Doherty, "The Road to Divided Government: Paved without Intention," in *Divided Government: Change, Uncertainty, and the Constitutional Order*, ed. Peter F. Galderisi (Lanham, Md.: Rowman & Littlefield, 1996). Cf. Morris P. Fiorina, *Divided Government,* 2d ed. (Needham Heights, Mass.: Allyn and Bacon, 1996).

5. Harold Hotelling, "Stability in Competition," *The Economic Journal* 39 (1929), 41–57.

6. Duncan Black, *A Theory of Committees and Elections* (New York: Cambridge University Press, 1958).

7. There are additional assumptions, including the symmetric and single-peaked preferences of voters, universal turnout, and an odd number of voters.

8. Anthony Downs, *An Economic Theory of Democracy* (New York: Harper and Row, 1957).

9. Randall Calvert, "Robustness of the Multidimensional Voting Model: Candidates' Motivations, Uncertainty, and Convergence," *American Journal of Political Science* 29 (1985): 69–95. Donald A. Wittman, "Candidate Motivations: A Synthesis of Alternatives," *American Political Science Review* 77 (1983): 142–57.

10. For example: Melvin J. Hinich and Michael C. Munger, *Ideology and the Theory of Political Choice* (Ann Arbor: University of Michigan Press, 1994). David Lalman, Joe Oppenheimer, and Piotr Swistak, "Formal Rational Choice Theory: A Cumulative Science of Politics," in *Political Science: The State of the Discipline II*, ed. Ada W. Finifter (Washington, D.C.: American Political Science Association, 1993). Martin J. Osborne, "Spatial Models of Political Competition under Plurality Rule: A Survey of Some Explanations of the Number of Candidates and the Positions They Take," *Canadian Journal of Economics* 28 (1995): 261–301.

11. James M. Enelow and Melvin J. Hinich, *The Spatial Theory of Voting: An Introduction* (New York: Cambridge University Press, 1990).

12. Stephen D. Ansolabehere, James M. Snyder Jr. and Charles Stewart III, "Candidate Positioning in U.S. House Elections" (unpublished manuscript, Massachusetts Institute of Technology, 1998). Benjamin I. Page, *Choices and Echoes in Presidential Elections* (Chicago: University of Chicago Press, 1978). John L. Sullivan and Daniel Richard Minns, "Ideological Distance between Candidates: An Empirical Examination," *American Journal of Political Science* 20 (1976): 439–68. Gerald C. Wright Jr. and Michael B. Berkman, "Candidates and Policy in United States Senate Elections," *American Political Science Review* 80 (1986): 567–88.

13. Keith T. Poole and Howard Rosenthal, *Congress: A Political-Economic History of Roll Call Voting* (New York: Oxford University Press, 1997).

14. Downs, *An Economic Theory of Democracy*.

15. David R. Mayhew, *Congress: The Electoral Connection* (New Haven, Conn.: Yale University Press, 1974), 13.

16. Richard F. Fenno Jr., *Home Style: House Members in Their Districts* (Boston: Little, Brown, 1978).

17. Morris P. Fiorina, *Representatives, Roll Calls, and Constituencies* (Lexington, Mass.: Lexington Books, 1974), 7.

18. John H. Aldrich, *Why Parties? The Origin and Transformation of Political Parties in America* (Chicago: Univeristy of Chicago Press, 1995). John G. Geer, "Rules Governing Presidential Primaries," *Journal of Politics* 48, no. 1 (1986): 1006–25. Warren E. Miller and M. Kent Jennings, *Parties in Transition* (New York: Russell Sage Foundation, 1986). Austin Ranney, "Turnout and Representation in Presidential Primary Elections," *American Political Science Review* 74 (1972): 685–96. Richard M. Scammon and Ben J. Wattenberg, *The Real Majority* (New York: Coward, McCann, and Georghegan, 1970). Cf. Barbara Norrander, "Ideological Representativeness of Presidential Primary Voters," *American Journal of Political Science* 33 (1989): 570–87.

To provide some justification, consider 1992 National Election Study data based on respondents' reports of their positions on the standard ideology measure that runs from "most liberal" (1) to "most conservative" (7). Democratic primary voters had a mean placement of 3.87, Republican primary voters had a mean of 4.73, and the mean of general-election voters was between the other two at 4.32. These differences are likely more pronounced at the congressional level, though the NES has never asked whether respondents voted in congressional primaries.

19. Note that this is polarization only with regard to the general electorate; extreme positions are actually moderate if primary voters are the reference group.

20. Ingemar Hansson and Charles Stuart, "Voting Competitions with Interested Politicians: Platforms Do Not Converge to the Preferences of the Median Voter," *Public Choice* 44 (1984): 431–41. Sullivan and Minns, "Ideological Distance between Candidates." Wright and Berkman, "Candidates and Policy in United States Senate Elections."

21. Aldrich, *Why Parties?*

22. Fenno, *Home Style*.

23. This is also similar to Fiorina's (*Representatives, Roll Calls, and Constituencies*) "two constituencies" thesis. (Samuel Huntington, "A Revised Theory of American Party Politics," *American Political Science Review* 44 [1950]: 669–77. David C. King, "Party Competition and Polarization in American Politics" [paper presented at the annual meeting of the Midwest Political Science Association, Chicago, 1998]. Catherine R. Shapiro, David W. Brady, Richard A. Brody, and John A. Ferejohn, "Linking Constituency Opinion and Senate Voting Scores: A Hybrid Explanation," *Legislative Studies Quarterly* 15, no. 4 [November 1990]: 599–623).

24. Donald P. Green and Ian Shapiro, *Pathologies of Rational Choice Theory* (New Haven, Conn.: Yale University Press, 1994).

25. Robert A. Bernstein, *Elections, Representatives, and Congressional Voting Behavior* (Englewood Cliffs, N.J.: Prentice Hall, 1989). One might add that many congressional primaries are not even contested. In 1992, 52% of representatives and 42% of senators won their primaries because no one ran against them.

26. Warren E. Miller and Donald E. Stokes, "Constituency Influence in Congress," *American Political Science Review* 57 (1963): 45–57.

27. Fiorina, *Representatives, Roll Calls, and Constituencies*, 33.

28. Fenno, *Home Style*. Mayhew, *Congress*.

29. R. Douglas Arnold, *The Logic of Congressional Action* (New Haven, Conn.: Yale University Press, 1990), 37.

30. Fenno, *Home Style*, 10.

31. Fenno, *Home Style*; Thomas E. Mann, *Unsafe at Any Margin: Interpreting Congressional Elections* (Washington, D.C.: American Enterprise Institute, 1978).

32. Miller and Stokes, "Constituency Influence in Congress," 54.

33. M. Daniel Bernhardt and Daniel E. Ingberman, "Candidate Reputatons and the 'Incumbency Effect,'" *Journal of Public Economics* 27 (1985): 47–67. Robert S. Erikson, "Roll Calls, Reputations, and Representation in the U.S. Senate," *Legislative Studies Quarterly* 25 (1990): 623–43. Hinich and Munger, *Ideology and the Theory of Political Choice*.

34. Fenno, *Home Style*.

35. The 1992 data are part of a larger collection from House and Senate incumbents analyzed in Barry C. Burden, "Candidates' Positions in Congressional Elections" (Ph.D. diss., Ohio State University, 1998).

36. Other information about the member, such as name, party, or region, is ignored at this stage.

37. Poole and Rosenthal, *Congress: A Political-Economic History*.

38. See James M. Snyder, "Artificial Extremism in Interest Group Ratings," *Legislative Studies Quarterly* 17 (1992): 319–46.

39. David W. Rohde. *Parties and Leaders in the Postreform House* (Chicago: University of Chicago Press, 1991).

40. Mayhew, *Congress*, 61.

41. Barry C. Burden, Gregory A. Caldeira, and Tim Groseclose, "Measuring the Ideologies of U.S. Senators: The Song Remains the Same," *Legislative Studies Quarterly* 25 (2000): 237–58. John W. Kingdon, *Congressmen's Voting Decisions*, 3d ed. (Ann Arbor: University of Michigan Press, 1989).

42. Members from Louisiana and Virginia were dropped because of those states' unusual nominating procedures. Other members were also omitted if they failed to vote on at least 50 roll calls.

43. Members who lost their primaries or who were seeking another office are not included here.

44. For example: Gary C. Jacobson, "Strategic Politicians and the Dynamics of House Elections, 1946–1986," *American Political Science Review* 83 (1989): 773–93.

45. Donald Philip Green and Jonathan S. Krasno, "Salvation for the Spendthrift Incumbent: Reestimating the Effects of Campaign Spending in House Elections," *American Journal of Political Science* 32 (1988): 884–907.

46. Paul S. Herrnson, *Congressional Elections: Campaigning at Home and in Washington,* 2d ed. (Washington, D.C.: Congressional Quarterly Press, 1998).

47. The predictions come from the October 24, 1992, issue of *Congressional Quarterly Weekly Report* and take on values of –3 (Safe Republican), –2 (Republican Favored), –1 (Leans Republican), 0 (No Clear Favorite), +1 (Leans Democratic), +2 (Democrat Favored), and +3 (Safe Democratic).

48. Julius Turner, "Primary Elections as the Alternative to Party Competition in 'Safe' Districts," *Journal of Politics* 15 (1953): 197–210.

49. Huntington, "A Revised Theory," 669–77. David C. King, "Party Competition."

50. Barry C. Burden, "Candidates' Positions in Congressional Elections."

51. Hinich and Munger, *Ideology and the Theory of Political Choice.*

52. R. Michael Alvarez, *Information and Elections* (Ann Arbor: University of Michigan Press, 1996).

53. Downs, *An Economic Theory of Democracy.*

54. Peter Aranson and Peter C. Ordeshook, "Spatial Strategy for Sequential Elections," in *Probability Models of Collective Decision Making*, ed. R. Niemi and H. Weisberg (Columbus, Ohio: Merrill, 1972). Guillermo Owen and Bernard Grofman, "Two-Stage Electoral Competition in Two-Party Contests: Persistent Divergence of Party Positions with and without Expressive Voting" (paper presented at the annual meetings of the Public Choice Society, Long Beach, Calif., 1995, 1997).

8

The Effects of Electoral Rules on Congressional Primaries

Kristin Kanthak and Rebecca Morton

The 1992 California Senate race between Democrat Barbara Boxer and Republican Bruce Herschensohn was argued by some to be a case in which the ideological differences between the two candidates were stark. Herschensohn, a Los Angeles television and radio commentator, wrote speeches for Richard Nixon, supported Ronald Reagan for president, opposed abortion, argued for a flat-rate income tax, and favored offshore oil drilling in California. Boxer, a member of the House of Representatives, led women to oppose the nomination of Clarence Thomas to the Supreme Court because of charges of sexual harassment, denounced the Persian Gulf War, and had the record for voting for more spending than any other member of the House. Boxer ended up winning the race 48 percent to Herschensohn's 43 percent (other candidates received 9 percent of the vote) after news leaked that Herschensohn attended nightclubs with nude dancing.

Republican moderate Tom Campbell found the race frustrating. He had competed for the nomination against Herschensohn and lost—Herschensohn had defeated him 38 percent to 36 percent in the Republican primary (Sonny Bono received 17 percent of the vote). Campbell believed that he could have defeated Boxer, that his positions were closer to the median voter in the electorate, and that Herschensohn had lost when Republicans could have won the general election.

IF YOU CAN'T WIN, CHANGE THE RULES

Campbell decided to take action—he decided to change the rules governing how the Republican Party nominated candidates. He believed that the system the party used to select candidates disadvantaged moderates like him and hurt the party

116

electorally. A change in the rules, he believed, would favor moderates. Campbell took his campaign to the public at large and succeeded in getting California to pass in March 1996 a referendum changing the rules.

What were these rules, and why did Campbell think changing the rules would matter? Specifically, Campbell's efforts led California to adopt a variant of the open primary system, a system whereby voters can choose the primary in which they wish to vote on election day, regardless of their prior party affiliation. The specifics of the California change are more fully explored by Elisabeth Gerber in chapter 10. Here, we consider the theory and the empirical evidence behind Campbell's belief by discussing the types of primary systems used in congressional contests across the states and how these types may affect candidate and voter behavior in congressional elections.

ELECTORAL REGULATIONS AND CANDIDATE NOMINATIONS

In U.S. politics, two major electoral coalitions—two political parties, the Democrats and the Republicans—largely dominate governing coalitions. One of the main reasons for this dominance is generally believed to be the effect of winner-take-all, single-member legislative elections, commonly called Duverger's Law. It is a stylized fact that this important aspect of our electoral system has allowed our two major parties to control so extensively the outcomes of congressional elections. The dominance is striking—in the past fifty years only three members of Congress have not been either a Democrat or a Republican.

Yet other aspects of our electoral rules also have significant effects on congressional elections, effects that are often overlooked. Most of the electoral rules govern the process by which candidates achieve general election ballot access (candidate nomination procedures) and the extent to which voters participate in that process. In this chapter we explore this process and how these rules can and do affect congressional primaries. Existing research on this subject is divided. Gerber and Morton[1] contend that primary election systems that have easier rules for allowing voter participation result in candidates choosing policy positions closer to general electorate voter preferences. King,[2] however, suggests that openness can lead candidates to appeal to extremist single-issue voters, with candidates taking positions that are farther from the general electorate voter preferences.

We believe that the disagreement comes from grouping together primaries that have different requirements for voter participation. When we separate out these differences, we find that openness that allows mainly for independents and/or new voters to participate and for public crossover voting (voters must publicly declare a party affiliation in order to vote in that party's primary) is more likely to lead to candidates choosing moderate positions. But openness that allows for secret crossover voting (voters do not have to publicly declare a party affiliation) can lead to more extreme candidates winning. We find that these electoral rules can have an impact on the types of congressional candidates elected. Specifically, we find that, as Campbell suspected, opening up participation in primaries can benefit moderates. However, the effect depends on the degree of openness; and, in fact, when primaries are open to full participation by any voter, they can actually benefit extreme candidates.

In the next section, we review the types of primaries used in congressional elections and hypothesize the expected effects of each primary type on the positions of candidates elected. We then test our predictions using congressional data and find our hypotheses supported. We conclude with a discussion of the implications of research on candidate-nomination procedures for future congressional primaries.

CONGRESSIONAL PRIMARY ELECTION RULES

Candidates can run for Congress as nominees of a major or a minor political party or as an independent. The states vary in the hurdles that candidates must jump to run as a candidate from a political party. In Louisiana, for example, candidates who wish to run under a political party's label face few hurdles, only a small filing fee. The parties there do not have primary elections, and the elections are "nonpartisan." Thus, in Louisiana, there can be and often is more than one candidate bearing the same party label in the election. That is, all candidates, regardless of party affiliation or independent status, face each other in a first-stage election, and there is no general election if a candidate gets over 50 percent of the vote. If the candidate with a plurality of the vote does not receive more than 50 percent, the two top vote receivers face each other in a runoff election.[3] These two candidates can bear the same party label or different party labels.

In the other forty-nine states, for a congressional candidate to run in a general election under a party label, he or she must receive the nomination of that party. If the nomination is not contested, this may simply involve receiving support from a convention or from other party leaders. But if the nomination is contested, the competing candidates for the nomination must face each other in a partisan convention fight and/or partisan primary election to decide who will be the party nominee in the general election.[4]

Congressional partisan primaries differ across the states regarding whether party membership is required for participation and how party membership is defined. There are four different variants of defining who can participate in a party's primary: pure-closed, semiclosed, semiopen, and pure-open. The title of each system gives some clues as to how it varies in voter participation. In general, in *pure-closed primary systems* voters register a party affiliation in advance of the election. Voters who affiliate as Democrats can vote only in the Democratic primary, for example. Voters who do not choose a party affiliation in advance are not allowed to vote in the primary election at all. States vary in how early voters must declare their party affiliation. In New Hampshire, for example, voters need to declare affiliation only ten days in advance, while in New York, voters must declare their affiliation one year in advance. For the period of our empirical study (1982–90), eighteen states used closed primaries: Arizona, California, Colorado, Connecticut, Delaware, Florida, Kansas, Kentucky, Maryland, Nebraska, Nevada, New Hampshire, New Mexico, New York, North Carolina, Pennsylvania, South Dakota, and West Virginia.

Semiclosed primary systems are closed primary systems that allow new or unaffiliated voters to vote in a party's primary without declaring affiliation in advance. Hence, some voters can choose to vote in the primary on election day, but those who have previously affiliated and/or registered as voters cannot. Six states have semiclosed primary systems for the period 1982–90: Maine, Massachusetts, New Jersey, Oklahoma, Oregon, and Rhode Island.

Semiopen and *pure-open primary systems*, in contrast, allow *all* voters to choose a party primary preference on election day. In semiopen primaries, the decision is made publicly—all voters must request publicly the ballot of a particular party or otherwise declare a membership in that political party (at least for election day) to receive a party's ballot. Fourteen states used semiopen primaries in the period 1982–90: Alabama, Arkansas, Georgia, Illinois, Indiana, Iowa, Mississippi, Missouri, Ohio, South Carolina, Tennessee, Texas, Virginia, and Wyoming.[5] In pure-open primary systems, voters make the decision about which party's primary to vote in privately. Nine states used pure-open primaries in the period 1982–90: Hawaii, Idaho, Michigan, Minnesota, Montana, North Dakota, Utah, Vermont, and Wisconsin. Berdahl describes how these private primaries work:

> Under the Wisconsin open primary, for example, the voter is asked no questions about his party affiliation, but is handed the ballots of all parties, which are separately printed but fastened together; he detaches the ballot of the party with which he desires to affiliate, votes it and drops it in the ballot box, and drops the others in a box for waste ballots. Thus the voter has chosen membership in a particular party, but no one else need know which party it is, and he is free to change his affiliation at any time.[6]

Semiopen and pure-open primaries also can vary in another dimension—the ease with which voters can choose a party's primary by office in the same election. Typically, there is more than one nomination contest on a ballot. For example, voters may be deciding who a party's nominee will be for governor as well as lieutenant governor, for senator as well as representative. In standard semiopen and pure-open primaries, a voter's choice of party primary will apply to all the nomination contests on the ballot. But in blanket systems, voters can choose contest by contest which party's primary to participate in—perhaps voting in the Democratic primary for governor and the Republican primary for lieutenant governor. Two states had blanket primary systems during the period 1982–90: Alaska and Washington. These blanket systems may involve public declarations of party affiliation and be semiopen, as is currently (2000 election) the case in California. Moreover, Alaska's Republican Party currently restricts participation to registered Republicans and unaffiliated voters, making that blanket system a variant of semiclosed and semiopen. However, for the period of our study, both Alaska and Washington operated pure-open primary systems.

In table 8.1 we summarize the types of primary systems used from 1982 to 1996. Because a number of states changed their primary systems in the 1990s, we use data from 1982 to 1990 in our empirical analysis.

HOW PRIMARY SYSTEMS AFFECT CONGRESSIONAL CANDIDATES' POLICY POSITIONS

Nonpartisan Elections

It is well known that in two-candidate elections in which candidates are maximizing their probability of winning and in which voter preferences are nicely behaved, candidates will converge at the policy position most preferred by the median voter in the general electorate, as the Hotelling-Downsian model predicts.[7] If there are more than two candidates, the analysis is more complicated and many equilibria can exist, depending on the assumptions made about voters and candidates. However, when nonpartisan elections are used in congressional races, such as those in Louisiana, the candidates face a majority requirement as discussed earlier. This means that if a candidate does not receive more than 50 percent of the vote in the first stage of the election, then he or she is in a two-candidate race with his or her closest opponent; and we would expect these two candidates to be drawn to positions close to the median voter. This is true even if the two candidates are from the same political party. Nonpartisan congressional elections, then, should lead candidates choosing moderate positions close to the median voters in their general electorates.

Pure-Closed Primary Systems

How does competing in a primary affect a candidate's position? A number of formal theoretical models have analyzed the effects of closed primary elections on the positions candidates choose.[8] Typically, these models assume that voters in primaries are more extreme than the general electorate, that the median or decisive voter in each party's primary is more extreme than the median voter in the elec-

Table 8.1: **Primary System Type, U.S. States, 1982–1996**

State	Primary System	State	Primary System
AL	Semiopen	MT	Pure-open
AK	Blanket	NE	Pure-closed (1982–94)
	Pure-open 1982–90		Semiclosed 1996 (Independents)
	Semiclosed (Republicans 1992–96)		
AZ	Pure-closed	NV	Pure-closed
AR	Semiopen	NH	Pure-closed 1982–90
			Semiclosed 1992–96
			(previously unaffiliated)
CA	Pure-closed	NJ	Semiclosed (previously unaffiliated)
CO	Pure-closed 1982–90	NM	Pure-closed
	Semiclosed 1992–96		
	(previously unaffiliated)		
CT	Pure-closed	NY	Pure-closed
DE	Pure-closed	NC	Pure-closed 1982–94
			Semiclosed 1996 (Republicans)
FL	Pure-closed	ND	Pure-open
GA	Semiopen	OH	Semiopen
HI	Pure-open	OK	Semiclosed (Independents)
ID	Pure-open	OR	Pure-closed 1982–90
			Semiclosed 1992–96
			(Republicans)
IL	Semiopen	PA	Pure-closed
IN	Semiopen	RI	Semiclosed (previously unaffiliated)
IA	Semiopen	SC	Semiopen
KS	Pure-closed 1982–90	SD	Pure-closed
	Semiclosed 1992–96 (previously unaffiliated)		
KY	Pure-closed	TN	Semiopen
LA	Nonpartisan	TX	Semiopen
ME	Semiclosed (previously unaffiliated)	UT	Pure-open
MD	Pure-closed	VT	Pure-open
MA	Semiclosed (previously unaffiliated)	VA	Semiopen
MI	Pure-open	WA	Blanket Pure-open
MN	Pure-open	WV	Pure-closed 1982–90
			Semiclosed 1992–96
			(Republicans)
MS	Semiopen	WI	Pure-open
MO	Semiopen	WY	Semiopen

Source: Alexander J. Bott. *Handbook of United States Election Laws and Practices* (New York: Greenwood, 1990); state election officials.

torate. Candidates in the primaries, then, choose policy positions "as if" they are maximizing the expected utility or preferences of their respective party's decisive or median voter. When candidates must choose their policy positions with uncertainty about the nature of the preferences of voters in the general election, the policy positions that the candidates will choose may diverge substantially from the standard convergent Hotelling-Downsian predicted position, and they choose positions close to the ideal points of the decisive voter in their parties' primaries.[9]

Semiclosed Primary Systems

What happens, however, if primaries are not closed but are semiclosed, semiopen, or pure-open? Consider first the effect of semiclosed primaries. In semiclosed primaries, voters who are previously unaffiliated and/or new voters can choose to vote in a party's primary. If it is assumed that these voters are more moderate than the partisan voters in a closed primary, then allowing them to vote in a semiclosed primary should make the decisive voter in the primary more moderate and should result in candidates choosing more moderate positions.[10] Hence, we expect that in semiclosed primaries candidates will choose more moderate positions than in closed primaries.

Semiopen and Pure-Open Primary Systems

Semiopen and pure-open primaries are more complicated. In these primaries, not only can unaffiliated and/or new voters choose in a party's primary, but even members of other political parties can vote in a party's primary. When a voter chooses to vote in the primary of a party different from the party she or he normally votes in or identifies with, a voter is engaged in what has been called "crossover voting." Crossover voting can be either "sincere" or "strategic." Sincere crossover voting occurs when a voter crosses over to vote for a candidate he or she would like to see win the general election (because that candidate is the voter's most preferred candidate who can possibly win).[11] Strategic crossover voting occurs when a voter crosses over to vote for a candidate who she or he believes is more likely to lose in the general election to his or her preferred candidate in the voter's own party. The key is that sincere crossover voting is designed to increase the likelihood that the candidate who receives the crossover vote will win the general election, whereas strategic crossover voting is designed to increase the likelihood that another candidate in the voter's own party will win the general election.

Generally we think of sincere crossover voters as moderate voters, and thus sincere crossover voting would shift the decisive voter in a party's primary to a more moderate position and, as a result, would favor moderate candidates. In contrast, strategic crossover voters are more likely to vote for extremist candidates, advantaging these candidates. Following this reasoning, semiopen and pure-open primaries may lead to more moderate candidates if sincere crossover is substantial but may not if strategic crossover is likely. Strategic crossover voting is complicated, however, because it requires that voters act in concert to vote for a candidate they do not prefer. It requires a substantial degree of coordination of voters and a surety among the voters that the outcome of their own primary does not depend on their votes. The coordination may be easier in semiopen primaries than in pure-open primaries, in which strategic crossover voters can see that others are also engaging in this behavior and therefore they can act as a group. However, if strategic crossover is something of which one is ashamed (perhaps because the voter does not want to express what may be seen as public support for a party with extreme candidates the voter does not prefer), voters may be more reluctant to cross over strategically in semiopen primaries than they would in pure-open ones. Thus, it is difficult to predict the effect of publicness on strategic crossover.

Regardless of the type of open primary, empirical evidence suggests that strategic crossover voting is rare,[12] although there are many notorious examples of strategic crossover from the party machine age when coordinated voting choices could be more easily organized.[13] This suggests that semiopen and pure-open primaries, like semiclosed primaries, are more likely to favor moderate candidates, assuming that sincere crossover voters are moderates and that candidates elected from these states will have more moderate positions relative to the median voter in their states than in states with closed primaries. Gerber and Morton[14] find empirical support for this argument. They show that in states with more open primary systems (combining some of the aforemention types, which will be discussed later), members of Congress choose more moderate positions relative to the median voters in their districts than do members elected from states with closed primary systems.

DO OPEN PRIMARIES ATTRACT EXTREMISTS?

Our analysis so far assumes that opening up primary elections by allowing new and/or unaffiliated voters (as in semiclosed primaries), voters willing to publicly cross over (as in semiopen primaries), or voters who privately cross over (as in pure-open primaries) brings more moderates into the primary election and that candidates then choose more moderate positions. However, others contend that opening up primary elections actually brings in more extreme voters and causes candidates to choose more divergent positions. King, for example, notes that political practitioners make the opposite argument: "Phil Sharp (who served in the House for 20 years) and Mickey Edwards (16 years in the House) . . . argue [open primaries] are more divisive than closed primaries because candidates play to the wingnuts who can be brought to the polls on single issues, like gun control, rent control, abortion, and union rights."[15] In fact, King tests this hypothesis and finds that when he compares the average divergence of members of Congress from their district median voters in semiopen and pure-open primaries to the average divergence in closed primaries for the 103rd, 104th, and 105th Congresses, the average member selected from closed primaries is more moderate (although, members selected from semiclosed primaries are the most moderate in the 104th and 105th Congresses).

Who is right? Does openness lead to moderation, as Gerber and Morton[16] found and as Campbell believed in California, or does it lead to extremism, as suggested by King[17] and the political practitioners he quotes? The data analyses of Gerber and Morton and of King are inadequate to address this question fully. First, both studies lump together semiopen and pure-open primaries. Yet, the requirement of making a public declaration may substantially influence voter participation choice, as Geer[18] notes, and voters in semiopen systems may be significantly different from voters in pure-open primary systems. King's argument may hold for primary systems in which voters are not required to make any public declaration, whereas the contention of Gerber and Morton may apply to semiopen primaries. Furthermore, Gerber and Morton also combine blanket primaries with nonpartisan elections, which are fundamentally different systems. In the next section, we reanalyze the Gerber and Morton study, separating out in finer detail these differences in primary systems to determine more adequately the effects of primary openness on the relative extremeness of candidates.

EMPIRICAL ANALYSIS

Hypotheses and Estimation Equations

The debate in the preceding section can be summarized into the following competing hypotheses:

- *Hypothesis 1:* (Gerber and Morton) Candidates in more open primaries choose positions more moderate than do those in closed primary systems.
- *Hypothesis 2:* (King) Candidates in more open primaries choose positions more extreme than those in closed primary systems.
- *Hypothesis 3:* (Combined Gerber-Morton and King) The relationship between openness and candidate policy positions is nonlinear. Increasing openness, as in semiclosed primaries, may lead candidates to choose moderate positions; but as openness increases to pure-open systems, candidates become more extreme than in closed primaries.

To test among these three hypotheses, we use data from U.S. congressional elections from 1982 to 1990. Our dependent variable in the analysis is the policy position of the winning congressional candidate, *Winner Ideology*$_{it}$ from each congressional district i ($i = 1$ to 434) at time t ($t = 1$ to 5). We estimate these positions using the winning candidate's ADA score averaged over the two years immediately following the election, correcting for abstentions.[19]

Gerber and Morton estimate the following equation to test whether differences in candidate nomination procedures affect candidate policy positions:

Equation I

$$Winner\ Ideology_{it} = \beta_0 + \beta_1 District\ Ideology_i + \beta_2 District\ Ideology_i^2 + \beta_3 Party_{it} + \beta_4 Semiclosed_i * Party_{it} + \beta_5 Open_i * Party_{it} + \beta_6 NP/Blanket_i * Party_{it} + u_{1it}$$

Where *District Ideology* is measured as the average of the district's Mondale and Dukakis votes, *District Ideology*^{2} is this variable squared (to capture the nonlinear relationship between this measure and the median voter position in the district, see Gerber and Morton[20] for a discussion); *Party* is coded as -1 for Republicans and 1 for Democrats; *Semiclosed* is scored as 1 if a state used semiclosed primaries, 0 if otherwise; *Open* is scored as 1 if a state used semiopen or pure-open primaries, 0 if otherwise; and *NP/Blanket* is scored as 1 if a state used nonpartisan elections or blanket primaries, 0 if otherwise.

Gerber and Morton use the party variable to measure the symmetric effect that the different types of primaries are expected to have on members of Congress' positions depending on the member's party membership, that is, for Democrats, extreme positions are high values of ADA scores, and for Republicans, extreme positions are low values of ADA scores. Thus, we expect that if, for example, semiclosed primaries lead to more moderate positions relative to the median voter in a district, then the variable will lower Democratic member ADA scores and raise Republican member ADA scores.

As noted for Equation I, Gerber and Morton's and King's empirical estimations combine semiopen and pure-open primaries in one variable and nonpartisan elections and blanket primaries in another variable. First, we wish to investigate the extent to which this lumping together masks the nonlinear relationship between openness and moderation that we expect. We estimate the following equation with new dummy variables for the different types of candidate nomination systems:

Equation II

$$Winner\ Ideology_{it} = \beta_0 + \beta_1 District\ Ideology_i + \beta_2 District\ Ideology_i^2 + \beta_3 Party_{it} + \beta_4 Semiclosed_i * Party_{it} + \beta_5 Semiopen_i * Party_{it} + \beta_6 Pure\text{-}Open_i * Party_{it} + \beta_7 Blanket * Party_{it} + \beta_8 Nonpartisan_i * Party_{it} + u_{1it}$$

EMPIRICAL RESULTS: OVERALL EFFECTS OF
PRIMARY SYSTEM DIFFERENCES

The second column of table 8.2 reports the results of the estimation of Equation II. To interpret the regression coefficients, negative coefficients indicate that increases in the independent variable lead to candidates choosing more moderate positions relative to the median voter position in their district, and positive coefficients indicate that increases in the independent variable lead to candidates choosing more extreme positions relative to the median voter in their district. The null case is a candidate selected from a pure-closed primary state. We find that indeed there is a significant difference between the effects of semiopen primaries and pure-open ones. Candidates who are selected from semiclosed, semiopen, and nonpartisan states are significantly more likely to have moderate positions relative to their districts' median voters than are those selected from pure-closed primary states. Those selected from nonpartisan states are the most moderate relative to their districts' median voters, as the theory would predict. This evidence suggests that opening up primaries in some cases does result in candidates choos-

Table 8.2: Pooled Cross-Section Time-Series Regression Coefficients (Ordinary Least Squares) Relating Winner's ADA Score and Primary System Type, U.S. Congressional Districts, 1982–90

Independent Variable	OLS Results		OLS Results	
District Ideology	3.00**	(0.18)	2.99**	(0.17)
District Ideology Squared	−0.02**	(0.00)	−0.02**	(0.00)
Party	22.57**	(0.62)	23.67**	(1.03)
Semiclosed * Party	−4.32**	(1.40)	−4.58**	(1.56)
Semiopen * Party	−5.04**	(0.84)	−2.17**	(0.89)
Pure-Open * Party	4.07**	(1.12)	3.12**	(1.17)
Nonpartisan * Party	−14.95**	(2.76)	−6.34**	(2.79)
Blanket * Party			−5.58**	(2.65)
Runoff * Party			−6.79**	(1.65)
Trend * Party			0.51**	(0.25)
Open-Seat * Party			2.38*	(1.35)
Presidential * Party			−1.50**	(0.72)
South * Party			−4.05**	(1.69)
New England * Party			−1.59	(1.80)
Constant	−46.64**	(4.47)	−44.85**	(4.35)
Adjusted R Squared	0.77	0.78		
Observations	2170		2170	

*Significant at .1 level, two-tail test; standard errors in parentheses.

**Significant at .05 level, two-tail test; standard errors in parentheses.

ing more moderate positions. Pure-open primaries, in contrast, lead candidates to select more extreme positions than do pure-closed primaries. This suggests that openness as in pure-open primaries, in which voters can choose which primary to vote in secretly, does lead candidates to select extreme positions, as King contends.

Our results may reflect the omission of other factors that may be correlated with primary election systems and that are likely to affect the policy positions of candidates. In the third column of table 8.2, we report regression results that attempt to control for some of these effects, some of which turn out to be significant.

- First, we noted earlier that some variants of pure-open and semiopen primaries use a system that allows voters to crossover according to the office—blanket primaries. We include *Blanket * Party* to evaluate whether this advantages moderate candidates. We find that it is significantly negative, suggesting that blanket primaries lead to more moderate candidates.

- Second, a number of states that have partisan primaries also use majority requirements. We include *Runoff * Party* to control for this effect. This is significantly negative, suggesting that regardless of the primary election system, majority requirements do lead to candidates choosing more moderate positions relative to the median voters in their districts.

- Third, a number of scholars have argued that members of Congress have become more polarized since the early 1970s. To control for a possible effect of increasing polarization, we add the variable *Trend * Party*, which is scored *Party * t*, where $t = 1, 2, 3, 4, 5$. We find evidence that members of Congress are becoming more polarized over time, choosing more extreme positions.

- Fourth, because incumbents may be more able to provide district voters with private district-specific benefits, these candidates may be allowed by their voters to choose more extreme positions because the voters may be willing to accept deviations from their preferences in exchange for these pork barrel benefits. Thus, we might expect that members of Congress selected in open-seat races will choose positions closer to the median voter. We find no support for this, as *Open Seat * Party*'s coefficient has the wrong sign and is significantly different from zero at a 10 percent confidence level.

- Fifth, in presidential election years, more voters may choose to participate, and the greater participation may lead to candidates choosing positions closer to the median voters in their districts. We do find support for this, as *President * Party* is significantly negative.

- Following Gerber and Morton, we also add in two regional variables that might affect the degree of moderation, *South * Party* and *New England * Party*. We find that while members of Congress selected from southern states do choose more moderate positions, there is no significant difference among those selected from New England states.

EMPIRICAL RESULTS: PARTY SPECIFIC EFFECTS OF
PRIMARY SYSTEM DIFFERENCES

While our results support the contention that the effect of openness on candidate positions is nonlinear, it is likely that the effects of openness will also vary by major party, that is, during the period of our study, Democratic members of Congress were in the majority and thus had more control over ultimate policy decisions within Congress. This may mean that the relationship between primary system and congressional policy positions is fundamentally different for the two parties. To test the extent to which this is true, we estimate separate regressions by party, which are reported in table 8.3. Note that in this table the Democratic coefficients have the same interpretation as in table 8.2: positive coefficients mean that increases in an independent variable increases extremism in candidate's positions relative to the district's median voters, while negative coefficients indicate that increases in an independent variable increases moderation in candidate's positions relative to the district's median voters. Republican coefficients, however, have the opposite signs for moderation and extremism (positive coefficients indicate a moderation effect of the independent variable, and negative coefficients indicate an extremist effect of the independent variable).

Table 8.3: Pooled Cross-Section Time-Series Regression Coefficients, *DV* = Winner's ADA Score, Democrats and Republicans, U.S. Congressional Districts, 1982–1990

Independent Variable	Democrats		Republicans	
District Ideology	2.65**	(0.22)	−1.42**	(0.46)
District Ideology Squared	−0.02**	(0.00)	0.03**	(0.01)
Semiclosed	−4.68**	(1.92)	14.68**	(1.92)
Semiopen	−4.96**	(1.09)	−3.95**	(1.07)
Pure-Open	4.57**	(1.48)	−2.68**	(1.34)
Nonpartisan	−16.28**	(3.34)	−7.76**	(3.45)
Blanket	−1.04	(3.34)	13.98**	(3.03)
Runoff	−8.45**	(1.98)	−5.37**	(2.08)
Trend	0.89**	(0.30)	0.21	(0.30)
Open-Seat	1.37	(1.76)	−2.72*	(1.48)
Presidential	−3.59**	(0.87)	−1.69**	(0.86)
South	−10.20**	(2.07)	−0.39	(2.02)
New England	10.07**	(2.28)	19.96**	(2.10)
Constant	−7.52	(6.38)	24.04**	(9.05)
Adjusted *R* Squared	0.56		0.49	
Observations	1302		868	

*Significant at .1 level, two-tail test; standard errors in parentheses.
**Significant at .05 level, two-tail test; standard errors in parentheses.

We find in table 8.3 that some of the variables have the same effect on both Democrats and Republicans. Semiclosed primaries cause both Democrats and Republicans to choose significantly more moderate positions, although the effect is greater for Republicans, and pure-open primaries cause both to choose more extreme positions, although the effect is insignificant for Republicans. However, there are some notable differences across parties. Democrats selected in semiopen primaries and nonpartisan elections and in the same years as presidential elections have significantly more moderate positions; for Republicans, these differences lead to more extreme positions. The regional differences also have converse effects, with Democrats, but not Republicans, being significantly more moderate in the South. In New England states, the data show Democrats more extreme and Republicans more moderate. This, no doubt, reflects regional preferences, differences not sufficiently captured by the district ideology measures.

CONCLUSION

Tom Campbell advocated changing California's nomination procedures because he thought the changes would cause candidates to choose moderate positions by opening up California's closed primaries to more voters. Previous empirical evidence on the effect of openness on candidate policy positions disagrees over the effect of openness—Gerber and Morton show that openness can result in candidates choosing more moderate positions, while King finds that open primaries can actually have the opposite effect, resulting in candidates choosing more extreme positions than in closed primaries. In an effort to resolve this discrepancy in the literature, we make a distinction suggested by Geer, between semiopen and pure-open primary systems. We also separate out nonpartisan elections from blanket primaries to explore the effects of these two different systems on candidate policy positions.

By doing so, we find that the level of difficulty in switching party labels on election day can create differences in the level of extremism of the candidates. Semiclosed and semiopen primaries lead to more moderate candidates than do closed primaries in general, while pure-open primaries actually lead to more extreme candidates than do closed primaries. Nonpartisan elections and blanket primaries also lead to more moderate candidates. Furthermore, we find that there are substantial differences in the effects of different primary rules by political party, particularly for the semiclosed, semiopen, and blanket variants.

Our results, then, suggest that it is problematic to lump together various primary election systems when studying their effects on candidate choices. Indeed, subtle differences in the rules surrounding primaries can create large differences on candidate policy choices. Opening up closed primaries on a limited basis can cause candidates to choose significantly more moderate positions, but too much openness, as in pure-open primaries, can result in candidates who choose even more extreme positions than those selected in pure-closed primaries.

We explore briefly in this chapter one theoretical explanation as to why openness may have this nonlinear effect—semiclosed and semiopen primaries attract independents and moderates who vote sincerely for moderate candidates (thus advantaging them), and pure-open primaries attract extremist voters (thus advantaging extreme candidates). But, we see our analysis as only a first step in exploring the effects of these detailed differences both theoretically and empirically. Our empirical evidence suggests that there are fundamental differences in the nature of political competition by primary system and that future research on congressional elections should consider how these differences work to have these effects.

NOTES

1. Elisabeth R. Gerber and Rebecca B. Morton, "Primary Election Systems and Representation," *Journal of Law, Economics, and Organization* 14, no. 2 (1998): 304–24.

2. David C. King, "Party Competition and Polarization in American Politics" (paper presented at the annual meetings of the Midwest Political Science Association, Chicago, 1998, and at the MIT Conference on Parties and Congress, Cambridge, Mass., 1999).

3. Often the first stage in nonpartisan elections is called a "primary," although it is really a general election because it potentially can lead to the selection of the elected official. In *Foster v. Love*, 522, U.S. 67, 118 S. Ct. 464 (1997), the U.S Supreme Court addressed the issue of whether the first stage should be viewed as a general election. Federal election law requires that the date of all presidential elections and of the biennial election for all congressional seats be on a single November day (2 U.S.C. §§1, 7; 3 U.S.C. § 1). When Louisiana adopted nonpartisan elections for Congress, in 1978, the state held the first stage of the elections in October, having the runoff elections, when required, on the federal election date. Yet, over 80% of the state's contested congressional elections actually were settled in October, with one candidate (usually the incumbent) selected in the first stage by receiving more than 50% of the vote. The Supreme Court found that Louisiana's statute conflicted with federal law to the extent that it is applied to select a congressional candidate in October; the Louisiana nonpartisan first-stage elections are now held in November.

4. Some states (such as Virginia) allow for conventions to replace primaries, and others (such as Connecticut) require that candidates first receive a certain percentage of the vote in a convention to be on the primary ballot.

5. John F. Bibby [*Politics, Parties, and Elections in America*, 4th ed. (Belmont, Calif.: Wadsworth, 2000)] labels Iowa, Ohio, and Wyoming as semiclosed primary states because although voters can change party membership on election day, this is technically different from registering publicly for election day, as in semiopen primaries (since the presumption is that a voter is a member of the party whose primary he or she voted in in the last election or registered as a member of in the last election). We categorize semiclosed primaries as those in which only new or unaffiliated voters can choose a primary on elec-

tion day and semiopen primaries as those in which all voters can choose to do so, but they must choose a primary publicly. Because Iowa, Ohio, and Wyoming allow all voters the option of choosing on election day, we contend that they are fundamentally different from the other semiclosed states and that in operation they are like the semiopen states.

6. Clarence A. Berdahl, "Party Membership in the United States," *American Political Science Review* 36 (1942): 22.

7. See Melvin J. Hinich and Michael C. Munger, *Analytical Politics* (Cambridge: Cambridge University Press, 1994) for details.

8. James S. Coleman, "Internal Process Governing Party Positions in Elections," *Public Choice* 11 (1971): 35–60. James S. Coleman, "The Positions of Political Parties in Elections," in *Probability Models of Collective Decision Making*, ed. R. Niemi and H. Weisberg (Columbus, Ohio: Merrill, 1972). Peter Aranson and Peter C. Ordeshook, "Spatial Strategy for Sequential Elections," in *Probability Models of Collective Decision Making*, ed. R. Niemi and H. Weisberg. Donald A. Wittman, "Candidates with Policy Preferences: A Dynamic Model," *Journal of Economic Theory* 14 (1977): 180–89. Donald A. Wittman, "Candidate Motivations: A Synthesis of Alternatives," *American Political Science Review* 77 (1983): 142–57. Donald A. Wittman, "Spatial Strategies When Candidates Have Policy Preferences," in *Advances in the Spatial Theory of Voting,* ed. J. Enelow and M. Hinich (Cambridge: Cambridge University Press, 1991). John H. Aldrich, "A Downsian Spatial Model with Party Activism," *American Political Science Review* 77 (1983): 974–90. John H. Aldrich and Michael D. McGinnis, "A Model of Party Constraints on Optimal Candidate Positions," *Mathematical and Computer Modelling* 12 (1989): 437–50.

9. Gerber and Morton ("Primary Election Systems") review this literature. Rebecca Morton ("Incomplete Information and Ideological Explanations of Platform Divergence," *American Political Science Review* 87, no. 2 [1993]: 382–92) shows using laboratory elections that uncertainty can cause candidates to diverge as predicted.

10. William H. Flanigan and Nancy H. Zingale (*Political Behavior of the American Electorate,* 9th ed. [Washington, D.C.: Congressional Quarterly Press, 1998]: 114–15) present evidence that on the key issues that divide the two major parties, independent and unaffiliated voters' preferences are at moderate positions.

11. A voter also may sincerely cross over to vote for a second preferred candidate because his or her first preference has no chance of winning.

12. See R. Michael Alvarez and Jonathan Nagler, "Analysis of Crossover and Strategic Voting," Social Science Working Paper 1019, California Institute of Technology, 1997.

13. See Berdahl, "Party Membership," for a discussion of strategic crossover in New Jersey before World War II.

14. Gerber and Morton, "Primary Election Systems."

15. King, "Party Competition," 32.

16. Gerber and Morton, "Primary Election Systems."

17. King, "Party Competition."

18. John G. Geer, "Rules Governing Presidential Primaries," *Journal of Politics* 48, no. 1 (1986): 1006–25.

19. The Speaker of the House does not vote. Therefore he does not have a measurable policy position and is excluded from our study.

20. Gerber and Morton, "Primary Election Systems."

9

Explaining the Ideological Differences between the Two U.S. Senators Elected from the Same State: An Institutional Effects Model

Bernard Grofman and Thomas L. Brunell

Taking into account institutional realities such as party primaries, the role of party activists, and national party images that impact on party competition over multiple constituencies,[1] work done subsequently, both theoretical[2] and empirical,[3] has shown that although the centrist pressures identified by Downs[4] are quite real, in two-party competition a considerable degree of party divergence is to be expected.

We focus our attention for this chapter on U.S. senators elected from the same state. We offer an institutional explanation both of when we can expect divided Senate delegations and of the expected ideological differences between senators from the same state of the same and opposite parties.[5] Like Gerber and Morton,[6] the critical distinction we draw is between closed and open primaries.[7]

In the usual closed primary situation, it has been shown theoretically that, ceteris paribus, candidates of each party are likely to be located quite near the median voter of their own party, albeit shifted somewhat in the direction of the overall median voter.[8] Thus, for the usual type of closed primary, candidates of opposite parties are expected to be rather different ideologically, because each is largely mirroring their own party's median voter,[9] and the Democratic median voter is known to be to the left of the Republican median voter in all fifty states.[10] In contrast, if there is an open primary in a state, this generates centripetal pressures on the candidates of each party vis-à-vis the overall median voter, because the primary electorate will no longer be so purely partisan in composition as a reult of the possibility of crossover participation from supporters of the other party.[11]

In their study of U.S. House elections, Gerber and Morton[12] find strong support for the hypothesis that, ceteris paribus, the average ideological extremism of the winners will be greater in closed primaries than in open ones. They explain this finding by the fact that "greater participation by voters outside the party reduces control over candidate nominations by extreme party members and is therefore expected to produce candidates with policy positions closer to the ideal point of the general electorate median voter."[13] The belief that open primaries foster the selection of more moderate candidates is not just a notion confined to the ranks of Public Choice scholars. It is also the common wisdom of political activists and journalists.

In March 1996, California voters authorized by referendum (Proposition 198) the use of an open primary (more particularly, a so-called "blanket primary") for the state. In the *Los Angeles Times*, February 23, 1997, in an op-ed piece, the chair of California's Republican Party is quoted as saying that the new primary rules "would sap the creativity from politics by punishing candidates from the ideological wings of the party and favoring those of the more moderate, and mushy, middle." The staff writer of a later bylined story on the new primary rules accepted this view and opined that "moderate candidates are expected to be favored in an open primary because they have the best chance of attracting voters from other parties."[14]

Here we build on the ideas about the impact of primary type in Gerber and Morton[15]—ideas that inspired the writing of this chapter—by complementing their 1998 analysis of the impact of primary type on ideological extremism in elections to the U.S. House of Representatives, with a study of U.S. Senate elections. We focus in large part on the impact of primary type on ideological differences between senators of the same and of opposite parties elected from the same state, and we look also at the likelihood of divided Senate delegations as a function of primary type.

As noted previously, we distinguish between two types of primary elections: open and closed. Open primaries are those in which voters can choose the party primary in which they want to participate—a Democrat can choose to vote in the Republican primary if he or she so desires. Closed primaries, on the other hand, are restricted to registered partisans—only voters registered in a party can participate in the primary election. There are many subtleties to the specific laws in each of the states.

We expect that, ceteris paribus, in states with open primaries, when senators of opposite parties are elected, the ideological differences between them will be less, on average, than is true for senators of opposite parties elected in states with closed primaries.

On the other hand, in states with open primaries, the presence of crossover voting should increase (at least somewhat) the standard deviation of the ideological composition of the primary electorates, especially that in the party primary of the party whose candidate is most likely to win. This increase in standard deviation of the primary electorate's ideological composition should lead to an increase in the variance across elections in the ideological positions of the nominees chosen by the party. Thus, ceteris paribus, in states with open primaries, when senators of the same party are elected, the ideological differences between them should be greater, on average, than is true for senators of the same party elected in states with closed primaries.[16]

If there is a dominant party and its candidates reasonably reflect the preferences of the overall median voter, it is very unlikely that that party's senatorial candidates will be defeated. Because open primaries more readily permit competition for the overall median voter to take place within the party primaries prior to the general election, we would expect that, ceteris paribus, states with open primaries are less likely to have divided Senate delegations than are states with closed primaries.[17]

The combination of these three hypotheses with the fact that the ideological difference manifested in roll-call-voting behavior between senators of the same party from the same state is far less than that between senators of opposite parties from the same state[18] leads us to an important final hypothesis. On balance, ceteris paribus, the ideological differences between senators elected from states that use closed primaries should be greater, on average, than is true for senators elected in states with open primaries.

There are two reasons for this. First, states with open primaries should be less likely to be divided, thus giving rise to only slight differences, on average, between the state's senators. Second, even when states with open primaries are divided in their senatorial delegation, the differences between senators of opposite parties in the open primary states will be less than the differences in the closed primary states. These two effects reinforce each other; and the countervailing effect, namely that senators of the same party from open primary states will be slightly less alike in voting behavior than is true for senators of the same party from closed primary states, is not nearly as important in its overall impact on ideological differences as a function of primary type.[19]

Now we turn to a test of these four hypotheses.

DATA ANALYSIS

We have gathered the relevant data, partisan makeup and Americans for Democratic Action (ADA) scores for senators from all fifty states for the years 1971 to 1996. Hypothesis 1 simply states that states with closed primaries will have more mixed Senate delegations (1 senator from each party). Table 9.1 is a cross tabulation of the type of primary that a state uses to nominate its senators and whether the state has a divided delegation. The hypothesis is clearly supported in our range of data. Both primary types have nearly equal number of observations over our sample period—there are 432 observations with closed primaries and 468 obser-

**Table 9.1: Number of Divided and Unified Senate
Delegations by Primary Type, 1971–1996**

	Unified Delegation	*Divided Delegation*
Closed primaries	202	230
Open primaries	291	177

Chi-square = 22.14
Probability < .001

vations with open primaries. Of those 468 with open primaries, only 177 had divided Senate delegations (37.8 percent). But of the 432 observations for closed primary states, fully 53.2 percent (230) had divided delegations to the Senate. A chi-square test indicates statistical significance at below the .001 level.

Hypotheses 2 and 3 deal with the degree of ideological difference between the two senators in each state. Clearly, in those states with divided delegations, the distance between the two senators will be greater than in those states with a unified delegation. But here we seek to go further than that observation to include as variables both whether the two senators are of the same party and what type of primary election a state uses to elect nominees. Hypothesis 2 states that open primary states with divided Senate delegations will have less ideological difference, measured by the absolute value of adjusted ADA score differences, than will closed primary states with divided delegations. We use the adjusted data for ADA scores as described in Groseclose, Levitt, and Snyder.[20] Table 9.2 uses adjusted ADA scores for each senator and primary type data to breakdown the ideological distance between senators. Again we use data from 1971 to 1996. The pattern is quite clear; those states with open primaries and split Senate delegations have less ideological distance between the two senators on average than do divided delegations in states with closed primaries. States using a closed primary average 46.21 difference, while open primary states average 43.54 difference, a divide of about 7 points on the 100-point ADA scale (the *t*-test indicates statistical significance at the .10 level).

**Table 9.2: Average Ideological Difference between Senators in States by Primary
Type and Whether Delegation Is Unified or Divided Overall (1971–1996)**

Primary Type	*Senate Delegation*	*Average Ideological Difference*	*Number of Observations*
Closed	Unified	12.9	201
Open	Unified	10.6	290
Closed	Divided	33.7	227
Open	Divided	22.5	177

Our next hypothesis deals with only those states with a unified Senate delegation. The average distance between two senators of the same party is only 13.13 points on the adjusted ADA scale. So the difference we are trying to explain is quite small. Hypothesis 3 states that open primary states with unified Senate delegations will have greater ideological differences than will closed primary states with unified delegations.

Table 9.2 shows that the evidence indicates that this hypothesis is not true. In those states with open primaries and two senators from the same party, the average ideological difference is 10.6, while closed primary states with unified delegations averaged 12.9.

We also tested Hypotheses 2 and 3 individually for nine Congresses in our data set. Table 9.3 presents the results. The hypothesis dealing with unified delegations is only supported in two of the nine Congresses (99th and 100th Congresses). On the other hand the hypothesis dealing with divided delegations is upheld in seven of the nine. Thus, while we cannot conclude that the primary type has the expected effect when Senate delegations are unified, we feel justified in concluding that our theory about the relationship between primary type and divided delegations is true.

According to Hypothesis 4, the ideological differences between senators with closed primaries should be greater on average than that for senators from open primary states. Table 9.4 breaks down ideological divisions between representatives by primary type. The hypothesis is again fully supported by the data. The average difference between the ADA score of one senator in a state relative to the other senator is 33.7 in states with closed primaries, compared to only an average of 22.5 points in open primary states. This difference is statistically significant beyond the .01 level.

We also include a regression model to further establish the relationship be-

Table 9.3: Test of Hypotheses 2 and 3 for Each Congress

Congress	Years	Unified Delegation Open > Closed	Divided Delegaton Closed > Open
96	1979–80	No	Yes
97	1981–82	No	Yes
98	1983–84	No	Yes
99	1985–86	Yes	Yes
100	1987–88	Yes	Yes
101	1989–90	No	No
102	1991–92	No	Yes
103	1993–94	No	Yes
104	1995–96	No	No

Table 9.4: Average Ideological Difference between Senators in a State by Primary Type

Primary Type	Average Ideological Difference	Number of Observations
Closed	30.5	428
Open	23.2	467

$t = 4.73$, 893 df, probability $< .001$. Ideology is measured using adjusted ADA scores (*see* Timothy Groseclose, Steven D. Levitt, and James M. Snyder Jr., "Comparing Interest Group Scores across Time and Chambers: Adjusted ADA Scores for the U.S. Congress," *American Political Science Review* 93 [March 1999]: 33–50).

tween the type of primary in a state and the ideological cohesiveness of the senators. In table 9.5, the model indicates that after controlling for whether the delegation is divided (which obviously affects the dependent variable) and for the different Congresses, the primary type variable is negative, indicating that the space between the senators increases as we move from open to closed primaries. Thus, the effects of primary type significantly affect whether a state will elect a divided delegation, but beyond that primary type affects the nature of ideology of the senators as well. We also ran separate regressions for each Congress, and the results are still encouraging—the coefficient for the primary type is negative as hypothesized in seven of the nine Congresses (the 96th and 104th are the exceptions). In two of the remaining seven Congresses, the coefficient reaches statistical significance. We interpret these results as further support for our contention regarding a specific relationship between electoral institutions and the representation that is a direct outcome from these elections.

Table 9.5: Regression Model of Ideological Distance between Senators and the Effect of Primary Type

Constant	−34.76	(−1.63)
Primary type	−2.28*	(−2.06)
Divided delegation	33.43**	(29.96)
Congress	0.50*	(2.34)
N	895	
Adjusted R^2	.51	

*$p < .05$
**$p < .001$

Note: Entries are unstandardized regression coefficients with t-statistics in parentheses. The dependent variable is the absolute value of the difference between the adjusted ADA scores of the two senators in each state for each year. Primary type is a dichotomous variable coded "1" if the state uses a closed primary and "2" if it uses open. Divided delegation is also dichotomous, coded "0" if the two senators in the state are from the same political party and "1" if they are from different parties. Congress is coded 104 for the 104th Congress, etc.

CONCLUSION

In 1996, Morris Fiorina wrote that *"differences in nominating processes* [emphasis added] and contrasting perceptions of the comparative strengths of executive and legislative institutions can have nothing to do with split delegations since both senators of a state are nominated in the same manner and both are legislators."[21] The exact meaning of this quote is far from clear, but Professor Fiorina (probably simply due to imprecision in sentence wording) does seem to be suggesting that if two U.S. senators are elected under the same rules, there is no reason for those rules to impact on how different they are from one another (ideologically or in terms of party). Clearly, if Fiorina meant this (and we doubt that he did), the data we have provided in this chapter show that he was wrong. Primary rules do impact both on whether a state will have a divided delegation and on how different the elected senators will be from each other. Those states with closed primaries are more likely to have a divided delegation and because of this are more apt to have greater ideological difference between the two senators of that state. We also hypothesized that primary type will have the opposite effect for unified delegations; the data do not support that contention. Indeed, more times than not, closed primary states have greater ideological difference for unified delegations as well.

Of course the difference in primary type is not the only factor affecting the ideological difference (similarity) between two senators from a state. Other research has linked the likelihood of mixed Senate delegations to demographic heterogeneity of a state,[22] to policy balancing,[23] and to long-term partisan realignments.[24] Other important factors include whether the state allows straight party vote with one lever,[25] as well as the proportion of independents among registered voters.[26]

NOTES

1. See the following reviews of how institutional complexities may be taken into account in spatial models: James M. Enelow and Melvin J. Hinich, eds., *Advances in the Spatial Theory of Voting* (New York: Cambridge University Press, 1990). Bernard Grofman, ed., *Information, Participation, and Choice: "An Economic Theory of Democracy" in Perspective* (Ann Arbor: University of Michigan Press, 1993). Bernard Grofman, "Toward an Institution-Rich Theory of Political Competition, with a Supply-Side Component," in *Information, Participation, and Choice: "An Economic Theory of Democracy" in Perspective*, ed. Bernard Grofman (Ann Arbor: University of Michigan Press, 1993). Melvin J. Hinich and Michael C. Munger, *Ideology and the Theory of Political Choice* (Ann Arbor: University of Michigan Press, 1995).

2. For example, Peter Aranson and Peter C. Ordeshook, "Spatial Strategy for Sequential Elections," in *Probability Models of Collective Decision Making*, ed. R. Niemi and H. Weisberg (Columbus, Ohio: Merrill, 1972). James S. Coleman, "The Positions of Political Parties in Elections," in *Probability Models of Collective Decision Making,* ed. R. Niemi

and H. Weisberg. Alberto Alesina, "Credibility and Policy Convergence in a Two-Party System with Rational Voters," *American Economic Review* 78 (1988): 796–805. Rebecca Morton, "Incomplete Information and Ideological Explanations of Platform Divergence," *American Political Science Review* 87, no. 2 (1993): 382–92. David Baron, "Electoral Competition with Informed and Uninformed Voters," *American Political Science Review* 88, no. 1 (March 1994): 33–47. Guillermo Owen and Bernard Grofman, "Two-Stage Electoral Competition in Two-Party Contests: Persistent Divergence of Party Positions with and without Expressive Voting" (presented at the annual meeting of the Public Choice Society, Long Beach, California, 1995).

3. Charles Bullock and David Brady, "Party, Constituency, and Roll Call Voting in the U.S. Senate," *Legislative Studies Quarterly* 8 (1983): 29–43. Morris P. Fiorina, *Representatives, Roll Calls, and Constituencies* (Lexington, Mass.: Lexington Books, 1974). Bernard Grofman, Robert Griffin, and Amihai Glazer, "Identical Geography, Different Constituencies, See What a Difference Party Makes," in *Developments in Electoral Geography*, ed. R. J. Johnston, F. Shelley, and P. Taylor (London: Croom Helm, 1990). Keith T. Poole and Howard Rosenthal, "The Polarization of American Politics," *Journal of Politics* 46 (1984): 1061–79. Catherine R. Shapiro, David W. Brady, Richard A. Brody, and John A. Ferejohn, "Linking Constituency Opinion and Senate Voting Scores: A Hybrid Explanation," *Legislative Studies Quarterly* 15, no. 4 (November 1990): 599–623.

4. Anthony Downs, *An Economic Theory of Democracy* (New York: Harper and Row, 1957).

5. A variety of other reasons have been offered for party divergence, such as the "two constituencies thesis that heterogeneity in the electorate contributes to divided Senate delegations and strong differences between the two senators if they happen to be of opposite parties" (Bullock and Brady, "Party, Constituency, and Roll Call Voting; cf. Gi-Ryong Jung, Lawrence W. Kenny, and John R. Lott Jr., "An Explanation for Why Senators from the Same State Vote Differently So Frequently," *Journal of Public Economics* 54 [1994]: 65–96), incumbency-related effects (see, e.g., Scott L. Feld and Bernard Grofman, "Incumbency Advantage, Voter Loyalty, and the Benefit of the Doubt," *Journal of Theoretical Politics* 3, no. 2 [1991]: 115–37), and realignment (Thomas L. Brunell and Bernard Grofman, "Explaining Divided Senate Delegations 1788–1996: A Realignment Approach," *American Political Science Review* 92 June 1998: 391–99). See general review in Bernard Grofman, "In Two Party Competition, Why Do We Have So Much Party Divergence?: A Review and Synthesis of a Baker's Dozen's Worth of Proffered Explanations" (unpublished manuscript, School of Social Sciences, University of California, Irvine, 1997). The literature on voter policy balancing (e.g., Alberto Alesina, and Howard Rosenthal, *Partisan Politics, Divided Government, and the Economy* (New York: Cambridge University Press, 1995). Elisabeth R. Gerber and Adam Many, "Incumbency-Led Ideological Balancing: A Hybrid Model of Split-Ticket Voting," [paper presented at the annual meeting of the Midwest Political Science Association, 1996]) may also be relevant to understanding this issue. We offer our institutional focus as complementary to that of other approaches.

6. Elisabeth R. Gerber and Rebecca B. Morton, "Primaries and Strategic Voting," (unpublished manuscript, Department of Political Science, University of California, San Diego, 1995). Gerber and Morton, "Primary Election Systems," *Journal of Law Economics and Organization* 14, no. 2 (1998): 304–24.

7. We may classify party primaries in a number of different ways; and it is common for authors to distinguish, for example, between closed and semiclosed primaries and among

several types of open primaries; for example, those where all voters may vote in whichever primary they choose and may defer that choice until election day, those where voters may vote for some offices in one primary and for other offices in the other primary (blanket primaries), and those where candidates of both parties run on the same primary ballot, with the two top vote getters, regardless of party affiliation, entering into a subsequent runoff if no candidate receives a majority in the primary (nonpartisan primary [a.k.a. jungle primary]). Here, however, to maintain reasonable cell sizes for purposes of hypothesis testing, we have kept to the simplest possible dichotomy. We list in the appendix the classification of each of the 50 states according to dichotomized primary type. Our classification is the same as that in Gerber and Morton ("Primary Election Systems," 304–24). However, we have done some further preliminary analyses not reported here in which we look to see if more finely tuned distinctions among primary types would be advantageous in developing and testing more precise hypotheses. Because of small n's for certain primary types, our general answer so far is no.

8. The shift toward the overall median can be expected to be greater if there is a large number of independents in the electorate (Shapiro, Brady, Brody, and Ferejohn, "Linking Constituency Opinion," 599–623).

Aranson and Ordeshook, "Spatial Strategy." Coleman, "The Positions of Political Party." Owen and Grofman, "Two-Stage Electoral Competition." Gerber and Morton, "Primaries and Strategic Voting." Gerber and Morton, "Primary Election Systems."

9. The ideological position of the candidates in any constituency is a function not merely of that candidate's party, but also of the ideological characteristics of the voters in that constituency; for example, a typical Democrat in a conservative constituency is to the right of a typical Democrat in a liberal constituency (Bernard Grofman, William Koetzle, Michael McDonald, and Thomas Brunell, "A New Look at Split-Ticket Outcomes for House and President: The Comparative Midpoints Model," *Journal of Politics* 62, no.1 [2000]: 34–50). As we show here, it is also a function of the institutional incentives for party convergence/divergence.

10. To establish the finding that Republican median voters are uniformly to the right of Democratic median voters in each state, Grofman, Koetzle, McDonald, and Brunell ("A New Look at Split-Ticket Outcomes") classify voters according to the seven-point party ID scale (with leaners classed with identifiers) and look at state-level data from the 1988–90–92 NES Senate study. These data yield sample sizes of well over a hundred for all states.

11. Picking the lesser of two evils is, we believe, a much more common strategy in terms of motivating crossover voting in open primaries than is deliberately seeking to ensure the nomination of a weak candidate of the opposite party, especially because we would anticipate that the likelihood of crossover voting is greatest when one party tends to dominate the state's senatorial politics and voters of the other party cross over to vote in its primary. Compare with the following: Christopher Hanks and Bernard Grofman, "Turnout in Gubernatorial and Senatorial Primary and General Elections in the South, 1922–90: A Rational Choice Model of the Effects of Short-Run and Long-Run Electoral Competition on Turnout," *Public Choice* 94, no. 3–4 (1998): 407–21; and Bernard Grofman and Theodore Arrington, "Party Registration Choices as a Function of Political Competition: A Test of a Strategic Model of 'Hidden Partisanship'" (unpublished manuscript, School of Social Sciences, University of California, Irvine, 1996).

12. Gerber and Morton, "Primaries and Strategic Voting." Gerber and Morton, "Primary Election Systems."

13. Gerber and Morton, "Primary Election Systems."

14. Dave Lesher, "Bill Proposes Changes in New Open Primary Law," *Los Angeles Times*, March 1, 1997, p. A1.

15. Gerber and Morton, "Primaries and Strategic Voting."

16. Of course, the magnitude of this effect may not be that large, especially if crossover voting is limited in scope. The evidence from the handful of studies that have been done suggests that many voters never shift between primaries; however, voter turnout in primaries may be higher, ceteris paribus, in states with open primaries than in states with closed primaries (see literature review in Gerber and Morton, "Primary Election Systems").

17. If the identifiers of one party outnumber the identifiers of the other party, it might appear that the preponderant party's candidate would essentially always win, because, ceteris paribus, the candidate of the party whose voters comprise a clear preponderance of the electorate should be more likely to be closer to the overall median voter. However, this is too simplistic. Bernard Grofman, Samuel Merrill, Thomas Brunell, and William Koetzle ("The Power of Ideologically Concentrated Minorities," *Journal of Theoretical Politics* 11, no. 1 [1999]: 57–74) have shown that we also need to take into account the ideological concentration of supporters of the two parties. If the minority party's supporters have a much lower standard deviation with respect to ideology than is true for the larger party, then the candidate of the minority party may still be closer to the overall median voter than is the candidate of the preponderant party. Thus, a constituency, such as a state, can be much more competitive than the relative balance of party identifiers in it would seem to indicate. In this chapter, however, we shall focus on institutional effects associated with primary type rather than on variance considerations or other factors.

18. Poole and Rosenthal, "The Polarization of American Politics." Grofman, Griffin, and Glazer, "Identical Geography."

19. Studying senators of the same and of opposite parties from a given state under various types of primary rules provides us a kind of "partial" natural experiment. Because one of our comparisons is between senators of the same state, we do not need to worry as much about constituency factors that may produce differences in electoral outcomes. Of course, as noted earlier, electoral constituency and geographic constituency need not coincide.

20. Timothy Groseclose, Steven D. Levitt, and James M. Snyder Jr., "Comparing Interest Group Scores across Time and Chambers: Adjusted ADA Scores for the U.S. Congress," *American Political Science Review* 93 (March 1999): 33–50.

21. Morris P. Fiorina, *Divided Government*, 2d ed. (Needham Heights, Mass.: Allyn and Bacon, 1996), 43.

22. Bullock and Brady, "Party, Constituency, and Roll Call Voting."

23. Fiorina, *Divided Government*.

24. Brunell and Grofman, "Explaining Divided Senate Delegations."

25. Nineteen states permitted voters to vote some type of a straight party ticket with one mark in the 1996 election. See Richard G. Smolka, ed. Election Administration Reports, February 24, 1996.

26. Martin P. Wattenberg, *The Decline of American Political Parties, 1952–1992* (Cambridge, Mass.: Harvard University Press, 1994).

APPENDIX 9–A

Classification of States by Primary Type

Closed Primaries	*Open Primaries*
Arizona	Alabama
California	Alaska
Colorado	Arkansas
Connecticut	Georgia
Delaware	Hawaii
Florida	Idaho
Kansas	Illinois
Kentucky	Iowa
Maine	Louisiana
Maryland	Michigan
Massachusetts	Minnesota
Nebraska	Mississippi
Nevada	Missouri
New Hampshire	Montana
New Jersey	North Dakota
New Mexico	Ohio
New York	South Carolina
North Carolina	Tennessee
Oklahoma	Texas
Oregon	Utah
Pennsylvania	Vermont
Rhode Island	Virginia
South Dakota	Washington
West Virginia	Wisconsin
	Wyoming

Source: Bott (1990), Table 1.3, pages 22–25.

10

California's Experience with the Blanket Primary

Elisabeth R. Gerber

In March 1996, California voters passed Proposition 198 (Prop 198), the Open Primary Initiative. The initiative requires the state to replace its closed primary system for nominating federal, statewide, and state legislative candidates with a "blanket primary" system. Under the blanket primary, all candidates are listed on a single ballot, and voters choose a single candidate for each office, regardless of the party of the voter or of the candidate.[1] The candidate from each party who receives the greatest number of votes becomes that party's nominee. This system is also used in Alaska and Washington State.

Prop 198 passed with little fanfare. Proponents spent less than a million dollars collecting signatures and campaigning for the initiative, and opponents spent a mere $50,000. Since Prop 198's passage, however, much money and resources have been devoted to an intense battle over the measure's legal future. In the course of the initiative campaign and litigation, several issues have been raised that are critical for understanding both the normative/legal and positive/political science aspects of modern primaries. In this chapter, I use Prop 198 as a case study for discussing these legal and political science issues.

I begin by providing some background information about the political context from which Prop 198 emerged. I then discuss some of the most important legal issues that arose during the Prop 198 litigation. These include questions such as: What are the constitutional rights of political parties? What is the state's interest in regulating parties? What is the state's interest in regulating primary elections? Who speaks for the party—elected representatives, party officials, rank-and-file members, regular citizens, or the courts? What happens when the interests of those constituents come into conflict? I do not purport to provide definitive answers to these questions. Rather, my goal is simply to sketch the contours of the debate by laying out the positions articulated by each side.

I next consider a number of social scientific questions brought out in the initiative campaign and subsequent litigation. These include: Does the blanket primary result in strategic voter behavior? Does it result in higher levels of citizen participation? Does it enhance feelings of citizen involvement and efficacy? Does it result in more competitive elections? Does it advantage moderate candidates? Does it advantage women, minorities, or minor party candidates? Does it weaken the political parties? Unlike the normative/legal issues I consider in the preceding section, which are primarily theoretical, these issues are empirical in the sense that they debate what the actual consequences of the blanket primary will be. I therefore assess these arguments by considering some of the empirical evidence from California's first blanket primary in June 1998.[2] I end by discussing recent developments and the likely future of the blanket primary in California.

PROPOSITION 198

Proposition 198 was the brainchild of a coalition of public officials, candidates for elected office, and citizen activists. For many years, observers have hypothesized that California's closed primaries resulted in the nomination and the election of highly ideological candidates.[3] The (highly simplified) argument is that by limiting participation in the closed primary to registered partisans, candidates from both parties need only appeal to a relatively homogenous, hard-core, partisan segment of the electorate.[4] Candidates who share these partisans' ideological positions are nominated and ultimately elected, with little pressure to reflect moderate or centrist interests.

Empirically, there is some evidence that California's elected representatives were ideologically extreme. California's partisan congressional delegations were some of the most extreme in the country, with the state's 1996 mean Republican NOMINATE score substantially above the party average and the mean Democratic NOMINATE score substantially below.[5] California's state legislative delegations were also reputed to be highly ideological and extreme compared to voters in the state. Of course, the causal linkage between electoral institutions and these empirical regularities is a tenuous one (which I will describe in more detail later), but to ideologically centrist candidates and reformers, the possibility of opening nominations to a wider electorate had great appeal.

The campaign to support Prop 198 received most of its financial contributions from a handful of moderate candidates, especially State Senate candidate Tom Campbell, whose campaign contributed $97,787 to Prop 198, and former State Senator Becky Morgan, whose campaign contributed $146,326.[6] The campaign also enjoyed support from David Packard, Bill Hewlett, and the Hewlett-Packard company, who together accounted for nearly half of all contributions received. Proponents argued that the blanket primary would give voters greater choice, increase voter participation, increase electoral competition, and weaken the power of political parties and special interests.[7] Supporting arguments in the official ballot pamphlet, the major source of information for most proposition voters,[8] were signed by former State Senator Becky Morgan, Professor Eugene Lee, former Chairman of the California Fair Political Practices Commission Dan Stanford, Independent State Senator Lucy Killea, and former State Controller Houston Flournoy.[9]

The campaign to oppose Prop 198 received all of its contributions from two sources—$50,000 from Rupert Murdoch and $48,847 from the California Republican Party.[10] Opponents argued that Democrats should not be able to select the Republican Party's nominees and vice versa, likening the blanket primary to allowing the football team of the University of California, Los Angeles (UCLA) to choose the head coach of the University of Southern California (USC). They argued that politicians and special interests would abuse the process by facilitating partisan "raiding" and that the law was unconstitutional. Ballot pamphlet arguments against Prop 198 were signed by Claremont Institute Senior Fellow Bruce Herschensohn, former State Attorney General John Van de Camp, acting director of the USC Unruh Institute of Politics Alison Dundes Renteln, California Republican Party Chairman John Herrington, and California Democratic Party Chairman Bill Press.[11] In the end, opponents spent only about half the amount raised in the campaign, no doubt seeing the futility of publicizing their politically unpopular position. On election day, March 26, 1996, Prop 198 received 59.51 percent of the vote in a low-turnout election.[12]

In the months that followed, the law was challenged in federal court by the California Democratic Party, the California Republican Party, the Libertarian Party, and the Peace and Freedom Party.[13] The defendant in the case was California Secretary of State Bill Jones. The State Attorney General's Office litigated the case and received financial and pro bono support from several supporting individuals and organizations. On November 24, 1997, the law was upheld in the Eastern District of California. The district court decision was appealed to the 9th Circuit Court and was affirmed on March 4, 1999.[14] On June 26, 2000, the U.S. Supreme Court overturned the law, declaring it an unconstitutional infringement of the parties' First Amendment rights.[15]

Legal Issues and Arguments

Several extremely interesting legal issues regarding political parties, elections, and the state's role in regulating candidate nominations were raised during the Prop 198 litigation. I will describe how each side in the case saw these issues. Note that while the Supreme Court ruled on some of these legal issues it did not address all of them, and many are likely to arise again in this and future cases concerning primary elections.

What Are the Constitutional Rights of Political Parties?

This question was central to the plaintiffs' challenge to the blanket primary. Plaintiffs argued that in a series of prior decisions, the U.S. Supreme Court had established a first amendment right of association for political parties. Most important, they argued that in *Tashjian v. Republican Party of Connecticut*, the Court ruled that the state could not compel the parties to change their requirements for participation in primaries, except to protect against certain forms of discrimination.[16] As such, they interpreted this decision as protecting the parties' interests in determining their own nomination rules. Defendants countered that the nature of the state's demands on the parties in the two cases were fundamentally different. In *Tashjian*, the state was trying to prohibit the parties from opening their nominations to nonmembers. In the current case, the state was trying to require the parties to expand participation. This interest in increasing participation, the defendants argued, outweighed any claim of the parties to determine their own nomination procedures.

What Is the State's Interest in Regulating Primary Elections?

The two sides saw primaries in very different lights. The plaintiffs cast primaries as private party affairs that should be the exclusive domain of the individual party organizations. The defendants cast primaries as integral first steps of the public electoral process. These differences, of course, have a long history in U.S. constitutional law and result from the ambiguous status of U.S. political parties as quasi-public, quasi-private institutions.

Given these differing views of primaries, it is not surprising that the two sides took very different positions on the state's role in regulating them. Since plaintiffs viewed primaries as private party affairs, they saw little role for state regulation. Since defendants viewed primaries as public elections, they saw a much greater role for the state.

Who Speaks for the Party?

Like many political reform issues, the blanket primary created a significant cleavage between the interests of elected representatives and party officials, on the one hand, and those of rank-and-file party members and regular citizens on the other. Political elites were uniformly opposed to the blanket primary.[17] The lawsuit involved the leadership of both major parties and nearly all of the minor parties in the state. Only the Reform Party remained silent on the issue, apparently because its leaders were divided.[18] Rank-and-file party members, by contrast, largely supported the blanket primary. Prop 198 passed in a closed primary election, where nearly all participants were registered partisans.[19] Poll results show that the measure received substantial support from all groups in the electorate, including major- and minor-party members and independents.[20]

This difference of opinion raises a very difficult issue: who speaks for the party—elected representatives, party officials, rank-and-file members, regular citizens, or the courts? And what happens when the interests of those constituents come into conflict? Plaintiffs argued that just as in representative government, rank-and-file party members delegate the authority to make decisions on behalf of the parties to their elected party officials. Defendants argued that rank-and-file members reserve the right to override party officials through established political channels (i.e., the initiative process) when their actions conflict with the membership's preferences.

Political Science Issues

Plaintiffs argued their case primarily on the legal issues. However, in the course of the initiative campaign and lawsuit, a number of positive/political science issues were also raised. I will discuss the position of Prop 198's supporters and opponents on each of these issues. Then, I will describe the empirical evidence from the 1998 California primary and other elections.

Does the Blanket Primary Result in Strategic Voter Behavior?

Like all "open" primaries, the blanket primary allows voters to more easily cross party lines in the primary. Cain and Gerber[21] consider three types of crossover behavior: (1) *Sincere crossover* voting involves crossing party lines to vote for one's most preferred candidate. (2) *Hedging* involves crossing party lines to vote for the most preferred candidate in the other party (but not the voter's top choice overall). (3) *Raiding* involves crossing party lines to vote for the candidate in the other party who will be the weakest opponent for the voter's preferred candidate. Under closed primaries, all three types of crossover behavior are difficult or impossible because partisans would need to reregister with the other party some specified period before the election. In California prior to 1998, this reregistration period was twenty-nine days. Under traditional open primaries, voters can choose on the day of the election the primary in which they wish to participate. However, there are opportunity costs associated with such decisions because crossing party lines for one race means that the voter is restricted to participating in that party's primary for all races in that election. Under blanket primaries, voters can cross party lines race by race, substantially reducing the difficulty of all three forms of crossover behavior.

Plaintiffs argued that the blanket primary would result in significant levels of all three types of crossover behavior. They downplayed distinctions between the three types, arguing that any time crossover voting occurs, nonmembers could be instrumental in determining a party's nominees. Plaintiffs produced evidence suggesting that vote margins in several races in 1996 were sufficiently slim that even small numbers of crossover voters could have swung the election outcomes. Defendants argued that while the overall levels of crossover voting could be high, few voters would be expected to engage in raiding because the informational demands are so high. Instead, most crossover voting would be of the less mischievous forms of sincere crossover and hedging. Defendants argued that sincere crossover and hedging were not so bad. Indeed, the whole point of the blanket primary, they argued, was to open the nomination process by facilitating these benign forms of crossover voting.

Several recent studies attempt to estimate the extent of crossover voting in the 1998 California primary. Analyzing polling data (from both preelection and exit polls) on votes and vote intentions in the gubernatorial and U.S. Senate races, Sides, Cohen, and Citrin find moderate levels of crossover voting, in the 7 to 12 percent range.[22] However, they find that the determinants of vote choice were nearly identical for crossover and noncrossover voters. In combination with their subsequent finding that many crossover voters continued to support the same candidate in the general election,[23] Sides, Cohen, and Citrin conclude that most of this crossover voting was sincere and probably did not affect the outcome of either race. Alvarez and Nagler[24] conducted an exit poll in five State Assembly districts. Because they specifically selected these five races as offering the most favorable conditions for crossover voting (i.e., only one primary was competitive, so members of the noncompetitive primary would have little incentive to vote in their own party's primary), we should not be surprised that they find higher levels of crossover voting overall. Indeed, they find that voters from the party with the uncontested primary crossed into the other party's primary at a rate of 15 percent, 24 percent, 28 percent, 29 percent, and 86 percent.[25] Salvanto and Wattenberg assessed crossover voting with yet another source of data.[26] They analyzed the actual absentee ballots cast in Los Angeles county. When one accounts for all of the choices a voter makes in a given election, the incidence of crossover voting is extremely high. Salvanto and Wattenberg found that only 46 percent of Democrats and 41 percent of Republicans cast a straight partisan ticket; others voted for at least one candidate from a different party. However, comparing these patterns to ticket splitting in the 1994 general election, they concluded that the blanket primary did not result in substantially different behavior. Indeed, they found that the overall incidence of ticket splitting in the 1994 general election was higher than in the 1998 primary. Most voters who crossed party lines in 1998 crossed over to vote for an incumbent.

Together, these studies show that while the incidence of crossover voting in the 1998 blanket primary was relatively low overall, it may have been quite important in a number of specific races. Most voters seemed to cross over to support their most preferred candidate in the other party.

Does It Result in Higher Levels of Citizen Participation?

Defendants argued that by extending participation to some 2.5 million previously excluded registered independents and minor-party voters, the blanket primary would increase voter participation.[27] And indeed, turnout (as a percent of eligible voting-age population) in the 1998 primary was approximately 6 points higher than in the 1994 primary (1998 turnout was 30.03 percent of eligible, 1994 turnout was 26.22 percent of eligible[28]). This result is despite a long-term trend of gradually declining turnout—in California and nationwide—over the past three decades.

There is also a second, potentially more important way that the blanket primary could increase participation. Although this reason was not articulated in the supporters' arguments, it is possible that changes in primary election laws might also increase turnout *in general elections*. There are at least two ways that moving to a blanket primary might spur general election turnout. To the extent that opening the nomination process to previously excluded independent and minor-party voters enhances their feelings of inclusiveness and efficacy, these voters may engage in more political activities of all sorts, including turning out at higher rates in the general election. To the extent that independent and minor-party voters form bonds with the candidates they support in the primary, they may be more likely to turn out to support their candidate in the general election. This second possibility is consistent with the findings by Sides, Cohen, and Citrin[29] and by Kousser[30] that voter loyalty to candidates supported in the primary is quite high.

Despite these possibilities, turnout (as a percent of eligible) in the 1998 general election was lower than in 1994: (41.43 percent of the eligible adult population participated in the 1998 general election, compared to 46.98 percent in 1994).[31] Note, however, that turnout in 1998 was nearly identical to that in1990 (with 41.05 percent turnout) and was similar to that in 1988 (with 43.38 percent). Thus, the blanket primary seemed to have little if any effect on participation in the general election.

Does It Result in More Competitive Elections?

A third empirical issue is whether the blanket primary results in more competitive elections. In their arguments in the official ballot pamphlet, Prop 198's proponents argued that it would. They noted that in many California legislative districts, partisan registration greatly favors one party. In these "safe" districts, the general election is virtually guaranteed to the nominee of the majority party; therefore, any real competition for the seat occurs in the primary. By opening participation in the primary to voters in the minority party (as well as to minor party members and independents), these voters will have a greater voice in selecting the district's representative. Candidates will also be forced to appeal to all voters in their districts and to compete for their votes. Defendants in the lawsuit made similar arguments.

Evidence on the effect of the blanket primary on competitiveness, however, is mixed. I first compare the competitiveness of U.S. House races in California between 1996 and 1998 by a number of measures.[32] When we measure competitiveness as the vote margin of the winning candidate over the second-place candidate, 1998 appears to be less competitive (i.e., winners win by greater margins). The average primary vote margin across all U.S. House races in 1998 was 80.01 percentage points, compared to 74.37 in 1996. When we limit our analysis to contested races, the difference between 1998 and 1996 is even greater (average winner's margin of 47.39 in 1998, 36.54 in 1996). The picture is similar for open-seat races as well (average winner's margin of 50.48 in 1998, 44.17 in 1996).

A second measure of competitiveness is the number of races decided by less than some margin. Again focusing on U.S. House races, there were fewer competitive races by this measure in 1998 than in 1996. In 1998, there were 38 contested primaries (with more than one candidate), compared to 42 in 1996; 8 primary races were decided by less than 20 percentage points in 1998, while 15 were decided by less than 20 points in 1996. Only five House primaries were decided by less than 10 points in 1998, whereas 10 were in 1996.

A third measure of competitiveness is the number of candidates vying for a party's nomination. And by this measure as well, House races were less competitive (i.e., there were fewer candidates) in 1998 than in 1996. In 1998, the average number of candidates in all races was 1.60, compared to 1.71 in 1996; in contested races it was 2.58, compared to 2.76 in 1996; and in open seats it was 2.60, compared to 4.00. Thus, U.S. House primaries under the blanket primary were decided by wider vote margins, less often decided by 20 (or 10) or fewer points, and were contested by fewer candidates.

There are, however, several important caveats to this analysis of the competitiveness of U.S. House primaries. First, 1998 was an extremely unusual year in terms of the national parties' strategies toward contesting races. Nationally, there was a record number of U.S. House races (152) in which a single candidate ran uncontested in the general election. In these races, the parties chose not to actively recruit and support candidates to challenge the incumbent. By contrast, only 18 House races were uncontested in the general election in 1996. This pattern indicates that the national parties changed from their prior practice of contesting most races to one of targeting a smaller number of races.

Second, although House primaries were, by these three measures, less competitive on average in 1998, the *relative* vote margin between the primary and the general was smaller in 1998. In other words, the most competitive primaries were more likely to be in races where the general election was also competitive. When a (nonopen) seat was contested in the general election (i.e., when a challenger ran against an incumbent in the general), the ratio of the primary to the general election vote margin was 5.0 in 1998; in 1996, this ratio was 5.43. This difference was much greater when at least one of the primaries was contested. When a (nonopen) seat was contested in the primary, the ratio of primary to general election vote margin was 2.46 in 1998, compared to 7.21 in 1996. This pattern fails to hold up, however, in open seats, where the primary to general election vote margin ratio is 5.39 in 1998 and 4.91 in 1996.

When we perform similar analyses of the competitiveness of State Assembly races, the results are again mixed. The average primary vote margin was greater in 1998 for all races and open seats (74.72 versus 71.32, and 48.34 versus 47.48, respectively) but was substantially smaller for contested seats (23.14 versus 28.07). More races were decided in 1998 by fewer than 10 points (18 versus 13). But the average number of candidates was still smaller in 1998 for all races, for contested races, and open-seat races.[33] Finally, the primary to general election vote margins are even smaller in 1998. For races contested in the general election, the primary to general election vote margin was 3.31 in 1998 and 13.94 in 1996. For races with at least one contested primary, the ratio was 1.16 in 1998 and 3.53 in 1996. And for open-seat races, the ratio was 9.74 in 1998 and 16.99 in 1996. Thus, Assembly primaries appear more competitive by some measures in 1998 and less competitive by other measures. The most competitive Assembly primaries took place in races with more competitive general election races.

Cho and Gaines[34] performed a similar analysis of the competitiveness of U.S. House races. Analyzing the Republican and the Democratic primaries separately, they compared the 1998 primary and general elections to 1992, 1994, and 1996. They, too, found mixed results, suggesting that the 1998 election was not clearly more competitive and that by some measures was less competitive than previous elections. Cho and Gaines also note the extremely high number of uncontested races in 1998. Then focusing on contested Republican primaries, they found that the average number of candidates, the average "effective" number of candidates, and the victors' margins over second-place finishers were generally similar for 1994, 1996, and 1998, with the 1992 election the most competitive by these measures. On the Democratic side, 1998 was slightly less competitive by these measures. Finally, in the general election, there were a greater number of uncontested races in 1998, but no other general patterns emerged. Given the mixed nature of these results, more elections and more analysis are clearly required to better understand the effects of the blanket primary on competitiveness.

Does It Enhance Feelings of Citizen Involvement and Efficacy?

In its election day exit poll, the *Los Angeles Times* asked voters a series of questions regarding their feelings about the blanket primary. Overall, responses were quite positive: 60 percent of all respondents agreed with the statement "The open primary allows me to vote for a candidate of my choice even if he or she is not in my party."[35] Agreement with this statement was shared by Democrats (59 percent), Independents (59 percent), Republicans (61 percent), whites (62 percent), blacks (58 percent), Latinos (56 percent), and Asians (53 percent). From the wording of the question and patterns of responses, however, it is not clear whether respondents were answering this question as a matter of fact or whether they were expressing favor toward the blanket primary because of this freedom of choice.

The next several questions in the *Times'* battery tapped more directly into voters' assessments of the blanket primary. And here, responses indicate some support for, or at least a general lack of opposition toward, the blanket primary. Only 31 percent of all respondents believed the blanket primary was "fairer because all voters can vote in candidate races." However, just 14 percent believed that "in a primary, only Democrats should vote for Democrats, etc." And only 8 percent reported that the "ballot was too confusing/list of names too long." Thus, while a minority of respondents believed that the blanket primary was fairer (presumably than the closed primary), a much smaller minority felt it was actually inappropriate, and very few felt it created problems for voters.

Will these neutral-to-positive election day feelings translate into lasting changes in citizens' attitudes toward elections and politics? Only time, and more surveys, will tell.

Does the Blanket Primary Advantage Moderate Candidates?

One of the major arguments made by proponents of Prop 198 and the defendants in the lawsuit was that the blanket primary would lead to the election of more moderate candidates. The basic logic of this argument is that by extending participation in a given party's primary to independents and members of other parties, centrist interests would be strengthened. This logic rests on a number of important assumptions. One is that members of each major party are distinct and ideologically polar. Thus, in the terminology of spatial modeling, the closed primary electorate median voter is relatively extreme ideologically, and extending participation shifts the decisive primary election median voter toward the center of the ideological spectrum. A second assumption is that independents are ideologically centrist. If they are extreme, then opening participation in the primary may shift the primary election median voter in either direction, depending on their relationship to each major party's electorate. A third assumption is that most crossover voting by other-party members will be of the sincere or hedging varieties.

Thus, moderate partisans and independents cross into the opposite party and support a moderate candidate. Plaintiffs countered that this third assumption was implausible—that raiding could be substantial. If so, then even if the first two assumptions are reasonable, the blanket primary could produce more ideologically extreme candidates.

A number of studies have tested whether the blanket primary advantages moderate candidates. Gerber and Morton[36] tested the effect of a number of different primary election laws on the ideological positions of winning U.S. House candidates between 1992 and 1996. They find that, compared to winning congressional candidates nominated under closed primaries, representatives from blanket primary systems are significantly more moderate, that is, Democrats are more conservative and Republicans are more liberal. They find, however, that the most moderate winners come not from the most open (blanket) primary systems, but rather from the more restrictive semiclosed primary systems.[37] These results are consistent with work by Grofman and Brunell,[38] which shows that open primary systems (including the blanket primary) are more likely to produce split-party U.S. Senate delegations. However, it is contrary to work by King,[39] which argues that open primaries lead to ideological polarization by encouraging policy specialization and targeted appeals to narrow constituencies.

While these previous studies have implications for California's conversion from a closed to an open primary, none focus on California exclusively. By contrast, work by Gerber[40] compares the rate at which moderate candidates were nominated and elected under the 1996 closed and 1998 blanket California primaries. Gerber finds that at the top of the ticket, the blanket primary seemed to have little impact on the ultimate election outcomes. In the U.S. House and State Assembly races, by contrast, the blanket primary did seem to advantage moderate candidates. Evaluating each of the open-seat, contested-challenger, and contested-incumbent House races, Gerber concludes that moderates were able to attract crossover support and to prevail in a number of districts. Comparing the 1998 Assembly primaries with 1996, she finds that moderates won half of all contested primaries in 1998, compared to 37 percent in 1996. The effect of the blanket primary was statistically significant in a model predicting the probability of a moderate winning his or her party's nomination, controlling for other candidate, district, and election characteristics. Thus, with the exception of King's evidence to the contrary, the blanket primary does seem to advantage moderate candidates.

Does the Blanket Primary Advantage Women, Minorities, or Minor Party Candidates?

Another consideration is whether the blanket primary advantages traditionally underrepresented candidates, such as women, minorities, or minor party candidates. Caul and Tate[41] argue that we should expect the blanket primary to disadvantage women candidates. They note that women tend to have less personal political capital than men in terms of prior political experience, incumbency, and personal wealth. Women therefore need strong parties to provide them with other resources (e.g., organizational resources, endorsements, expertise) that offset their initial disadvantage. To the extent that the blanket primary weakens the parties (a point to which I will return later), we expect that they will be less able to provide such resources and that women candidates will suffer.

In assessing the success of women candidates in blanket (and nonpartisan) congressional primaries across states, however, Caul and Tate find that women candidates do not, on average, fare worse than their closed or traditional open primary counterparts. It is important, though, that they do find that women who are successful in blanket and nonpartisan primaries are different in several respects: these women are more likely to be incumbents than successful women candidates under closed primaries, and they tend to have greater personal wealth. Thus, the blanket primary advantages (or at least does not disadvantage) women with the greatest levels of personal political capital.

Segura and Woods[42] consider the extent to which the blanket primary advantages or disadvantages minority candidates, particularly Latinos. Here, our predictions are less clear than in the case of women candidates. To the extent that minorities also lack the types of personal political capital identified by Caul and Tate,[43] we might expect the blanket primary to work to their disadvantage, by weakening the parties that provide them with important resources. To the extent that minorities can take advantage of greater opportunities for crossover voting, by appealing to members of their racial/ethnic group in other parties, we might expect the blanket primary to actually advantage minority candidates.

Indeed, Segura and Woods find that several Latino candidates were able to effectively appeal to substantial numbers of minority voters in the other party.[44] This was especially the case for moderate Latino Republican candidates in heavily Democratic districts with a Democratic incumbent. In these districts, the blanket primary meant that a Republican Latino candidate could pull support from Latino voters, most of whom are registered Democrats, to win the Republican nomination. Segura and Woods note that a record number of Republican Latinos were nominated in 1998. They argue that while few of these Latino Republicans were ultimately elected, the blanket primary may have helped the Republicans solve their "Latino problem" by helping Latino candidates reach out to Democratic Latino voters.

A third type of "underrepresented" candidate that I consider is the minor party candidate. For these candidates, the impact of the blanket primary is likely to be quite different. Unlike women and minority candidates, who have recently made substantial gains in terms of winning office, minor party candidates almost never win. Indeed, most research on the subject argues that winning a seat is not necessarily even the goal of minor party candidates; rather, it is to promote certain issues or positions.[45] Thus, the question of whether the blanket primary will prevent their parties from providing resources necessary for electoral success is irrelevant. We expect minor party candidates to care more about those effects of the blanket primary that are more relevant to their specific political goals. Collet argues that minor parties and minor party candidates have two related goals. He notes that "if minor parties in California merely aspire to persist as insular 'ideological entities,' then the blanket primary may be considered harmful, since the 'openness' of the new format allows for infiltration of outside voters and unendorsed candidates. However, if the goal of minor parties is to gain more visibility for their candidates and issues, the primary's 'openness' offers a significant opportunity for them to advance their electoral position in California."[46] He finds that minor party candidates received much greater voter support in 1998—in some cases twenty to thirty times greater. Thus, to the extent that minor party candidates hold the second goal of gaining visibility for their candidates and issues, the blanket primary seems to have advanced this goal. Collet also finds that in a survey conducted just after the 1998 California primary, most minor party candidates reported overall support for the blanket primary. The main exception is the Libertarian candidates, who opposed the blanket primary overall.

Does the Blanket Primary Weaken the Political Parties?

Finally, opponents of Prop 198 argued that even if none of the immediate potential consequences of the blanket primary came to bear, opening the nomination process to nonmembers would weaken the political parties. They argued that if nonmembers were allowed to participate in selecting the party's standard bearers, the party would lose its ability to control its message. The parties would then lose their raison d'être and hence their ability to attract members, contributions, and other sources of support. Plaintiffs in the lawsuit argued that this dilution of the party's message would be especially detrimental to minor parties, whose nominations could be swung by a small number of nonmember votes and whose members place an extremely high value on ideological purity.

Two bits of evidence suggest that these claims were exaggerated. First, the parties are alive and well, or at least as well as they ever have been, in California. Since at least the Progressive era, California has had a long tradition of weak parties *in the electorate*. Some of this weakness is probably due to reforms instituted by the Progressives themselves, such as nonpartisan local elections, cross-filing (eliminated in 1959), and the direct primary.[47] Some may also be due to Californians' "independent spirit."[48] However, at the same time, parties *in the legislature* have been quite strong, and there is little evidence that the blanket primary has weakened the parties in the legislature.[49]

A second bit of evidence speaking against the prediction that the blanket primary would weaken the political parties is the experience in other states, especially Washington. Experts for the defendants in the lawsuit argued that the blanket primary has not meant an end to the major parties in Washington, nor should it in California. Of course, there are many other important differences between Washington and California that might lead to different outcomes. However, if one wishes to argue that it is the blanket primary itself that would undermine California's parties, the fact that it did not undermine Washington's is problematic.

RECENT DEVELOPMENTS

One residual concern by the opponents of Prop 198 is the consequences of the reform for the presidential primary. In the course of the lawsuit, both major parties threatened not to seat the California delegation at their presidential nominating conventions if nonmembers participated in selecting the delegates. Whether the parties actually intended to follow through with these threats is debatable. Nevertheless, a number of proposals followed to address concerns about the acceptability of the blanket primary to the national parties. The first proposal originated in the legislature as SB 1505, which proposed a separate closed primary for the presidential primary. Since it amended sections of the election code originated by Prop 198, the bill required voter approval.[50] On the ballot in November 1998 as Proposition 3, the measure was defeated, receiving 46 percent of the statewide vote.[51]

With the defeat of Proposition 3, Secretary of State Bill Jones offered a second proposal for the presidential primary. Jones suggested that since there were already separate ballots (to select county party officials), the state could run the election as a blanket primary, allowing any voter to vote for any candidate, but could then count the votes for presidential candidates separately for voters from each party. The state parties could then send as delegates to the national conventions only those supporting candidates who were themselves supported by registered party members. Since this separate counting does not require changing requirements for participation or ballot format contained in the Prop 198 election code, it did not require a vote of the people. The Jones plan was used to conduct the March 2000 presidential primary.

CONCLUSION

California's blanket primary, and the lawsuit challenging the initiative that brought it about, provides a unique opportunity to examine the effects of electoral institutions on election dynamics. California's experience in 1998 suggests that the blanket primary lead to moderate-to-high levels of crossover voting; increased participation in the primary but not the general; received some support from voters;

and advantaged moderate candidates and Latinos. However, a number of questions remain unresolved, such as the effects on political competition, lasting turnout effects, and consequences for women and minor parties. And with the U.S. Supreme Court's decision invalidating the blanket primary, we may never know what the system's ultimate effects might have been.

NOTES

1. In fact, the parties still maintain separate ballots that are identical except for races for county party officials. Thus, voters must still reveal their party registration at their polling place.

2. Much of the evidence is drawn from chapters in an edited volume studying the 1998 California primary (Bruce E. Cain and Elisabeth R. Gerber, eds., *Voting at the Political Fault Line: California's Experiment with the Blanket Primary* [Berkeley: University of California Press, forthcoming]).

3. Elisabeth R. Gerber, "The Consequences of Primary Election Laws in the American States," expert report, *California Democratic Party v. Jones*, No. CIV S-96-2038 DFL, United States District Court for the Eastern District of California, 984 F. Supp. 1288.

4. For an academic version of this argument, see Elisabeth R. Gerber and Rebecca B. Morton, "Primary Election Systems and Representation," *Journal of Law, Economics, and Organization* 14, no. 2 (1998): 304–24.

5. D-NOMINATE computes each legislator's "ideal" point from his or her roll call votes on all nonunanimous votes (Keith T. Poole and Howard Rosenthal, "A Spatial Model for Legislative Roll Call Analysis," *American Journal of Political Science* 29, no. 2 [1985]: 357–84). Scores reported here are for the first (liberal-conservative) dimension. NOMINATE scores range from -1 (extreme liberal) to $+1$ (extreme conservative). The average NOMINATE score for California's House Democrats in the 105th Congress was -0.4268, while for all House Democrats it was much less liberal, at -0.3288. The average score for California's House Republicans in the 105th Congress was 0.4375, while for all House Republicans it was somewhat less conservative, at 0.4052. Party averages are computed excluding California representatives.

6. California Secretary of State, *Receipts and Expenditures by Committees Formed Primarily to Support or Oppose Ballot Measures*, Sacramento, 1996.

7. California Secretary of State, *Ballot Pamphlet*, Sacramento, 1996.

8. Shaun Bowler and Todd Donovan, *Demanding Choices* (Ann Arbor: University of Michigan Press, 1998).

9. California Secretary of State, *Ballot Pamphlet*.

10. California Secretary of State, *Receipts and Expenditures*.

11. California Secretary of State, *Ballot Pamphlet*.

12. Turnout was 29% of eligible, 39% of registered, and 47% of major-party registered voters (California Secretary of State, http://www.ss.ca.gov/elections, 1999).

13. *California Democratic Party v. Jones*, No. CIV S-96-2038 DFL, United States District Court for the Eastern District of California, 984 F. Supp. 1288.

14. *California Democratic Party v. Jones*, No. 97-17440, No. 97-17442, United States Court of Appeals for the Ninth Circuit, 169 F.3d 646.

15. *California Democratic Party v. Jones*, No. 99-401, United States Supreme Court.

16. *Tashjian v. Republican Party of Connecticut*, 479 U.S. 208 (1986).

17. Christian Collet ("Openness Begets Opportunity: Minor Parties and the First Blanket Primary in California," in *Voting at the Political Fault Line*, ed. Bruce E. Cain and Elisabeth R. Gerber) provides interesting evidence that most major- and minor-party candidates for office did not share this "official" view. In a survey of candidates for federal, statewide, and state legislative office in 1998, Collet found that many individual candidates saw the blanket primary as beneficial.

18. Collet, "Openness Begets Opportunity."

19. Under California's closed primaries, independents were provided special ballots that allowed them to vote only on the ballot measures and nonpartisan races. Anecdotal evidence suggests that participation by independents in California's closed primaries was insignificant.

20. Using data from the *Field Poll* (San Francisco: Field Institute, 1996), Shaun Bowler and Todd Donovan ("Political Reform via the Initiative Process," in *Voting at the Political Fault Line*, ed. Bruce E. Cain and Elisabeth R. Gerber) show that strong partisans were least likely to support Prop 198; independents, weak partisans, and minor-party members were most likely.

21. Bruce E. Cain and Elisabeth R. Gerber, "Explorations at the Fault Line," in *Voting at the Political Fault Line*, ed. Bruce E. Cain and Elisabeth R. Gerber.

22. John Sides, Jonathan Cohen, and Jack Citrin, "The Causes and Consequences of Crossover Voting in the 1998 California Elections," in *Voting at the Political Fault Line*, ed. Bruce E. Cain and Elisabeth R. Gerber.

23. See also Thad Kousser, "Crossing Over When it Counts," in *Voting at the Political Fault Line*, ed. Bruce E. Cain and Elisabeth R. Gerber.

24. R. Michael Alvarez and Jonathan Nagler, "Should I Stay or Should I Go? Sincere and Strategic Crossover Voting in California Assembly Races," in *Voting at the Political Fault Line*, ed. Bruce E. Cain and Elisabeth R. Gerber.

25. Note that AD49, where 86% of Republicans crossed over into the contested Democratic primary, is a strongly Democratic district with almost no chance of electing a Republican candidate.

26. Anthony M. Salvanto and Martin P. Wattenberg, "Peeking under the Blanket: A Direct Look at Crossover Voting in the 1998 Primary," in *Voting at the Political Fault Line*, ed. Bruce E. Cain and Elisabeth R. Gerber.

27. As of May 1998, 745,177 California voters were registered members of minor parties, and 1,804,284 were registered as "decline to state."

28. California Secretary of State, http://www.ss.ca.gov/elections, 1999.

29. John Sides, Jonathan Cohen, and Jack Citrin, "The Causes and Consequences of Crossover Voting in the 1998 California Elections," in *Voting at the Political Fault Line*, ed. Bruce E. Cain and Elisabeth R. Gerber.

30. Kousser, "Crossing Over When It Counts."

31. I compare turnout to the last midterm primary election, 1994. Turnout in the 1996 primary, a presidential election year, was higher than in either 1994 or 1998, as expected.

32. In my analysis of competitiveness, I use 1996 (rather than 1994) as the baseline year—1996 was the first year for which term limits had resulted in a complete turnover of the state legislature. Since there were several long-term incumbents still in the Assembly

in 1994, their relationships with voters might be quite different from those of the new representatives populating the state legislature by 1996. To facilitate comparison between the House and Assembly races, I also use 1996 as the base year for my analysis of House races.

33. The average numbers of candidates were 1.70 in 1998 versus 1.86 in 1996 for all races; 3.14 in 1998 versus 3.15 in 1996 for contested races; 2.63 in 1998 versus 2.77 in 1996 for open seats.

34. Wendy K. Tam Cho and Brian J. Gaines, "Candidates, Donors, and Voters in California's First Blanket Primary Elections," in *Voting at the Political Fault Line*, ed. Bruce E. Cain and Elisabeth R. Gerber.

35. The lead-in to this series of questions was worded as follows: "As you may know, this is California's first blanket or open primary in which voters may vote for any candidate running for office regardless of party affiliation. Do you think: (ACCEPTED ALL THAT APPLY)."

36. Gerber and Morton, "Primary Election Systems and Representation."

37. Under semiclosed primaries, independents and/or new voters are allowed to participate, but not members of other parties.

38. Grofman and Brunell, this volume (chapter 9).

39. David C. King, "Party Competition and Polarization in American Politics" (paper presented at the MIT Conference on Parties and Congress, Cambridge, Mass., 1999).

40. Elisabeth R. Gerber, "Strategic Voting and Candidate Policy Positions," in *Voting at the Political Fault Line*, ed. Bruce E. Cain and Elisabeth R. Gerber.

41. Miki Caul and Katherine Tate, "Thinner Ranks: Women Candidates and California's Blanket Primary," in *Voting at the Political Fault Line*, ed. Bruce E. Cain and Elisabeth R. Gerber.

42. Gary M. Segura and Nathan D. Woods, "Targets of Opportunity: California's Blanket Primary and the Political Representation of Latinos," in *Voting at the Political Fault Line*, ed. Bruce E. Cain and Elisabeth R. Gerber.

43. Caul and Tate, "Thinner Ranks."

44. Segura and Woods, "Targets of Opportunity."

45. Steven J. Rosenstone, Roy L. Behr, and Edward H. Lazarus, *Third Parties in America*, 2d ed. (Princeton, N.J.: Princeton University Press, 1996). Christian Collet, "Taking the 'Abnormal' Route: Backgrounds, Beliefs, and Political Activities of Minor Party Candidates," in *Multiparty Politics in America*, ed. Paul S. Herrnson and John C. Green (Lanham, Md.: Rowman & Littlefield, 1997). Collet, "Openness Begets Opportunity." Elisabeth R. Gerber and Rebecca B. Morton, "Electoral Institutions and Party Competition: The Effects of Nomination Procedures on Electoral Coalition Formation" (working paper, University of California, San Diego, 1999).

46. Collet, "Openness Begets Opportunity."

47. David Lawrence, *California: The Politics of Diversity* (Minneapolis/St. Paul, Minn.: West, 1995).

48. John C. Syer and John H. Culver, *Power and Politics in California*, 4th ed. (New York: Macmillan, 1992).

49. It is especially difficult to isolate the effect of the blanket primary on the strength of the parties in the legislature because the effects of term limits are being felt at the same time.

50. In California, the only way to amend a statute or a provision of the state constitution resulting from a voter initiative is with another popular vote, that is, an initiative or a referendum.

51. California Secretary of State, http://www.ss.ca.gov/elections, 1999.

Postscript 2000

Peter F. Galderisi

As this volume went to press, another national election cycle was completed. We need not detail the major story of that election. The long, contentious, and disputed presidential election outcome is well documented by now and makes for one of the most interesting electoral events in the twentieth century.

Lost in the details of that story, however, was the fact that other congressional elections, some just as close and contentious, were also taking place. Two races, one in Michigan's Eighth Congressional District, the other in Minnesota's Second, were not conceded until mid-December, while the last recounts of those elections were still under way, with the margins of victory fewer than one hundred and two hundred votes, respectively.

The razor-thin closeness of several races, including one in that most contentious of states, Florida, underlies the tenuous balance of power in both the U.S. Senate and the House.[1] Only after the final absentee ballots were counted in Washington State did we become aware of an even division of U.S. Senate seats for the first time in 120 years. Five Republican incumbents and one Democratic incumbent lost their bids for reelection. Each party also lost one open seat, resulting in a net gain of 4 seats for the Democrats. In the House, 18 seats changed party hands, with each party losing 6 open seats.[2] Two Democratic incumbents were defeated, as well as four Republicans—three in California alone, leaving the GOP with a narrow 221–212 edge.

The extraordinary reelection rate of House incumbents in the general election (over 98 percent) continues recent trends. Incumbents were equally successful in beating back or avoiding primary challenges, losing in only three districts. However, the lack of competition in general elections does not undermine the importance of the study of general election campaigns. By the same logic, a logic developed throughout this volume, we should similarly not ignore congressional primaries. Each has its own story, whether competitive or not, and each adds to our understanding of the power of incumbency, of the conditions for a loss of that power, and of the importance of activity in open seats.

Although few in number, the three primary defeats were not inconsequential, as they accounted for one-third of all incumbent losses. The three primary losses are also noteworthy in that they each have a different tale to tell and serve as useful examples of analyses presented throughout this volume. Each in a different way informs us that party organizations and activists can still influence nomination outcomes. One (Martinez-Solis) helps us to understand that even long-term incumbents are vulnerable in their primary races in districts where the opposition party has little chance of victory. The two others (Cook-Smith and Forbes-Seltzer) help us to understand the circumstances in which incumbents must simultaneously concern themselves with primary as well as general election challenges.

Nine-term Democratic incumbent Matthew Martinez (Calif.-31) was a former Republican who had won marginal victories in his first few races in the 1980s. He won reelection comfortably in the 1990s, with no primary opposition and with 70 percent of the general election vote in 1998. Although liberal on most issues and supported by many labor groups, he was more conservative than most Democrats in his district on several social and environmental issues. Democratic activists faulted him for ignoring his district during his tenure and for taking easy reelection as a given. Challenged in the Democratic portion of California's blanket primary by a quality, state party–backed candidate, State Senator Hilda Solis, Martinez lost by a wide 62 percent to 9 percent margin. Solis comfortably won this now heavily Democratic district in the general election with 80 percent of the vote (no Republican had entered the primary race).[3] Embittered by his defeat, lame-duck Congressman Martinez switched his party designation to Republican for the rest of his term.

In Utah's Second District, two-term incumbent Republican Congressman Merrill Cook needed to wage two campaigns simultaneously. As with many incumbents, Cook needed to bolster his credentials in the state's most competitive district to avoid any challenge from a well-placed Democrat. Cook, as a member of the House Transportation and Infrastructure Committee, touted his ability to increase funding for Interstate 15 and other projects in anticipation of Salt Lake City's 2002 Winter Olympics. Having long been a thorn in the side of Utah's Republican organization (he had on several occasions undermined GOP victories with his independent bids, and then, as a Republican representative, gained notoriety for his emotional and sometimes public verbal tirades against state Republican officials), he also needed to work against any significant challenge first in the district convention and then, if necessary, in a runoff primary. Knowing that a party almost never holds on to a competitive House seat when it denies an incumbent renomination, and believing that Cook was the strongest candidate that the Republicans could field, U.S. House Republican leaders came to Utah and endorsed Cook. Most state Republican leaders reluctantly, and halfheartedly, backed away from any direct challenge. Even his flyers pronouncing his opposition to the loss of U.S. control over the Panama Canal, however, were insufficient to carry him through the convention without a fight from the party's more conservative flank.

With his own finances severely depleted (he had depended on them for previous victories), he lost the subsequent runoff primary (41 percent to 59 percent) to Derek Smith, a wealthy businessman who, like Cook in his earlier elections, was able to finance most of his own campaign. Smith subsequently lost the general election to Jim Matheson (41 percent to 56 percent), the son of the late and very popular governor Scott Matheson.

New York's First District presents perhaps the most interesting tale of party influence over the nominating process. Three-term Republican incumbent Michael Forbes had won reelection comfortably in 1998 in a district that had increasingly sided with the Democratic Party, particularly on social issues (Clinton's 1996 margin of victory was 15 percent). Perhaps because of his district's changing partisan dynamics, but more likely because of his many procedural and policy battles with House GOP leaders (he early on criticized Newt Gingrich's speakership), Forbes switched to the Democratic Party in 1999. This desertion understandably led Forbes to anticipate a strong Republican challenge in the general election. Congressman Forbes unfortunately never made it that far. Despite spending over $1.4 million during his primary campaign (some, if not most, in obvious anticipation of his general election fight), he was upset in the Democratic primary by a challenger with little political experience, 70-year-old retired librarian Regina Seltzer. He lost by the slimmest of margins, 35 votes (at last count) out of roughly 12,000 cast. Seltzer had few resources at her disposal, but she was helped by a concentrated campaign by the Republicans, who attacked Forbes's record, reminding Democratic voters of his previous Republican and often conservative voting record. In such a low-turnout primary contest, GOP efforts were sufficient to undermine this incumbent's reelection success. The Republicans then went on to defeat the outfinanced Seltzer 56 percent to 40 percent.

Michael Forbes's primary expenditures prove that money may not always equate to victory, particularly if a party's resources are used against you. Money, however, will continue to become a major focus of the 2000 congressional elections as analysts begin to investigate FEC (Federal Election Committee) campaign documents. Preliminary estimates of congressional campaign spending in 2000 showed a roughly 40 percent increase over spending in 1998. Million-dollar campaigns for the House have become more the rule than the exception, with one campaign (Calif.-27) costing over $10 million. In West Virginia's open Second District, Democrat Jim Humphreys spent over $6 million of his own money, first in fending off three other candidates in the Democratic primary (he won with 43 percent of the vote), and then in narrowly losing the general election to Shelley Moore Capito, a state representative and daughter of the popular former governor Arch Moore. As with the presidential race, the Green Party's inroads (6 percent) into traditional Democratic constituencies certainly contributed to Humphrey's demise.

Senate races also ran high in expenditures. When all receipts are totaled, spending by the two major-party candidates for New York's open, high-profile Senate seat will probably exceed $100 million (including over $20 million spent by Republican Rudolph Giuliani, who dropped out of the race because of health and personal concerns). This $100 million does not include party spending not directly contributed or coordinated with the candidates, including GOP spending for anti-Democratic ads before a single candidate even announced any formal intention to run (and perhaps intended to discourage such announcements).

The most storied tale, however, will come from the Senate race in New Jersey, where Democrat Jon Corzine spent over $60 million, mostly from his own finances, roughly half going to win his primary battle against the better known and party organizational favorite, former Governor James Florio. Although Corzine's personal fortune enabled him to build up enough name recognition and favorability to defeat Florio 58 percent to 42 percent, it may have eventually become a liability by the time of the general election. His 4 percent victory over Congressman Bob Franks was much narrower than expected. Franks had himself won a close primary race with only 36 percent of the vote, a mere 2 percent above his closest GOP rival. We can only surmise that Franks's closely fought primary may have actually aided him in developing the statewide name recognition necessary to challenge such a well-financed general election opponent.[4]

One final comment is in order. We have every reason to expect a continuation of heightened activity by both candidates and parties and by interest groups in the next congressional election cycle. The evenly balanced party division in the House and Senate warrants that expectation. So do the increased opportunities for candidate recruitment and partisan gains in the House caused by the next round of reapportionment and redistricting. Twelve seats will move between 18 states, and most of the remaining states will also have to reconfigure district boundaries to accommodate population shifts chronicled by the 2000 Census. As a result of both reapportionment losses and partisan gerrymandering, some incumbents will invariably be faced with running against each other, sometimes in one party's primary. Other incumbents will be forced to run in drastically reconfigured districts, potentially reducing their safety. And if past postreapportionment elections are any indication, these reconfigurations will cause several incumbents to retire or to seek higher office, thereby increasing the number of open seats. Although we won't have a presidential election on which to focus, the congressional primaries and general elections of 2002 should be the most exciting and vigorously contested yet.

NOTES

I would like to thank the students in my honors U.S. institutions class for helping with the preparation for this postscript. Many of the figures cited are tentative, as final vote counts and expenditure data were not yet available.

1. In Florida's Twenty-second District, which covers parts of Palm Beach and Dade

Counties, long-term Republican incumbent Clay Shaw held on to his seat by fewer than 600 votes out of over 200,000 cast.

2. Seventeen total and five Republican open seats if we don't count California-31 (see following discussion).

3. The collective primary vote for both Democratic candidates exceeded 90 percent of all votes cast in that district's blanket nomination contest and was almost 84 percent of the total vote cast for Solis in the general election.

4. Other close races may have had the opposite effect, causing a depletion of the financial resources and party unity needed for a general election campaign. The Democratic primary in Pennsylvania's Fourth District seems to have followed this pattern.

Bibliography

Abramowitz, Alan. "Explaining Senate Election Outcomes." *American Political Science Review* 82 (1988): 385–403.

Aldrich, John H. "A Downsian Spatial Model with Party Activism." *American Political Science Review* 77 (1983): 974–90.

———. *Why Parties? The Origin and Transformation of Political Parties in America.* Chicago: University of Chicago Press, 1995.

Aldrich, John H., and Michael D. McGinnis. "A Model of Party Constraints on Optimal Candidate Positions." *Mathematical and Computer Modelling* 12 (1989): 437–50.

Alesina, Alberto. "Credibility and Policy Convergence in a Two-Party System with Rational Voters." *American Economic Review* 78 (1988): 796–805.

Alesina, Alberto, and Howard Rosenthal. *Partisan Politics, Divided Government, and the Economy.* New York: Cambridge University Press, 1995.

Alvarez, R. Michael. *Information and Elections.* Ann Arbor: University of Michigan Press, 1996.

Alvarez, R. Michael, David T. Canon, and Patrick Sellers. "The Impact of Primaries on General Election Outcomes in the U.S. House and Senate." Social Science Working Paper 932, California Institute of Technology, 1995.

Alvarez, R. Michael, and Jonathan Nagler. "Analysis of Crossover and Strategic Voting." Social Science Working Paper 1019, California Institute of Technology, 1997.

———. "Should I Stay or Should I Go? Sincere and Strategic Crossover Voting in California Assembly Races." In *Voting at the Political Vault Line: California's Experiment with the Blanket Primary*, ed. Bruce E. Cain and Elisabeth R. Gerber. Berkeley: University of California Press, forthcoming.

Ansolabehere, Stephen D., James M. Snyder Jr., and Charles Stewart III. "Candidate Positioning in U.S. House Elections." Unpublished manuscript, Massachusetts Institute of Technology, 1998.

Appleton, Andrew M., and Michael Buckley. "Washington: Christian Right Setbacks Abound." In *Prayers in the Precincts*, ed. John C. Green, Mark J. Rozell, and Clyde Wilcox. Washington, D.C.: Georgetown University Press, 2000.

Appleton, Andrew M., and Daniel S. Ward, eds. *State Party Profiles: A 50-State Guide to Development, Organization, and Resources.* Washington, D.C.: Congressional Quarterly Press, 1997.

Aranson, Peter, and Peter C. Ordeshook. "Spatial Strategy for Sequential Elections." In *Probability Models of Collective Decision Making*, ed. R. Niemi and H. Weisberg. Columbus, Ohio: Merrill, 1972.

Arnold, R. Douglas. *The Logic of Congressional Action.* New Haven, Conn.: Yale University Press, 1990.

Babson, Jennifer. "Explosive Infighting Takes Toll." *Congressional Quarterly Weekly Reports* 52 (1994): 2541.

Baer, Denise L., and David A. Bositis. *Elite Cadres and Party Coalitions.* New York: Greenwood, 1988.

Baron, David. "Electoral Competition with Informed and Uninformed Voters." *American Political Science Review* 88, no. 1 (March 1994): 33–47.

Barone, Michael, and Grant Ujifusa. *The Almanac of American Politics.* Washington, D.C.: National Journal, 1999.

Bartels, Larry M. *Presidential Primaries and the Dynamics of Public Choice.* Princeton, N.J.: Princeton University Press, 1988.

Beal, Merrill D., and Merle W. Wells, *History of Idaho.* Vol. 2. New York: Lewis Historical Publishing, 1959.

Berdahl, Clarence A. "Party Membership in the United States." *American Political Science Review* 36,(1942): 16–50, 241–62.

Bernhardt, M. Daniel, and Daniel E. Ingberman. "Candidate Reputations and the 'Incumbency Effect.'" *Journal of Public Economics* 27 (1985): 47–67.

Bernstein, Robert A. "Divisive Primaries Do Hurt: U.S. Senate Races, 1956–1972." *American Political Science Review* 71 (1977): 540–55.

———. *Elections, Representatives, and Congressional Voting Behavior.* Englewood Cliffs, N.J.: Prentice Hall, 1989.

Berry, Jeffrey, and Deborah Schildkraut. "Citizen Groups, Political Parties, and Electoral Coalitions." In *Social Movements and American Political Institutions*, ed. Anne Costain and Andrew S. McFarland. Lanham, Md.: Rowman & Littlefield, 1998.

Bibby, John F. *Politics, Parties, and Elections in America*, 4th ed. Belmont, Calif.: Wadsworth, 2000.

Bibby, John F., and L. Sandy Maisel. *Two Parties—or More? The American Party System.* Boulder, Colo.: Westview, 1999.

Black, Duncan. *A Theory of Committees and Elections.* New York: Cambridge University Press, 1958.

Blum, John Morton. *The Republic Roosevelt.* New York: Atheneum, 1970.

The Book of the States. Chicago: Council of State Governments (various years).

Boots, Ralph Simpson. *The Direct Primary in New Jersey.* Ph.D. diss., Columbia University, 1917.

Born, Richard. "The Influence of House Primary Election Divisiveness on General Election Margins, 1962–1976." *Journal of Politics* 43 (1981): 640–61.

Bott, Alexander J. *Handbook of United States Election Laws and Practices.* New York: Greenwood, 1990.

Bowler, Shaun, and Todd Donovan. *Demanding Choices*. Ann Arbor: University of Michigan Press, 1998.

———. Political Reform via the Initiative Process." In *Voting at the Political Vault Line: California's Experiment with the Blanket Primary*, ed. Bruce E. Cain and Elisabeth R. Gerber. Berkeley: University of California Press, forthcoming.

Bradley, Martin B., and Norman M. Green Jr., *Churches and Church Membership in the United States 1990*. Atlanta, Ga.: Glenmary Research Center, 1992.

Brickner, Isaac M. "Direct Primaries versus Boss Rule." 1909. In *Selected Articles on Direct Primaries*, 3d ed., ed. C. E. Fanning. Minneapolis, Minn.: Wilson, 1911.

Brunell, Thomas L., and Bernard Grofman. "Explaining Divided Senate Delegations 1788–1996: A Realignment Approach." *American Political Science Review* 92 (June 1998): 391–99.

Brunell, Thomas L., William Koetzle, John DiNardo, Bernard Grofman, and Scott L. Feld. "The $R2 = .93$. Where Then Do They Differ? Comparing Liberal and Conservative Interest Group Ratings." *Legislative Studies Quarterly* 24 (February 1999): 87–99.

Buell, E. H., Jr. "Divisive Primaries and Participation in Fall Presidential Campaigns: A Study of the 1984 New Hampshire Primary Activists." *American Politics Quarterly* 14 (1986): 376–90.

Buenker, John D. "The Urban Political Machine and the Seventeenth Amendment." *Journal of American History* 56 (1969): 305–22.

Bullock, Charles S., III and David Brady. "Party, Constituency, and Roll-Call Voting in the U.S. Senate." *Legislative Studies Quarterly* 8 (1983): 29–43.

Bullock, Charles S., III and Loch K. Johnson. *Runoff Elections in the United States*. Chapel Hill: University of North Carolina Press, 1992.

Burden, Barry C. "Candidates' Positions in Congressional Elections." Ph.D. diss. Ohio State University, 1998.

Burden, Barry C., Gregory A. Caldeira, and Tim Groseclose. "Measuring the Ideologies of U.S. Senators: The Song Remains the Same." *Legislative Studies Quarterly* 25 (2000): 237–58.

Burden, Barry C., and David C. Kimball. "A New Approach to the Study of Ticket Splitting." *American Political Science Review* 92 (1998): 533–44.

———. *Divided Loyalties: Congressional Elections and Split-Ticket Voting*. Book manuscript, 1999.

Cain, Bruce E., and Elisabeth R. Gerber. "Explorations at the Fault Line: California's Blanket Primary Experiment." In *Voting at the Political Vault Line: California's Experiment with the Blanket Primary*, ed. Bruce E. Cain and Elisabeth R. Gerber. Berkeley: University of California Press, forthcoming.

California Secretary of State. *Ballot Pamphlet*. Sacramento, 1996.

———. *Receipts and Expenditures by Committees formed Primarily to Support or Oppose Ballot Measures*. Sacramento, 1996.

————. http: //www.ss.ca.gov/elections (1999).

Calvert, Randall. "Robustness of the Multidimensional Voting Model: Candidates' Motivations, Uncertainty, and Convergence." *American Journal of Political Science* 29 (1985): 69–95.

Caul, Miki, and Katherine Tate. "Thinner Racks: Women Candidates and California's Blanket Primary." In *Voting at the Political Vault Line: California's Experiment with the Blanket Primary*, ed. Bruce E. Cain and Elisabeth R. Gerber. Berkeley: University of California Press, forthcoming.

Cho, Wendy K. Tam, and Brian J. Gaines. "Candidates, Donors, and Voters in California's First Blanket Primary Elections." In *Voting at the Political Vault Line: California's Experiment with the Blanket Primary*, ed. Bruce E. Cain and Elisabeth R. Gerber. Berkeley: University of California Press, forthcoming.

Coleman, James S. "Internal Process Governing Party Positions in Elections." *Public Choice* 11 (1971): 35–60.

————. "The Positions of Political Parties in Elections." In *Probability Models of Collective Decision Making,* ed. R. Niemi and H. Weisberg. Columbus, Ohio: Merrill, 1972.

Collet, Christian. "Taking the 'Abnormal' Route: Backgrounds, Beliefs, and Political Activities of Minor Party Candidates." In *Multiparty Politics in America*, ed. Paul S. Herrnson and John C. Green. Lanham: Rowman & Littlefield, 1997.

————. "Openness Begets Opportunity: Minor Parties and the First Blanket Primary in California." In *Voting at the Political Vault Line: California's Experiment with the Blanket Primary*, ed. Bruce E. Cain and Elisabeth R. Gerber. Berkeley: University of California Press, forthcoming.

Comer, John. "Another Look at the Effects of the Divisive Primary." *American Politics Quarterly* 4, no. 1 (1976): 121–28.

Cox, Gary W. "Centripetal and Centrifugal Incentives in Electoral Systems." *American Journal of Political Science* 34 (1990): 903–35.

Cox, Gary W., and Michael C. Munger. "Closeness, Expenditures, and Turnout in the 1982 U.S. House Elections." *American Political Science Review* 83 (1989): 217–31.

Cox, Gary W., and Jonathan N. Katz. "Why Did the Incumbency Advantage in U.S. House Elections Grow?" *American Journal of Political Science* 40 (1996): 478–97.

Downs, Anthony. *An Economic Theory of Democracy.* New York: Harper and Row, 1957.

Eismeier, Theodore J., and Philip H. Pollock III. "Money in the 1994 Elections and Beyond." In *Midterm: Elections of 1994 in Context*, ed. Philip A. Klinker. Boulder, Colo.: Westview, 1996.

Enelow, James M., and Melvin J. Hinich. *The Spatial Theory of Voting: An Introduction.* New York: Cambridge University Press, 1990.

Enelow, James M., and Melvin J. Hinich, eds. *Advances in the Spatial Theory of Voting.* New York: Cambridge University Press, 1990.

Epstein, Leon. *Political Parties in the American Mold.* Madison: University of Wisconsin Press, 1986.

Erickson, Robert S. "Roll Calls, Reputations, and Representation in the U.S. Senate." *Legislative Studies Quarterly* 25 (1990): 623–43.

"Exit Poll." *Los Angeles Times*, June 2, 1998.

Ezra, Marni. "The Benefits and Burdens of Congressional Primary Elections." Ph.D. diss., American University, 1996, and paper prepared for presentation at the 1996 annual meeting of the Midwest Political Science Association, Chicago, April 18–20, 1996.

———. "A Reexamination of Congressional Primary Turnout." *American Politics Quarterly.* Forthcoming.

Federal Election Commission. *Federal Elections 96: Election Results for the U.S. President, the U.S. Senate, and the U.S. House of Representatives.* Washington, D.C.: Federal Election Commission. At http://www.fec.gov/pubrec/cover.htm (1997).

Federal Election Commission. *Federal Elections 98.* Washington, D.C.: 1999.

Feld, Scott L., and Bernard Grofman. "Incumbency Advantage, Voter Loyalty, and the Benefit of the Doubt." *Journal of Theoretical Politics* 3, no. 2 (1991): 115–37.

Fenno, Richard F., Jr. *Home Style: House Members in Their Districts.* Boston: Little, Brown, 1978.

Field Poll 9601. San Francisco: Field Institute, 1996.

Fiorina, Morris P. *Representatives, Roll Calls, and Constituencies.* Lexington, Mass.: Lexington Books, 1974.

———. *Divided Government.* 2d ed. Needham Heights, Mass.: Allyn and Bacon, 1996.

Flanigan, William H., and Nancy H. Zingale. *Political Behavior of the American Electorate*, 9th ed., Congressional Quarterly Books (1998): 114–15.

Fort, Rodney, W. Hallagan, C. Morong, and T. Stegner. "The Ideological Component of Senate Voting: Different Principles or Different Principals?" *Public Choice* 76 (1991): 39–57.

Galderisi, Peter F. "Is the Direct Primary a Threat to Party Maintenance? The Divisive Primary Revisited, Again." Paper delivered at the annual meeting of the Midwest Political Science Association, Milwaukee, April 28–May 1, 1982.

Galderisi, Peter F., and Benjamin Ginsberg. "Primary Elections and the Evanescence of Third-Party Activity in the United States." In *Do Elections Matter?* ed. Benjamin Ginsberg and Alan Stone. Armonk, N.Y.: M. E. Sharpe, 1986.

Geer, John G. "Rules Governing Presidential Primaries." *Journal of Politics* 48, no. 1 (1986): 1006–25.

———. "Assessing the Representativeness of Electorates in Presidential Primaries." *American Journal of Political Science* 32 (1988): 929–45.

Gerber, Elisabeth R. "The Consequences of Primary Election Laws in the American States." Expert report, *California Democratic Party v. Jones*, San Diego, 1997.

―――. "Strategic Voting and Candidate Policy Positions." In *Voting at the Political Vault Line: California's Experiment with the Blanket Primary*, ed. Bruce E. Cain and Elisabeth R. Gerber. Berkeley: University of California Press, forthcoming.

Gerber, Elisabeth R., and Adam Many. "Incumbency-Led Ideological Balancing: A Hybrid Model of Split-Ticket Voting." Paper presented at the annual meeting of the Midwest Political Science Association, Chicago, 1996.

Gerber, Elisabeth R., and Rebecca B. Morton. "Primaries and Strategic Voting." Unpublished manuscript, Department of Political Science, University of California, San Diego, 1995.

―――. "Primary Election Systems and Representation." *Journal of Law, Economics, and Organization*, 14, no. 2 (1998): 304–24.

―――. "Electoral Institutions and Party Competition: The Effects of Nomination Procedures on Electoral Coalition Formation." Working paper, University of California, San Diego, La Jolla, 1999.

Goldenberg, Edie N., and Michael W. Traugott. *Campaigning for Congress*. Washington, D.C.: Congressional Quarterly Press, 1984.

Green, Donald Philip, and Jonathan S. Krasno. "Salvation for the Spendthrift Incumbent: Reestimating the Effects of Campaign Spending in House Elections." *American Journal of Political Science* 32 (1988): 884–907.

Green, Donald Philip, and Ian Shapiro. *Pathologies of Rational Choice Theory*. New Haven, Conn.: Yale University Press, 1994.

Green, John C., James L. Guth, and Kevin Hill. "Faith and Election: The Christian Right in Congressional Campaigns 1978–1988." *Journal of Politics* 55 (1993): 80–91.

Green, John C., James L. Guth, Lyman A. Kellstedt, and Corwin E. Smidt. "Evangelical Realignment: The Political Power of the Christian Right." *Christian Century* 112, no. 21 (1995): 676–79.

―――. "A Defeat, Not a Debacle." *Christian Century* 15, no. 36 (1998): 1238–45.

Green, John C., James L. Guth, Corwin E. Smidt, and Lyman A. Kellstedt. *Religion and the Culture Wars*. Lanham, Md.: Rowman & Littlefield, 1996.

Green, John C., James L. Guth, and Clyde Wilcox. "Less Than Conquerors: The Christian Right in State Republican Parties." In *Social Movements and American Political Institutions*, ed. Anne N. Costain and Andrew S. McFarland. Lanham, Md.: Rowman & Littlefield, 1998.

Green, John C., Mark J. Rozell, and Clyde Wilcox, eds. *Prayers in the Precincts: The Christian Right in the 1998 Elections*. Washington, D.C.: Georgetown University Press, 2000.

Grofman, Bernard, ed. *Information, Participation, and Choice: "An Economic*

Theory of Democracy" in Perspective. Ann Arbor: University of Michigan Press, 1993.

Grofman, Bernard. "Toward an Institution-Rich Theory of Political Competition, with a Supply-Side Component." In *Information, Participation and Choice: "An Economic Theory of Democracy" in Perspective*, ed. Bernard Grofman. Ann Arbor: University of Michigan Press, 1993.

———. "In Two-Party Competition, Why Do We Have So Much Party Divergence?: A Review and Synthesis of a Baker's Dozen's Worth of Proffered Explanations." Unpublished manuscript, School of Social Sciences, University of California, Irvine, 1997.

Grofman, Bernard, and Theodore Arrington. "Party Registration Choices as a Function of Political Competition: A Test of a Strategic Model of 'Hidden Partisanship.'" Unpublished manuscript, School of Social Sciences, University of California, Irvine, 1996.

Grofman, Bernard, Robert Griffin, and Amihai Glazer. "Identical Geography, Different Constituencies, See What a Difference Party Makes." In *Developments in Electoral Geography*, ed. R. J. Johnston, F. Shelley, and P. Taylor. London: Croom Helm, 1990.

Grofman, Bernard, Samuel Merrill, Thomas Brunell, and William Koetzle. "The Power of Ideologically Concentrated Minorities." *Journal of Theoretical Politics* 11, no. 1 (1999): 57–74.

Grofman, Bernard, William Koetzle, Michael McDonald, and Thomas Brunell. "A New Look at Split-Ticket Outcomes for House and President." *Journal of Politics* 62, no. 1 (2000): 34–50.

Groseclose, Timothy, and Keith Krehbiel. "Golden Parachutes, Rubber Checks, and Strategic Retirements from the 102d House." *American Journal of Political Science* 38 (1994): 75–99.

Groseclose, Timothy, Steven D. Levitt, and James M. Snyder Jr. "Comparing Interest Group Scores across Time and Chambers: Adjusted ADA Scores for the U.S. Congress." *American Political Science Review* 93 (March 1999): 33–50.

Guth, James L., and John C. Green. "Politics in the Promised Land: The Christian Right at the Grassroots." In *Research in the Social Science Study of Religion*, ed. Monty L. Lynn and David O. Moberg. Greenwich, Conn.: JAI Press, 1993.

Hacker, Andrew. "Does a 'Divisive' Primary Harm a Candidate's Election Chances?" *American Political Science Review* 59 (1965): 105–10.

Handlin, Oscar. *Al Smith and His America*. Boston: Little, Brown, 1958.

Hanks, Christopher, and Bernard Grofman. "Turnout in Gubernatorial and Senatorial Primary and General Elections in the South, 1922–90: A Rational Choice Model of the Effects of Short-Run and Long-Run Electoral Competition on Turnout." *Public Choice* 94, no. 3–4 (1998): 407–21.

Hansson, Ingemar, and Charles Stuart. "Voting Competitions with Interested Politicians: Platforms Do Not Converge to the Preferences of the Median Voter." *Public Choice* 44 (1984): 431–41.

Herrnson, Paul S. *Congressional Elections: Campaigning at Home and in Washington.* Washington, D.C.: Congressional Quarterly Press, 1995.

———. *Congressional Elections: Campaigning at Home and in Washington.* 2nd ed. Washington, D.C.: Congressional Quarterly Press, 1998.

Herrnson, Paul S., and James G. Gimpel, "District Conditions and Primary Divisiveness in Congressional Elections." *Political Research Quarterly* 48, no. 1 (1995): 117–34.

Hertzke, Allen D. *Echoes of Discontent.* Washington, D.C.: Congressional Quarterly Press, 1993.

Hinich, Melvin J., and Michael C. Munger. *Ideology and the Theory of Political Choice.* Ann Arbor: University of Michigan Press, 1995.

———. *Analytical Politics.* Cambridge: Cambridge University Press, 1994.

Hotelling, Harold. "Stability in Competition." *The Economic Journal* 39 (1929), 41–57.

Huckshorn, Robert J. *Political Parties in America.* 2d ed. Monterey, Calif.: Brooks/Cole, 1984.

Huntington, Samuel. "A Revised Theory of American Party Politics." *American Political Science Review* 44: (1950) 669–77.

Hutmacher, J. Joseph. "Charles Evans Hughes and Charles F. Murphy: The Metamorphosis of Progressivism." *New York History* (1965): 25–40.

Jackson, John S., III, and Nancy L. Clayton. "Leaders and Followers: Major Party Elites, Identifiers, and Issues, 1980–92." In *The State of the Parties,* ed. John C. Green and Daniel M. Shea. Lanham, Md.: Rowman & Littlefield, 1996.

Jacobson, Gary C. *Money in Congressional Elections.* New Haven, Conn.: Yale University Press, 1980.

———. "Strategic Politicians and the Dynamics of House Elections, 1946–1986." *American Political Science Review* 83 (1989): 773–93.

———. *The Electoral Origins of Divided Government: Competition in U.S. House Elections, 1946–1988.* Boulder, Colo.: Westview, 1990.

———. *The Politics of Congressional Elections.* 4th ed. Boston: Allyn and Bacon, 1996.

Jacobson, Gary C., and Michael A. Dimock. "Checking Out: The Effects of Bank Overdrafts on the 1992 House Elections." *American Journal of Political Science* 38 (1994): 601–24.

Jacobson, Gary C., and Samuel Kernell. *Strategy and Choice in Congressional Elections.* New Haven, Conn.: Yale University Press, 1981.

———. *Strategy and Choice in Congressional Elections.* 2d ed. New Haven, Conn.: Yale University Press, 1983.

Jewell, Malcolm E. *Parties and Primaries: Nominating State Governors.* New York: Praeger, 1984.

Jewell, Malcolm E., and David M. Olson. *Political Parties and Elections in American States*, 3d ed. Chicago: Dorsey, 1988.

Johnson, Donald Bruce, and James R. Gibson. "The Divisive Primary Revisited: Party Activists in Iowa." *American Political Science Review* 68 (1974): 67–77.

Jung, Gi-Ryong, Lawrence W. Kenny, and John R. Lott Jr. "An Explanation for Why Senators from the Same State Vote Differently So Frequently." *Journal of Public Economics* 54 (1994): 65–96.

Kenney, Patrick. "Sorting Out the Effects of Primary Divisiveness in Congressional and Senatorial Elections." *Western Political Quarterly* 41 (1988): 765–77.

Kenney, Patrick, and T. W. Rice. "The Effect of Primary Divisiveness in Gubernatorial and Senatorial Elections." *Journal of Politics* 46 (1984): 904–15.

———. "The Effect of Contextual Forces on Turnout in Congress and Primaries." *Social Sciences Quarterly* 67 (1986): 329–36.

———. "The Relationship between Divisive Primaries and General Election Outcomes." *American Journal of Political Science* 31 (1987): 31–44.

———. "Presidential Prenomination Preferences and Candidate Evaluations." *American Political Science Review* 82, no. 4 (1988): 1309–19.

Key, V. O. *American State Politics: An Introduction.* New York: Knopf, 1956.

Kiewiet, D. Roderick, and Langche Zeng. "An Analysis of Congressional Career Decisions, 1947–1986." *American Political Science Review* 87 (1992): 928–41.

King, David C. "The Polarization of American Parties and Mistrust of Government." In *Why People Don't Trust Government*, ed. Joseph S. Nye Jr., Philip D. Zelikow, and David C. King. Cambridge, Mass.: Harvard University Press, 1997.

———. "Party Competition and Polarization in American Politics." Paper presented at the annual meeting of the Midwest Political Science Association, Chicago, 1998, and at MIT Conference on Parties and Congress, 1999.

Kingdon, John W. *Congressmen's Voting Decisions.* 3d ed. Ann Arbor: University of Michigan Press, 1989.

Kousser, J. Morgan. *The Shaping of Southern Politics.* New Haven, Conn.: Yale University Press, 1974.

Kousser, Thad. "Crossing Over When It Counts." In *Voting at the Political Vault Line: California's Experiment with the Blanket Primary*, ed. Bruce E. Cain and Elisabeth R. Gerber. Berkeley: University of California Press, forthcoming.

Krasno, Jonathan S., and Donald Phillip Green. "Preempting Quality Challengers in House Elections." *Journal of Politics* 50, no. 4 (1988): 920–36.

Lalman, David, Joe Oppenheimer, and Piotr Swistak. "Formal Rational Choice Theory: A Cumulative Science of Politics." In *Political Science: The State of the Discipline II*, ed. Ada W. Finifter. Washington, D.C.: American Political Science Association, 1993.

Lawrence, David. *California: The Politics of Diversity.* Minneapolis/St. Paul, Minn.: West, 1995.

Lengle, James I. "Divisive Presidential Primaries and Party Electoral Prospects, 1932–1976." *American Politics Quarterly* 8, no. 3 (1980): 261–77.

Lengle, James I., Diana Owen, and Molly W. Sonner. "Divisive Nominating Mechanisms and Democratic Party Electoral Prospects." *Journal of Politics* 57, no. 2 (1995): 370–83.

Lesher, Dave. "Bill Proposes Changes in New Open Primary Law." *Los Angeles Times*, March 1, 1997, p. A1.

Lovejoy, Alan Fraser. *La Follette and the Establishment of the Direct Primary in Wisconsin, 1890–1904.* New Haven, Conn.: Yale University Press, 1941.

Lowi, Theodore J., and Joseph Romance. *A Republic of Parties? Debating the Two-Party System.* Lanham, Md.: Rowman & Littlefield, 1998.

Luce, Robert. "Does Our Ballot Law Fortify the Boss?" *State Service Magazine* (July 1918).

Magleby, David B., and Candice J. Nelson. *The Money Chase: Congressional Campaign Finance Reform.* Washington, D.C.: Brookings Institution, 1990.

Maisel, L. Sandy. *From Obscurity to Oblivion: Running in the Congressional Primary.* Rev. ed. Knoxville: University of Tennessee Press, 1982.

———. *Parties and Election in America: The Electoral Process,* 3d ed. Lanham, Md.: Rowman & Littlefield, 1999.

Maisel, L. Sandy, Cary T. Gibson, and Elizabeth J. Ivry. "The Continuing Importance of the Rules of the Game: Subpresidential Nominations in 1994 and 1996." In *The Parties Respond: Changes in American Parties and Campaigns,* 3d ed., ed. L. Sandy Maisel. Boulder, Colo.: Westview, 1998.

Maisel, L. Sandy, Elizabeth J. Ivry, Benjamin D. Ling, and Stephanie G. Pennix. "Reexploring the Weak-Challenger Hypothesis: The 1994 Candidate Pools." In *Midterm: Elections of 1994 in Context,* ed. Philip A. Klinker. Boulder, Colo.: Westview, 1996.

Maisel, L. Sandy, and Walter J. Stone. "Determinants of Candidate Emergence in U.S. House Elections: An Exploratory Study." *Legislative Studies Quarterly* 22 (1997): 79–96.

Mann, Thomas E. *Unsafe at Any Margin: Interpreting Congressional Elections.* Washington, D.C.: American Enterprise Institute, 1978.

Mann, Thomas E., and Raymond E. Wolfinger. "Candidates and Parties in Congressional Elections." *American Political Science Review* 74 (1980): 617–32.

Martin, Boyd A. *The Direct Primary in Idaho.* Palo Alto, Calif.: Stanford University Press, 1947.

Mayer, William G. *The Divided Democrats: Ideological Unity, Party Reform, and Presidential Elections.* Boulder, Colo.: Westview, 1996.

Mayhew, David R. *Congress: The Electoral Connection.* New Haven, Conn.: Yale University Press, 1974.

McAdams, John C., and John R. Johannes. "Determinants of Spending by House Challengers 1974–84." *American Journal of Political Science* 31 (1987): 457–83.

McCormick, Richard L. "Prelude to Progressivism: The Transformation of New York State Politics, 1890–1910." *New York History* (1978): 253–73.

———. *From Realignment to Reform.* Ithaca, N.Y.: Cornell University Press, 1981.

Merriam, Charles E., and Louise Overacker. *Primary Elections.* Chicago: University of Chicago Press, 1928.

Meyer, Ernst. *Nominating Systems.* Madison, Wisc.: By the author, 1902.

Miller, Penny M., Malcolm E. Jewell, and Lee Sigelman. "Divisive Primaries and Party Activists: Kentucky, 1979 and 1983." *Journal of Politics* 50, no. 2 (1988): 459–70.

Miller, Warren E., and M. Kent Jennings. *Parties in Transition.* New York: Russell Sage Foundation, 1986.

Miller, Warren E., and Donald E. Stokes. "Constituency Influence in Congress." *American Political Science Review* 57 (1963): 45–57.

Morton, Rebecca. "Incomplete Information and Ideological Explanations of Platform Divergence." *American Political Science Review* 87, no. 2 (1993): 382–92.

Norrander, Barbara. "Ideological Representativeness of Presidential Primary Voters." *American Journal of Political Science* 33 (1989): 570–87.

O'Donnell, Norah M. "Capps 53 Percent Win Cheers Democrats, Restores Old Record of 53 Women in House." *Roll Call* 43, no. 65 (1998): 1, 28.

Oldfield, Duane. *The Right and the Righteous: The Christian Right Confronts the Republican Party.* Lanham, Md.: Rowman & Littlefield, 1996.

Ornstein, Norman, Thomas Mann, and Michael J. Malbin. *Vital Statistics on Congress, 1989–90.* Washington, D.C.: American Enterprise Institute, 1991.

———. *Vital Statistics on Congress 1999–2000.* Washington, D.C.: American Enterprise Institute, 2000.

Osborne, Martin J. "Spatial Models of Political Competition under Plurality Rule: A Survey of Some Explanations of the Number of Candidates and the Positions They Take." *Canadian Journal of Economics* 28 (1995): 261–301.

Owen, Guillermo, and Bernard Grofman. "Two-Stage Electoral Competition in Two-Party Contests: Persistent Divergence of Party Positions with and without Expressive Voting." Paper presented at the annual meetings of the Public Choice Society, Long Beach, California, 1995, 1997.

Page, Benjamin I. *Choices and Echoes in Presidential Elections.* Chicago: University of Chicago Press, 1978.

Petrocik, John R., and Joseph Doherty. "The Road to Divided Government: Paved without Intention." In *Divided Government: Change, Uncertainty, and the Constitutional Order*, ed. Peter F. Galderisi. Lanham, Md.: Rowman & Littlefield, 1996.

Pierson, James E., and Terry B. Smith. "Primary Divisiveness and General Election Success: A Re-examination." *Journal of Politics* 37 (1975): 555–62.

Pollock, James K. *The Direct Primary in Michigan, 1909–1935.* Ann Arbor: University of Michigan Press, 1943.

Polsby, Nelson. *The Consequences of Party Reform.* Oxford: Oxford University Press, 1983.

Poole, Keith T., and Howard Rosenthal. "The Polarization of American Politics." *Journal of Politics* 46 (1984): 1061–79.

———. "A Spatial Model for Legislative Roll Call Analysis." *American Journal of Political Science* 29, no. 2 (1985): 357–84.

———. *Congress: A Political-Economic History of Roll Call Voting.* New York: Oxford University Press, 1997.

Powell, G. Bingham Jr. *Contemporary Democracies.* Cambridge, Mass.: Harvard University Press, 1982.

Ranney, Austin. "Turnout and Representation in Presidential Primary Elections." *American Political Science Review* 74 (1972): 685–96.

Rohde, David W. *Parties and Leaders in the Postreform House.* Chicago: University of Chicago Press, 1991.

Rosenstone, Steven J., Roy L. Behr, and Edward H. Lazarus. *Third Parties in America,* 2d ed. Princeton, N.J.: Princeton University Press, 1996.

Rozell, Mark J. "WISH List: Pro-Choice Women in the Republican Congress." In *After the Revolution: PACs, Lobbies, and the Republican Congress,* ed. Robert Biersack, Paul S. Herrnson, and Clyde Wilcox. Boston: Allyn and Bacon, 1999.

Rozell, Mark J., and Clyde Wilcox. *Interest Groups in American Campaigns.* Washington, D.C.: Congressional Quarterly Press, 1999.

———. *Second Coming: The New Christian Right in Virginia Politics.* Baltimore: Johns Hopkins University Press, 1996.

Rozell, Mark J., and Clyde Wilcox, eds. *God at the Grass Roots.* Lanham, Md.: Rowman & Littlefield, 1995.

———. *God at the Grass Roots 1996.* Lanham, Md.: Rowman & Littlefield, 1997.

Sabato, Larry. *The Democratic Party Primary in Virginia.* Charlottesville: University Press of Virginia, 1977.

Salisbury, Robert H. "Political Movements in American Politics." *National Journal of Political Science* 1 (1989): 15–30.

Salvanto, Anthony, and Marty Wattenberg. "Peeking under the Blanket: A Direct Look at Crossover Voting in the 1998 Primary." In *Voting at the Political Vault Line: California's Experiment with the Blanket Primary,* ed. Bruce E. Cain and Elisabeth R. Gerber. Berkeley: University of California Press, forthcoming.

Scammon, Richard M., and Alice V. McGillivray, eds. *America Votes 20* (1992). Washington, D.C.: Congressional Quarterly Press, 1993.

———. *America Votes 21* (1994). Washington, D.C.: Congressional Quarterly Press, 1995.

————. *America Votes 22* (1996). Washington, D.C.: Congressional Quarterly Press, 1997.

Scammon, Richard M., Alice V. McGillivray, and Rhodes Cook, eds. *America Votes 23* (1998). Washington, D.C.: Congressional Quarterly Press, 1999.

Scammon, Richard M., and Ben J. Wattenberg. *The Real Majority*. New York: Coward, McCann, and Georghegan, 1970.

Schantz, Harvey L. "Contested and Uncontested Primaries for the U.S. House." *Legislative Studies Quarterly* 4 (1980): 545–62.

Segura, Gary M., and Nathan D. Woods. "Targets of Opportunity: California's Blanket Primary and the Political Representation of Latinos." In *Voting at the Political Vault Line: California's Experiment with the Blanket Primary*, ed. Bruce E. Cain and Elisabeth R. Gerber. Berkeley: University of California Press, forthcoming.

Shapiro, Catherine R., David W. Brady, Richard A. Brody, and John A. Ferejohn. "Linking Constituency Opinion and Senate Voting Scores: A Hybrid Explanation." *Legislative Studies Quarterly* 15, no. 4 (November 1990): 599–623.

Sides, John, Jonathan Cohen, and Jack Citrin. "The Causes and Consequences of Crossover Voting in the 1998 California Elections." In *Voting at the Political Vault Line: California's Experiment with the Blanket Primary*, ed. Bruce E. Cain and Elisabeth R. Gerber. Berkeley: University of California Press, forthcoming.

Smolka, Richard G. (ed.) *Election Administrative Reports*, February 24. Washington, D.C.: Maric, 1996.

Snyder, James M. "Artificial Extremism in Interest Group Ratings." *Legislative Studies Quarterly* 17 (1992): 319–46.

Soper, J. Christopher, and Joel Fetzer. "The Christian Right and the Republican Party in California: Necessarily Yoked," in *Prayers in the Precincts*, ed. John C. Green, Mark J. Rozell, and Clyde Wilcox. Washington, D.C.: Georgetown University Press, 2000.

Southwell, Priscilla L. "The Politics of Disgruntlement: Nonvoting and Defection among Supporters of Nomination Losers, 1968–1984." *Social Science Journal* 8, no. 1 (1986): 81–95.

————. "Prenomination Preferences and General Election Voting Behavior." *Social Science Journal* 31, no. 1 (1994): 69–77.

Standing, William H., and James A. Robinson. "Inter-Party Competition and Primary Contesting: The Case of Indiana." *American Political Science Review* 48 (1954).

Stone, Walter J. "Prenomination Candidate Choice and General Election Behavior: Iowa Presidential Activists in 1980." *American Journal of Political Science* 28 (1984): 361–78.

————. "The Carryover Effect in Presidential Elections." *American Political Science Review* 80, no. 1 (1986): 271–78.

———. "On Party Switching among Presidential Activists: What Do We Know?" *American Journal of Political Science* 35, no. 3 (1991): 598–607.

Stone, Walter J., Lonna Rae Atkeson, and Ronald B. Rapoport. "Turning On or Turning Off? Mobilization and Demobilization Effects of Participation in Presidential Nomination Campaigns." *American Journal of Political Science* 36, no. 3 (1992): 665–91.

Stone, Walter J., and L. Sandy Maisel. "The Not-So-Simple Calculus of Winning: Potential House Candidates' Nomination and General Election Chances." Paper presented at the annual meeting of the American Political Science Association, Atlanta, September 1999. Available at www.socsci.colorado.edu/CES/home.html.

Stone, Walter J., L. Sandy Maisel, and Cherie Maestas. "Candidate Emergence in U.S. House Elections." Paper presented at the annual meeting of the American Political Science Association, Boston, September 3–6, 1998. Available at www.socsci.colorado.edu/CES/home.html.

Stone, Walter J., L. Sandy Maisel, Cherie Maestas, and Sean Evans. "A New Perspective on Candidate Quality in U.S. House Elections." Paper presented at the annual meeting of the Midwest Political Science Association, Chicago, April, 1998. Available at www.socsci.colorado.edu/CES/home.html.

Sullivan, John L., and Daniel Richard Minns. "Ideological Distance between Candidates: An Empirical Examination." *American Journal of Political Science* 20 (1976): 439–68.

Syer, John C., and John H. Culver. *Power and Politics in California.* 4th ed. New York: Macmillan, 1992.

Tourelle, Ellen, ed. *The Political Philosophy of Robert M. La Follette as Revealed in His Speeches and Writings.* Madison, Wisc.: Robert M. La Follette, 1920.

Turner, Julius. "Primary Elections as the Alternative to Party Competition in 'Safe' Districts." *Journal of Politics* 15 (1953): 197–210.

Van Dongen, Rachel. "Even His Allies Question Use of 'Partial Birth' Ads." *Roll Call* 43, no. 76 (1998): 15, 18.

Ware, Alan. "Divisive Primaries: The Important Questions." *British Journal of Political Science* 9 (1979): 381–84.

Wattenberg, Martin P. *The Decline of American Political Parties, 1952–1992.* Cambridge, Mass.: Harvard University Press, 1994.

Westlye, Mark C. "The Effects of Primary Divisiveness on Incumbent Senators, 1968–1984." Paper presented at the annual meeting of the American Political Science Association, New Orleans, 1985.

White, Theodore. *Making of the President 1960.* New York: Atheneum, 1961.

Wilcox, Clyde. *Onward Christian Soldiers.* Boulder, Colo.: Westview, 1996.

Wilson, James Q. *The Amateur Democrat.* Chicago: University of Chicago Press, 1962.

Wittman, Donald A. "Candidates with Policy Preferences: A Dynamic Model." *Journal of Economic Theory* 14 (1977): 180–89.

———. "Candidate Motivations: A Synthesis of Alternatives." *American Political Science Review* 77 (1983): 142–57.

———. "Spatial Strategies When Candidates Have Policy Preferences." In *Advances in the Spatial Theory of Voting,* ed. J. Enelow and M. Hinich. Cambridge: Cambridge University Press, 1991.

Wright, Gerald C. Jr., and Michael B. Berkman. "Candidates and Policy in United States Senate Elections." *American Political Science Review* 80 (1986): 567–88.

Wright, John R. *Interest Groups and Congress: Lobbying, Contributions, and Influence.* Boston: Allyn and Bacon, 1996.

Index

About the Contributors

Thomas L. Brunell is assistant professor in the department of political science at Binghamton University (SUNY). His research focuses on U.S. Congress, elections, electoral systems, and the U.S. Census. He served as an American Political Science Association Congressional Fellow, class of 1998–99. His research has appeared in *American Political Science Review, Journal of Politics, Legislative Studies Quarterly, Party Politics,* and *Electoral Systems.*

Barry C. Burden is assistant professor of government at Harvard University. His research analyzes such issues as the turnout effects of third-party presidential candidates, the role that ideology and partisanship play in Congress, and the measurement of public opinion. He has published on these topics in *American Political Science Review, American Journal of Political Science,* and other journals and edited books. He is currently completing a coauthored manuscript entitled *Divided Loyalties: Congressional Elections and Split-Ticket Voting,* which examines the popular motivations behind divided government in the United States, and he is preparing an edited book on uncertainty in American politics.

Marni Ezra is assistant professor of political science at Hood College. Her areas of expertise are U.S. institutions and elections, with a specific focus on primary elections. Professor Ezra has published articles in a number of journals, including *Electoral Studies, American Politics Quarterly, PS,* and *Public Administration Review.* Her dissertation on congressional primary elections won a doctoral dissertation grant from the National Science Foundation.

Peter F. Galderisi is associate professor of political science at Utah State University. He has been a visiting professor at University of California, Santa Cruz, California State University, Fullerton, and UCLA. He is coeditor of *The Politics of Realignment: Party Change in the Mountain West* (1987) and editor of *Divided Government: Change, Uncertainty, and the Constitutional Order* (1996). He has written articles on public choice experimentation, redistricting, and realignment in the West.

Elisabeth R. Gerber is associate professor of political science at the University of California, San Diego. Gerber's research is concerned with the policy consequences of electoral laws and other political institutions. She has written numerous papers on the use of initiatives and referendums in California and other states and recently completed a book on the subject (*The Populist Paradox*, 1999). She is involved in a major study of electoral laws in the American states and their effects on election outcomes and representation. This work has resulted in numerous publications and lead to her involvement as an expert witness in the state of California's defense of Proposition 198, the Open Primary Act. Professor Gerber is completing a book on the implementation and enforcement of voter initiatives (with D. Roderick Kiewiet, Arthur Lupia, and Mathew D. McCubbins). Some of Professor Gerber's works are published in *American Political Science Review*, *American Journal of Political Science*, *Political Research Quarterly*, *Political Behavior,* and *Journal of Law, Economics, and Organization*. She received her Ph.D. from the University of Michigan in 1991.

Jay Goodliffe is assistant professor of political science at Brigham Young University, where his research interests include Congress, interest groups, and positive political theory. His primary subject of research is campaign finance in congressional elections, in particular the issue of war chests. His study of the 1998 Utah Second Congressional District Race will appear in *Outside Money: Soft Money and Issue Advocacy in the 1998 Congressional Elections* (2000). He received his Ph.D. from the University of Rochester.

John C. Green is professor of political science and director of the Ray C. Bliss Institute of Applied Politics at the University of Akron. His research interests include American parties and elections, with a special emphasis on the role of religion. He is coauthor of *The Diminishing Divide: Religion's Changing Role in American Politics* (2000) and *Religion and the Culture Wars* (Rowman & Littlefield, 1996) and coeditor of *The State of the Parties* (Rowman & Littlefield, 1999).

Bernard Grofman is professor of political science at the University of California, Irvine. He has been a fellow at the Center for Advanced Study in the Behavioral Sciences, Stanford, visiting professor at the University of Michigan and at the University of Washington, and guest scholar at the Brookings Institution. He has also been a visiting scholar at the University of Mannheim for three months in 1973 and visiting scholar in residence at Kansai University, Osaka, for one month in 1990. His past research dealt with mathematical models of group decision making and legislative representation and focused on electoral rules and redistricting. He has also been involved in modeling individual and group information processing and decision heuristics, and he has written on the intersection of law and social science, especially the role of expert witness testimony and the uses of statistical evidence. Currently he is working on comparative politics and political economy, with an emphasis on viewing the United States in comparative perspective.

Kristin Kanthak is assistant professor of political science at the University of Arizona. Her dissertation, "Legislative Power in the 20th Century," explores changes in the rules governing who received power in the House of Representatives during the 1900s. She was a former aide to Congressman Daniel Rostenkowski.

Michael Lyons is associate professor of political science at Utah State University. His research interests include the U.S. Congress and U.S. environmental policy. His most recent publication is "Political Self-Interest in U.S. Environmental Policy," in *Natural Resources Journal.* Together with Peter F. Galderisi he coauthored articles on congressional elections and coedited *The Politics of Realignment* (1987). He served as an American Political Science Association Congressional Fellow in the office of Representative Thomas Foley (D-Wash.), and as a delegate to the 1988 Democratic National Convention.

David B. Magleby is nationally recognized for his expertise on direct democracy, voting behavior, and campaign finance. He received his B.A. from the University of Utah in 1973 and his Ph.D. from the University of California, Berkeley. He is currently professor of political science and department chair at Brigham Young University. He has taught at the University of California, Santa Cruz, and the University of Virginia. His writings include *Direct Legislation* (1984), *The Money Chase: Congressional Campaign Finance Reform* (1990), *The Myth of the Independent Voter* (1992), *Outside Money: Soft Money and Issue Advocacy in the 1998 Congressional Elections* (2000), and several editions of an American government textbook, *Government by the People* (1999). He also published numerous articles in political science journals. He is immediate past-president of Pi Sigma Alpha, the national political science honor society.

L. Sandy Maisel is the William R. Kenan Jr. Professor of Government at Colby College. Former chair of the Legislative Studies and Political Organizations and Parties Organized Sections of the APSA and former president of the New England Political Science Association, Maisel's recent publications include *Parties and Elections in America: The Electoral Process* (3d ed., 1999) and editor and coauthor of *The Parties Respond: Changes in American Parties and Campaigns* (3d ed., 1998). He and Walter J. Stone are the principal co-investigators for the National Science Foundation–funded Candidate Emergence Study.

Rebecca Morton is professor of political science at the University of Houston. Professor Morton's articles have been published in numerous publications such as *American Political Science Review, American Journal of Political Science*, and *Journal of Law and Economics.* She is the author of *Methods and Models: A Guide to the Empirical Analysis of Formal Models in Political Science* (1999) and the coauthor of *Learning by Voting: Sequential Choices in Presidential Primaries and Other Elections* (2001).

Walter J. Stone is professor of political science and research associate of the Institute of Behavioral Sciences at the University of Colorado. The former editor of *Political Research Quarterly* and a frequent contributor to professional journals, he is also the author of *Nomination Politics: Party Activists and Presidential Choice* (1984) and *Republic at Risk: Self-Interest in American Politics* (1990).